ORLEY I. HOLTAN

Slippery Rock State College

INTRODUCTION
TO
THEATRE

A MIRROR TO NATURE

Prentice-Hall, Inc., Englewood Cliffs, New Jersey

Library of Congress Cataloging in Publication Data

HOLTAN, ORLEY I

   Introduction to theatre.

   Includes bibliographies.
   1. Theater.   2. Drama.   I. Title.
PN1655.H63   792   76–1885
ISBN   0-13-498741-1

FOR JUDITH,
just because

© 1976 Prentice-Hall, Inc., Englewood Cliffs, N.J.

Printed in the United States of America

10 9 8 7 6 5 4 3 2 1

Prentice-Hall International, Inc., *London*
Prentice-Hall of Australia Pty. Limited, *Sydney*
Prentice-Hall of Canada, Ltd., *Toronto*
Prentice-Hall of India Private Limited, *New Delhi*
Prentice-Hall of Japan, Inc., *Tokyo*
Prentice-Hall of Southeast Asia Pte. Ltd., *Singapore*

CONTENTS

PART THREE
THE THEATRE REFLECTS LIFE 133

8

9

10

11

PART FOUR
EVALUATING THE THEATRE 231

12

PREFACE

Many if not most textbooks designed for use in courses in introduction to theatre take a basically historical approach, or combine a historical approach with a general discussion of the practical aspects of theatre. This book attempts to take a different one. It is predicated on the assumption that many students enrolled in such courses may never have seen a play or, if they have that their theatre going experience is limited to a high school class play or to a musical performed by a local college or community theatre or by a professional touring group. It addresses itself chiefly to the questions, "what is theatre?" "what does theatre do?" "how does it work?" "what should the viewer expect from it?" It does not deal with history except as it relates to the above questions. The book is designed, therefore, primarily for such students and for a course in theatre appreciation. The author hopes that in so structuring this text that it will be equally useful as general background for future theatre majors.

The book views theatre as a communicative act which shares certain functions with the other arts and attempts to communicate similar messages. The structure and approach reflect this presupposition in that they show some affinities with various communication models and share an attitude that is becoming increasingly important in many disciplines — that all or a good part of man's behavior is communicative and symbolic. The first two chapters provide a general introduction to the arts and the theatre. The next five could be said to roughly parallel the first four terms of Burke's pentad: act, agent, agency, scene. The next four chapters deal at some length with the fifth term, purpose, and attempt to show how various forms and styles in the theatre have been responses to different experiences of life and have communicated different interpretations to it. The final chapter deals with criticism and attempts to provide some preliminary guidelines toward answering the question, "what is good theatre?"

No textbook will, of course, satisfy every instructor who adopts it or every student who reads it. This one was inspired by the author's experiences and problems in teaching the course to a particular set of students and was written because he feels that those students are probably quite typical. Nevertheless, he has tried to leave a good deal of leeway for the classroom instructor and to offer ideas and insights in the hope that, even if they are not agreed with, they will stimulate thought and discussion.

ACKNOWLEDGEMENTS

In writing any book one incurs a great many debts and in a book of this sort more than usual. I would like to express my appreciation to all those who furnished photographs and other material; most, if not all, of them are specifically mentioned in the captions or notes. I would also like to thank the editorial staff of Prentice-Hall for their dedicated work and excellent suggestions. An individual who deserves my belated thanks because he had more to do with forming my attitudes toward theatre than any other person is Dr. Henry G. Lee of Temple University. My chairman, Dr. Theodore Walwik, my colleagues in theatre, Mr. Milton Carless and Dr. Raymond Wallace, and my theatre students at Slippery Rock State College who have supported and encouraged me, served as a testing ground for many of the ideas expressed in this book and deserve my thanks as well. Lastly, my wife, Judith, probably the most brilliant woman I know, suggested the project in the first place and has continued to stimulate and encourage me.

ORLEY I. HOLTAN

PRENTICE-HALL SERIES IN THEATRE AND DRAMA
Oscar G. Brockett CONSULTING EDITOR

The Actor at Work, revised and enlarged
Robert Benedetti

Century of Innovation:
A History of European and American Theatre and Drama Since 1870;
Oscar G. Brockett and Robert R. Findlay

Children's Theatre: A Philosophy and a Method
Moses Goldberg

Creative Dramatics for the Classroom Teacher
Ruth Heinig and Lyda Stillwell

Creative Play Direction
Robert Cohen and John Harrop

Introduction to Theatre: A Mirror to Nature
Orley I. Holtan

Play Directing: Analysis, Communication, and Style
Francis Hodge

Playwriting: The Structure of Action
Sam Smiley

Theatre in High School: Planning, Teaching, Directing
Charlotte Kay Motter

Three Hundred Years of American Drama and Theatre
Garff B. Wilson

PART ONE

THE THEATRE AS ART

1

ART, THE THEATRE, AND MAN

ART SEEMS TO BE INHERENT and natural to man. Over two thousand years ago Aristotle said that man had an instinct for imitation. While modern psychologists might quarrel with his use of the term "instinct" the fact remains that man, uniquely among his fellow animals, feels that he must represent his life and experience, that he must give them visual and aural form as painting, sculpture, architecture, music, dance, theatre, literature. Though forms and styles may differ widely there seems to be no society beyond the most primitive that does not have some form of art. Furthermore, in the history of both Oriental and Western civilizations, art of some sort goes back to the very beginnings and is often linked with the mythical origins of the race. In the Western world we have discovered drawings upon the walls of caves that go all the way back to the stone age. Some form of dance, music and drama in the ancient Near East (Egypt, Crete, Greece) goes back perhaps a thousand years before Christ. The Japanese *Kojiki,* or *Record of Ancient Matters,* attributes the beginnings of dance and mime to the gods themselves. Art, then, is universal and it is ancient.

THE FUNCTIONS OF ART

Why does man produce and enjoy art; what does it do for him? There is no easy answer to these two questions. Philosophers have argued over the meaning and function of art for hundreds of years. Perhaps the safest course would be to say that there is no one single answer, but we can speculate about some of the possible answers. I would like to suggest that art does several things: it makes it possible for man to live a wider and richer life, it is a means by which man attempts to manage his environment and answer his deepest questions; it enables man to express the inexpressable, it allows man to communicate his ideas about experience in a uniquely forceful way. All of these functions may overlap and any single work of art may fulfill several functions both for the artist and for the consumer of the art.

All of us are aware that life can become rather humdrum, monotonous, and boring. Perhaps this humdrum quality of life becomes more obvious as we get older, but even for students there must be times when the daily routine of going to classes, writing papers, studying for exams, and even drinking beer or dating becomes dull and boring, and we look around for some variety or escape. In modern times the entertainment industry is organized to provide that escape, but art has also traditionally provided it. Through novels, stories, plays, music, painting, poetry, we can be temporarily lifted out of our humdrum world into a wider and richer one. This is most easy to see in the popular narrative arts; through the detective novel, the adventure movie or TV show, the love story, we can vicariously patrol the streets of Los Angeles in a squad car, we can ride with Custer or with the Indians, we can put ourselves in the place of the couple meeting and discovering that they love each other. We can, in fact, be caught up in and empathize with the events to the extent that we find ourselves responding physically. Our muscles tense as the hero fights it out with the villain or tears cloud our eyes as the heroine expires in her white hospital bed.

There is another and more immediate way in which art enhances and enriches life. The best way to understand this function of art is to imagine the complete absence of art. Imagine your room with no pictures on the walls, with no stereo, no radio, no television set, no books. Imagine all of the objects you use, your china, your silverware, ashtrays, etc., absolutely without decoration of any kind. Imagine your clothing to be of a dull and uniform color. It seems significant that prisoners or soldiers, who are frequently forced to live in drab, sterile environments, feel the impulse to decorate their living areas if in no other way than by pinning up the centerfold from *Playboy*. Perhaps without the various forms of art to provide enrichment of this sort much of life would become prison-like—drab, dull, and uninteresting.

You may have noticed that in the preceding the distinction between art and entertainment or decoration has been somewhat blurred. Surely art is more than the *Playboy* centerfold, or the popular movie, or the daisies stenciled on a set of plastic dishes. If it is not, why teach it in college? The trouble is that the dividing line between art and entertainment is not nearly so easily discovered as some people would have us believe. The history of all of the arts is full of examples of one generation's entertainment becoming another generation's art. In the nineteenth century Mark Twain was considered a popular journalist, lecturer, and writer of boys' books and his works were not thought worthy to be taught in college literature classes. Today, of course, *The Adventures of Huckleberry Finn* is considered an American classic. Similarly, in the eighteenth century many people of cultivated tastes felt that Shakespeare's plays were just too crude and barbaric to be considered as art and most productions of them were based upon rewritten and "improved" texts. Furthermore, entertainment, defined as the giving of pleasure, is a legitimate function of art and is part of what we mean when we say that it enhances and enriches life. If we do not immediately recognize this, the fault may lie in the way that we commonly think of both art and entertainment. We tend to think of art in the way that we think of certain foods or medicines—good for us but not necessarily pleasant or enjoyable. We tend to think of it also as something that is difficult to understand, that we have to learn about, that takes some effort to appreciate. Entertainment, on the other hand, we think of as something pleasant, something painless, something we merely sit back and enjoy. To a certain extent this common distinction is sound but it is not completely accurate as applied either to art or to entertainment. In general, good and serious art probably does take more effort to appreciate than does standard television fare, magazine illustrations or popular music, but there is no reason that art cannot be pleasant and enjoyable. At the same time, much that we regard as entertainment requires some effort to appreciate. To fully understand and enjoy the game of football, for example, may require considerable study of plays, formations, the duties of individual players, different coaching styles, etc. The point is that what we learn to enjoy seems to us to be entertaining and pleasurable whether it is watching football or watching ballet, playing golf, or writing poetry, and if we enjoy the activity we do not mind the effort involved in it. Nevertheless, while entertainment is one of the functions of art, it does not necessarily follow that all that entertains is art. The distinction between the two may lie in some of the other functions of art.

All of civilization can be seen as man's attempt to manage and control his environment. He exercises this control through a number of tools, but the most basic of those tools is the ability to symbolize. Through the use of symbols man can express not only his immediate feelings, reactions, and desires, he can also represent things that are not immediately present and that may not even exist. This is something that, as far as we now know, no other animal can do. The most common and obvious of man's symbol systems is language. But there are others. Body movements, pictures, statues, flags and emblems, uniforms and other forms of clothing, objects we use, all can function as symbols. This ability to symbolize, especially in the form of language lies at the base of all of man's other activities. From it he develops law, medicine, science, philosophy, government, technology. Through the use of this symbolizing capacity man has been able to answer a good many questions and to extend his control over a large portion of his surroundings. There are, however, certain aspects of his existence that man has not yet learned to control and certain questions that he has not been able to answer. He has not, for example, learned to control death. He has not eliminated evil from the world, nor has he satisfactorily explained why the innocent often suffer. He understands a great deal about the processes of nature, of birth and death, growth and decay, but he does not understand why. In attempting to deal with these eternal topics and to answer such questions as "Why are we here?" "Where are we going?" "Is there any purpose in existence?" man again turns to his symbolizing ability and develops myth, ritual, religion—and art. Instead of attempting to deal with such eternal questions on an intellectual level all of these activities do so sensually and emotionally. They may depend less exclusively on linguistic symbols and more on such things as objects, enactment, sounds, rhythms, colors, etc. The difference is between reading a philosophical book on ethics and seeing a dramatized struggle between good and evil, between reading a scientific treatise on the cycle of growth and decay in nature and being led to feel it through a poem, a painting, or a piece of music.

Many of the rituals of primitive man were, and in some parts of the world still are, designed to insure the changes of the season, the growth of crops, the presence of game and to mark or celebrate significant changes in the lives of human beings. Many of these rituals made use of song, dance, and a kind of drama in reenacting the events in the life of a god who ruled the seasons, the crops, or the game. Changes such as that from boyhood to manhood might be celebrated by a symbolic killing and resurrecting of the person undergoing the ceremony. The drawings of wild animals on the walls of caves referred to earlier were probably a kind of magic and were designed to capture the spirit of the animal so that he could be lured to the hunter who could then kill him. Thus, in primitive societies there is a close relationship between magic, ritual, religion, and art and among "civilized" peoples that relationship still exists, though it may not be as obvious. The ancient Greeks made statues of their gods. Medieval and Renaissance painting is full of religious symbolism much of which we may not perceive or understand unless we have made a special study of it. The great choral masses of Vivaldi, Bach, Mozart and other composers express man's religious awe and worship through music. Literature and theatre tend to depict human beings facing crises which embody the eternal questions and universal processes of existence, literature through the medium of words, and theatre through words plus enactment. All of this does not, of course, mean that artists, any more than philosophers, scientists, lawyers or politicians, are able to give us the final answers to these eternal questions, but only that the attempt to deal with them has always been one of the most important functions of art.

Language, as one of man's most basic tools, enables him to do a great many things. He can name and classify the things in his environment, he can make statements about them and he can preserve and pass on such information to others. Thus, he can attach the label "dog" to a particular animal and having done so he can classify other such animals when he meets them in the future. He can then formulate statements such as "Dogs bark" or "Dogs can be a great help in hunting." and thus convey to his fellow human beings information that is useful in dealing with dogs. We can make a wide variety of such statements, ranging from fairly concrete and verifiable ones such as "The sun is shining." to abstract and unverifiable ones such as "All men are created equal" or "Honesty is the best policy." The ability to apply such labels and formulate such statements makes it possible for man to symbolize a great deal of his experience with and knowledge of his surroundings. But there is a whole area of human experience in which discursive language does not seem sufficient. That is the area which the philosopher, Suzanne Langer, calls the life of the feelings. Try to describe, for example, what it feels like after a long hard winter, to come outdoors and find the sun shining, the snow melting away leaving puddles of water and patches of grass and a warm breeze blowing. We can make this kind of descriptive statement but it fails to express how we respond to that particular situation,—how it *feels* to us. Now consider the following poem by E. E. Cummings dealing with exactly these circumstances.

Chanson Innocente

*in Just
spring when the world is mud
luscious the little
lame balloonman*

whistles far and wee

*and eddie and bill come
running from marbles and
piracies and its
spring*

when the world is puddle-wonderful

*the queer
old balloonman whistles
far and wee
and bettyandisbel come dancing
from hop-scotch and jump-rope and*

*it's
spring
  and
    the
       goat-footed
balloonman whistles
far
and
wee.[1]*

Though some of the details of our own experience may be slightly different, most of us probably recognize that Cummings' poem conveys the *feeling* of spring better than pages of factual description.

Similarly, how do you describe how it feels to be in love, to look at the face of your first child, to hear of the death of someone dear to you? In short, ordinary language is not adequate to deal with the deeper feelings that we experience. It is exactly this "life of the feelings" that the philosopher, Suzanne Langer, says is the subject of art. Perhaps we cannot speak adequately about our love for that very special person but we can write a poem and many of us try to. Artists habitually try to express their feelings about things or how life feels by painting a picture, composing and/or performing a piece of music, writing a poem or a play. To the extent that they

Figure 1–1. The theatre deals with religion, the crucifixion scene from *Godspell*. (Slippery Rock State College, directed by Milton Carless, designed by Raymond Wallace. Company photographer, Michael F. Sunderman.)

are good and sensitive they either share our deepest feelings or cause us to share theirs.

Art can also function as a barometer for the social, economic, or political condition of the times. For example, America in the 1930s was in the grip of the Great Depression, the worst that the nation had ever suffered. Unemployment was high, wages low, poverty and hardship a reality, not for just parts of the society but for almost every American except the very few. Throughout the nation there was unrest; farmers in the Midwest and South demonstrated and rioted, there were strikes in the mines, the steel mills, and the automobile plants. Indeed, almost every industry was hit by labor troubles and violence on both sides was common. In February of 1934 there had been a taxi drivers' strike in New York, a relatively minor incident among the labor crises of the period. Clifford Odets, a young idealistic and socially conscious playwright, decided to use the incident as the basis for a play and thus as a symbol for the whole set of problems that were afflicting society. The play, *Waiting for Lefty*, was opened by the Group Theatre in 1935.

The play is set in a union hall as the taxi drivers debate the issue of whether or not to go out on strike. They are waiting for the return of Lefty, one of their leaders, who will bring them the reactions of the management to their demands. The debate is interspersed with a series of scenes depicting the problems and hardships of New York taxi drivers and their families. The audience response, as Harold Clurman describes it, was enthusiastic:

> The first scene of *Lefty* had not played two minutes when a shock of
> delighted recognition struck the audience like a tidal wave. Deep laughter,
> hot assent, a kind of joyous fervor seemed to sweep the audience toward the

stage. The actors no longer performed; they were being carried along as if by an exultancy of communication such as I had never witnessed in the theatre before. Audience and actors had become one. Line after line brought applause, whistles, bravos, and heartfelt shouts of kinship.[2]

At last, after a picture of the conditions of the working man during the period had been strongly presented, the message comes. But it is about, not from, Lefty. "Boys, Lefty ain't coming. He's dead. He was found in an alley, shot in the head." At this point the union leader turns to the audience and demands "Well, what's the answer?" and the audience leaped to its feet and responded with a spontaneous shout of "Strike, strike, strike!" Could Odets have conveyed his message with any greater impact by making a speech, or writing an editorial in a daily newspaper?

Artists like other human beings respond to the political, social, and economic events in the world around them. Their vocation, however, perhaps makes them more sensitive to those events than the ordinary person and at the same time provides them with a uniquely powerful means of communicating their reactions. Thus Beethoven responded in the *Eroica* symphony to Napoleon, as did Tchaikovsky in a different way in his *1812 Overture*. During the Spanish Civil War in 1936, Royalist planes bombed

Figure 1–2. The theatre deals with history. John Osborne's *Luther.* (Hilberry Theatre, Wayne State University, directed by N. Joseph Calarco, designed by Russell Paquette, costumes by Vic Leverett, lighting by Gary M. Witt.)

a small village called Guernica, killing many women and children. Picasso reacted to that event with a painting that remains a vivid picture of the horrors of war long after most people have forgotten the incident that inspired it. Two thousand years earlier the Athenians slaughtered and enslaved the inhabitants of the small island of Melos. Their only crime was the wish to remain neutral in the war between Athens and Sparta. Euripides was moved by this incident to write a play called *The Trojan Women* which remains a classic among antiwar plays and has much to say to us in the era of Vietnam, Cambodia, Cyprus, Biafra, and the war between Arabs and Israelis. The nature of the artists' comments about society and experience will be determined in large part by the conditions of their existence, the age in which the artists live and the kind of person they happen to be. They may be serious or comic, optimistic or pessimistic, conservative or radical, religious or atheistic, but however artists look at life and whatever they choose to say about it, their comments will, if they are great artists, carry unique impact and will often seem to apply not only to their own time and place but to all times and all places.

There is one function of art that we have not as yet discussed – the aesthetic experience. Perhaps we do not often talk about it because, though we know it when we experience it, it is almost impossible to find the words to describe it. In one way it is like the feeling of satisfaction that we get when we have eaten a superb meal, while in another way it is like the feeling of awe that we sometimes experience in church or while looking at a spectacular bit of scenery. Of course we do not get it from every work of art and all of us do not get it from the same form of art. Some of us may get it more readily from music, some from painting, some from poetry, some from theatre. Some of us may never get it at all, but if we do we are aware of a kind of elevation or transformation, heightening or satisfaction that goes beyond merely feeling that the thing we experienced was good. It may be the aim of every serious artist to create that effect in us, though obviously not every work of art succeeds in doing so.

ART AND THE THEATRE

Throughout its history the theatre has performed all of the functions discussed above and the live theatre and its variant forms, films, and television, continue to perform them for many people today. The theatre is both one of the most ancient and the most immediate of the arts. In the Western world its beginnings go back at least as far as the ancient Greeks, around 540 B.C. and perhaps even farther. It has gone through a great many changes over the years but the one constant that tends to make it such an immediate art is the performing of or acting out of events in the same dimension of space and time occupied by the audience. In the novel or short story or even in the story recounted orally the narrator always stands between the events and the audience. The story concerns what has

Figure 1–3. The theatre makes a political comment. Terence McNally's one-act satire on the draft, *Next.* (St. Olaf College, directed by Patrick Quade, designed by Dave Boelke.)

happened in the past and the actions must be recreated in the mind of the reader or hearer. In the theatre we see the actions occuring in front of our eyes. We cannot remove ourselves, contemplate, interrupt the action, go back and reread, or flip to the end of the book. We must allow the action to develop and once it is done it cannot be recalled and reexperienced except in memory.

Eric Bentley has defined theatre at its simplest level as A playing the part of B with C looking on.[3] A great deal of children's play might therefore be considered a kind of vestigial theatre, since the child pretends to be or takes on the role of someone else, though he typically plays for himself rather than for an audience. There are two ways, however, in which Bentley's definition, though it applies to most traditional theatre in the Western world, can be criticized. First of all, a number of theatre groups in the 1960s argued that impersonation or role playing is not essential to theatre. What is important, they say, is the performing of a series of actions or tasks, whether the actor does so in his own person or in that of someone else. This is a subject to which we shall return in a later chapter. Second, it is doubtful that the audience ever merely looks on. They always participate to some extent though the degree of that participation may vary according to the situation. Jazz musicians and fans used to speak of "making the scene" at a particular club or concert, implying that the presence and response of the audience as well as the particular combination of musicians on the stand created the music. In a similar sense actors and audience together "make the scene" at a live theatre production.

There is a kind of atmosphere or electricity that is created in the live theatre that flows back and forth between stage and audience, even if the audience watches silently. It is this two-way communication that distinguishes the live theatre from film and television for, while we may be caught up in and greatly moved by a film or a TV show, we cannot communicate with a picture and the picture cannot adapt its performance to our responses. In the theatre actors and audience are formed into a kind of sharing community and some modern groups have argued again that the separation between audience and performer ought to be broken down completely, so that the audience becomes an overt and active part of the performance. Furthermore they have argued that in addition to the other functions of art which we have discussed, the theatre ought to be concerned with creating a community, not only within the theatre for the span of the play but after the performance and outside the theatre.

To increase our appreciation of the theatre, like increasing our appreciation for food, drink, sport, or other forms of art, is to provide another element of pleasure that makes life richer and fuller. It is the aim of this book to increase that appreciation by helping its readers to understand what theatre attempts to do, how it does it, and how to judge whether it has been done well. Of course no book can do this by itself. Just as we can have no appreciation of music if we never hear any, we cannot appreciate the theatre unless we take every opportunity to see plays in performance, whether produced by professional companies, colleges and universities, community theatres, or high schools. Reading about the theatre can be a great help, but it is no substitute for experiencing it. If this book succeeds in its aim it should attract its readers into the theatre and should make theatre going a more pleasurable and rewarding activity for them.

Notes

[1]E. E. Cummings, *Poems, 1923–1954* (New York: Harcourt Brace and World, Inc., 1951). Reprinted by permission.

[2]Harold Clurman, *The Fervent Years* (New York: Hill & Wang, 1957), p. 138.

[3]Eric Bentley, *The Life of the Drama* (New York: Athenaeum, 1967), p. 150.

2

THE LANGUAGE OF THEATRE

ART COMMUNICATES. This much is common to all of the functions of art discussed in the previous chapter. Whether it involves a wider sense of life, an expression of emotion, the posing and the tentative answering of one of the eternal questions, or a propagandistic message concerning social, moral, economic or political issues, art communicates something.

Everyday communication begins with an impulse to convey or to express something. That something may be an emotion or a response to a physical sensation ("Damn it," "Ouch!" "I love you"); a bit of information ("Go three blocks and turn left"); a perception or an insight ("I think this part ought to go here"; "It seems to me your trouble is an inferiority complex"); or a quite abstract and complicated idea ("The square of the hypotenuse of a right triangle is equal to the sum of the squares of the other two sides"). That communication is carried on through a set of symbols which is arranged into a system or code. Signal flags, dots and dashes, the hand movements in sign language are all symbols and when we put them together in certain sequences they make up a code.

Most of man's everyday communication is carried on through a system of visible and audible symbols that we call language. It consists of a group of sounds that we arrange into sequences to form words, phrases, and sentences. The arrangements of those sounds and words must follow certain patterns that are accepted by the speakers of the language in order to convey meaning. Thus, the letters chri in English can be combined phonetically as /krI/ or /krai/ — but tbgxl cannot be combined phonetically at all. Similarly, a combination of words such as "I the horse in the barn some hay must give" makes sense but sounds very strange in English, though it would not sound at all strange in German. A combination such as "blue high birds the flying sky the in are" makes no sense and can be arranged to convey two different meanings. In speech this system is further supplemented by such nonverbal elements as stress, pitch, pause, loudness, body position, facial expression and gesture.

Art, too, begins with an impulse to express something, though what it is that the artist wants to express may not be absolutely clear to him at the outset. Like everyday communication each art has its special language made up of elements arranged in certain ways to convey a message. The painter, for example works with brushes, canvas, and paint and arranges color and line in spatial patterns. The musician works with sounds, represented on paper by musical notation, and arranges them sequentially in

15

time. We could describe each art in a similar manner. The individual art elements tend to be arranged in patterns that are more or less fixed. These patterns can be called artistic *conventions*. Artistic conventions tend to be much more flexible than languages. For example, a new perception or understanding of some aspect of reality, must be phrased according to the vocabulary and grammar of a common language. This tends to make the rate of change in language comparatively slow.

The artist can communicate most easily if he uses conventions that the audience understands. However, he may feel compelled to create a new set of conventions to express a new perception. The changes in artistic conventions can sometimes be quite sudden and drastic. One such drastic change is seen in the arbitrary breaking up of the picture planes in the work of the early cubists, Picasso and Braque (Picasso's "Ladies of Avignon" being a prime example). Similarly, composers at the beginning of the twentieth century occasionally included such things as factory whistles or sirens in their orchestrations to express their responses to the industrial age. Occasionally such drastic changes of convention have created strong reactions in the audience, as in the case of the riot that occurred when Stravinsky's "Rites of Spring" was first performed in Paris. The original artist may be ahead of the audience in their perceptions and a considerable period of time may be required for them to catch up with him. The Swedish playwright, August Strindberg, wrote a series of plays in the late nineteenth and early twentieth centuries that attempted to take the audience inside the mind of his central character and lead them to experience his fantasies, dreams, and hallucinations. These plays were generally received with hostility and puzzlement in his time and had to wait until the work of Freud and others had made the concept of the unconscious more commonly familiar to the mass audience. Today we quite easily accept scenes in plays and films that are projections of the character's mind and imagination.

Like the other arts theatre has its language made up of a variety of elements which are combined in various ways, according to certain conventions, to convey the message of the individual performance. As with the other arts those conventions have changed through the years as theatre artists have experienced reality in different ways; in our own time we probably have several sets of conventions coexisting side by side. Occasionally, as in the other arts, theatrical conventions have been drastically altered, sending theatre off in distinct new directions. In later chapters we will discuss some of those changes. Throughout the history of the theatre, however, certain elements have remained relatively constant. Those elements are: the actor, the script, a place to perform, some kind of scenic context, and an organizer of the production.

To break down the "vocabulary" of the theatre and discuss each of its individual elements, it might be well to start with the actor. This may seem a bit strange to many of us who think of plays as something to be read—a branch of literature that happens also to be designed for performance. We begin with the actor, however, for two reasons: acting precedes the written play in time and it is the one element without which we cannot have theatre.

The earliest origins of theatre are lost in prerecorded history. We first encounter it in a fairly highly developed form in ancient Greece about 540 B.C. We can only speculate about where it came from and how it developed to that point. One theory holds that it originated out of the kind of rituals that were mentioned in the previous chapter. Ceremonies dealing with the death and rebirth of the god, Dionysus, may first have come to include reenactment of various events in the story. This may have then been expanded to deal with the doings of other gods and secular heroes. By the time we find theatre among the ancient Greeks the ritual element has greatly diminished, Dionysus has almost completely disappeared and it has become a means of presenting a variety of different stories or series of events. If this theory is correct, the crucial step came at the point where the story of Dionysus began to be acted out rather than merely recited or sung. Another theory, not completely contradictory with the first, holds that theatre may have originated as a highly effective way of telling a story, though not necessarily one connected with the gods. We know that the earliest Greeks shared with many other semiprimitive peoples a rich oral tradition. Speaking, of course, originated long before writing and there are cultures existing even today that have never developed a written language. Yet these cultures possess an oral literature passed down from the elders of the tribe to the young and frequently recited or sung by "professional" story tellers. These story tellers have gone by various names, minstrel, bard, skald, etc. The semilegendary Homer, who is credited with composing the *Iliad* and the *Odyssey,* was probably one such story teller. We know also that in ancient Greece there was a class of professional story tellers known as *rhapsodes* who publicly recited the Homeric tales. Now it is just a step from *telling* a story to *acting* it and the good story teller tends at least partially to take on the character, actions, and speech patterns of the people in his story. Indeed, sometimes events almost demand to be shown rather than told, as Robert Edmond Jones points out in the following hypothetical story:

I am going to ask you to do the most difficult thing in the world – to imagine. Let us imagine ourselves back in the Stone Age, in the days of the cave man and the mammoth and the Altamira frescoes. It is night. We are all sitting together around a fire – Ook and Pow and Pung and Glup and little Zowie and all the rest of us. We sit close together. It is safer that way, if the wild beasts attack us. And besides, we are happier when we are together. We are afraid to be alone. Over on that side of the fire the leaders of the tribe are sitting together – the strongest men, the men who can run fastest and fight hardest and endure longest. They have killed a lion today. We are excited about this thrilling event. We are all talking about it. We are always afraid of silence. We feel safer when somebody is talking. . . .

The lion's kin lies close by, near the fire. Suddenly the leader jumps to his feet. "I killed the lion! I did it! I followed him! He sprang at me! I struck at him with my spear! He fell down! He lay still!"

He is telling us. We listen. But all at once an idea comes to his dim brain. "I know a better way to tell you. See! It was like this! *Let me show you!*"

In that instant drama is born.[1]

Thus, whether theatre originated out of ritual, as a natural extension of story telling, or from some other source it seems that the concept of acting out came first and only later did people sit down and deliberately write something to be acted.

Second, if we begin to define theatre by reduction—that is, by taking away all those things that we do not absolutely need in order to have theatre, we are left with only the actor. We can do without scenery, costumes, make-up, lights, properties, a theatre building, and a written script and still retain some kind of performance that we can call theatre, but if we take away the actor and leave the other elements we have nothing.

That enactment need not be based upon a written script can again be illustrated by reference both to theatre history and to contemporary practice. The ancient Greeks and the peoples who inhabited Italy before the dominance of Rome had forms of at least semi-improvised performances that are the forerunners of what we now know as comedy. In these, the humorous and frequently obscene dialogue must have been made up on the spur of the moment for the "gags" were often directed at members of the audience and at specific local situations. Some one thousand years later, in Renaissance Italy, there was an improvised form of theatre known as the *Commedia dell' Arte,* in which the actors played a set of stock characters from show to show and worked from a story outline, making up the specific dialogue as they went along. Today improvised theatre has become quite common again, especially among experimental groups, and there have been, in recent years, comedy troupes that quickly build a skit based upon suggestions shouted from the audience.

Even words are not absolutely necessary to tell a story or to convey a mood. One way to test this is to turn on your television set, turn the sound way down and see how much of the story you can follow without the dialogue. Of course you will miss some of it but a great deal is conveyed merely by action and facial expression. The mimist, Marcel Marceau, does a skit in which he acts all the characters in a courtroom scene, without a word of dialogue. Those who have seen it can testify that they have no trouble in understanding what is going on and almost seem to hear the dialogue, though none is spoken.

In spite of the fact that a *written* script is not necessary for a performance, some kind of script probably always exists and is, therefore, an important element in the theatre's language. Every performance follows a pattern of some sort and develops toward some kind of conclusion. If it did not the audience would be likely to become bored, confused, or angry and the performers would not know when to quit. The majority of such scripts are written in advance and contain dialogue for actors to memorize, but some, especially among modern experimental groups, are developed in rehearsal and others are improvised during performance. Even improvisations may tend to follow a standard pattern, especially as they are repeated several times. The actors in the *Commedia* played the same characters in a variety of standard situations, so that while the dialogue may not have been written down and memorized, it probably tended to become somewhat fixed after the show had been performed a few times. The contemporary comedy troupes referred to earlier can probably anticipate quite accurately the kinds of suggestions that they will get from the audience and therefore have at least a general idea of the structure of the skit. A script, then, defined as a pattern of development or an organizing principle is probably present in every production, improvised or not.

The majority of Western theatre has been based upon written scripts which exist separately from the performance and can be read as literature. It is important, however, that we remember that the script or written play is only the starting point for the performance and cannot be completely experienced on the printed page. An analogy may be helpful here. Music is not music until it is played. Beethoven's "Ninth Symphony" or Hoagy Carmichael's "Stardust" are merely incomprehensible marks on a piece of paper and do little or nothing for us until musicians perform them. It is harder to see this distinction with plays because while few of us can read music we can all read words. No musician, however, even though he can read the notation, would argue that music exists independently in the written score. In the same way we have not experienced the real potential of a play until we have seen it performed.

The analogy with music is helpful in another way too. The musical score indicates for the musicians what they are to play but not, except for some broad limitations, how. It will contain the notes, the key signature and a notation as to tempo, but within those limitations the musicians still have considerable freedom of interpretation. In some forms of music, such as jazz, they may depart from the written score altogether and build their own improvisations upon the chord structure. The same is true to a considerable degree of the text of a play. The actors must normally say the words in the script, but they have considerable freedom as to the meaning put on them through facial expression, loudness, rate, tone of voice and so on. To a degree the actor must portray the character as written but still has a considerable amount of latitude to interpret that character. An actor who plays Macbeth must act out the encounter with the witches, the plot to murder Duncan, the betrayal of Banquo, the slaying of Macduff's wife and children, and the final battle in which he gets killed. Nevertheless, one actor may see him as a ruthless, power hungry man who occasionally lacks the courage he needs to carry through his ambitions while another may see him as a basically decent man who is led astray by the promise of glory and the urgings of a ruthless wife. John Gielgud's Hamlet, Laurence Olivier's Hamlet and Richard Burton's Hamlet will all contain a certain core that is Shakespeare's, but each will also contain a large element that is Gielgud's, Olivier's or Burton's. The greatest dramatic characters may be those that allow the most leeway for such interpretation.

Another element of the theatre's language is the actor's and the audience's space — the stage, the performance area, the theatre building. We are accustomed to seeing a play occur on a raised stage while the audience sits in rows in the auditorium, separated by some distance from the action. We are used, furthermore, to having the stage brightly lighted while the audience sits in darkness and to being able to separate stage from audience by a curtain which opens and closes each act. This arrangement, however, is only one of many possible ones, and a comparatively recent development at that. It is equally possible for the audience to sit or stand all the way or most of the way around the action, to be above it, or to be right in the middle of it. A theatre, reduced to its essentials, is simply a place where actors and audience can assemble and hold a performance. It need not therefore be a building designed for theatre or even be indoors, but can be a room, a hall, a railroad coach or a park. Some modern groups have been experimenting with "found space" — performance areas that are not theatres as we normally define that word but that make possible interesting relationships between actor and audience.

We are also accustomed to sitting quietly in the theatre, registering our response only through applause at the appropriate times or, if the show is a comedy, through laughter. Thus, we might be shocked if we were sitting at the Kabuki-za in Toyoko to see a spectator stand up and shout encouragement or abuse at the actor, almost exactly as he would if he were at a baseball game. Such conduct, however, would not have shocked an Elizabethan audience which probably behaved in much the same way. Ancient Greek audiences, according to at least one scholar, used to drum their heels on the stone or wooden benches of their theatres to indicate disapproval of an actor or a play, and fights and disturbances apparently were common enough so that there were severe legal penalties against them. Anyone who has ever attended a children's play has seen that the children will often stand up and shout advice or warnings to the players, sometimes to the point of almost drowning the actors' voices. Black audiences, too, carry into the theatre the tradition of their church where audible responses to the preaching are expected and encouraged. Thus, at a black play one is apt to hear shouted comments and responses which encourage rather than annoy the performers. Some modern groups have attempted to encourage overt vocal and even physical participation by the spectators in the action of the play often justifying this by arguing, as suggested in the previous chapter, that theatre is a communal activity with its roots in participatory ritual. Thus, variety of both physical and psychological relationships are possible between spectator and performer and the two affect each other. The physical relationship tends to create a certain psychological one and a particular psychological relationship may demand a different kind of physical arrangement.

A performance can take place anywhere where actors and audience can assemble — in a bare room or an open outdoor space, using the natural light of the sun and with the performers wearing their everyday clothing. By far the majority of theatre performances, however, are more elaborate than that, adding to the elements of performance, script and actor-audience space, additional elements such as scenery, lighting, costume, make-up, properties and sound effects. Though we can do without all of these things and still retain a core that we can call theatre, they are not frills or superficialities. Where they are employed they are an integral part of the final product that is the theatrical performance and of the effect upon the audience which is the aim of the performance. Each can contribute to the performance in a variety of ways, depending upon the theatrical conventions at work in it. Scenery can provide a background for the actor, can function as something for him to use, can help to convey the mood or meaning of the play, or can create a total environment in which the actor seems to live. Lighting can merely make the actors visible or it can create the illusion of place, time of day or year, or it can function metaphorically to help convey the play's meaning, or it can create mood. Costume can serve to set the actor apart from the audience, to enhance or minimize his natural stature or attractiveness or to identify his character in terms of age, class, life-style, locale or period in history. Make-up can similarly beautify the actor or make him uglier or help to identify his character in terms of age, health, social status, race and even, sometimes, sex. Properties function as objects for the actor to use, as details to create an illusion of place and time, as a means of telling us about the people who use them or are surrounded by them, or even as symbols to help convey the play's meaning. Sound effects can similarly create the illusion of place, circumstances, and time, or can function powerfully to create mood. All of these things which we collectively call the technical elements have performed all or some of these functions at different periods in the theatre's history.

It is clear that someone must function to bring together and organize the actors, the script, the theatrical space, and the technical elements so that they function as a complete performance. Today that person is the director and he is frequently thought of as the master artist of the theatre — the guiding hand and mind who is responsible for the final production. The director, thought of in this way, is a relatively new development in the theatre. Even before the director, however, somone — the playwright, the leading actor, the stage manager — probably had to organize the production and make sure that all the elements worked reasonably well together.

We have spent a considerable amount of time breaking the theatre down into its separate elements and we shall consider each of them separately in subsequent chapters. It is important to remember, however, that the performed play is not merely the combination or composite of these individual elements. It is a separate thing which includes but transcends them. Perhaps if we return to our earlier analogy with language we can make this point clearer. The word "dog" is not just a combination of the sounds "duh," "aw" "guh," None of these single elements has meaning in itself; they can be combined in one other way in English to convey a distinctly different meaning and each of them can appear in a variety of other combinations. Suzanne Langer has argued that the work of art is itself a symbol with its own unique meaning, one that is not simply the sum of the individual meanings of the elements contained in it. Each performed play is, therefore, a symbol, a vision of life, and the individual elements are combined in a particular way to communicate that meaning.

Notes

[1]Robert Edmond Jones, *The Dramatic Imagination* (New York; Theatre Arts Books 1941), pp. 45–46.

Suggested Readings

BENTLEY, ERIC. *What Is Theatre*. Boston: Beacon Press, 1956. Note pp. 235–270.

JONES, ROBERT EDMOND. *The Dramatic Imagination*. New York: Duell Sloan and Pearce, 1941.

KIRBY, MICHAEL. *The Art of Time*. New York: E. P. Dutton & Co., 1969.

KNOBLER, NATHAN. *The Visual Dialogue*. New York: Holt, Rinehart & Winston, Inc., 1966.

PART TWO

THE ELEMENTS OF THEATRE

3

THE ACTOR

143011

FOR MOST PEOPLE the first thing that probably comes to mind when they think of the theatre is the actor. Indeed, if, as Bentley said, theatre is at its simplest level A playing the part of B with C looking on, it is right that the actor should be the first thing they think of. All arts, in one way or another, attempt to convey the artist's feelings, his understanding of reality, his experience in the world around him. Each art attempts to do this in a different way, through a different medium. The novelist and the poet use words, the composer sounds, the painter pigments and canvas, the sculptor stone or metal. The medium of the theatre is enactment. We can have theatre, as we said in the previous chapter, without the technical elements, without a theatre building, even without a written script; we cannot have theatre without acting. Here is one of the chief differences, too, between the live theatre and film. It is possible to have an interesting and effective film without acting, even without human beings, but this cannot be done in the theatre. The closest we come to it, perhaps, is in the Japanese puppet theatre, but even there the puppets resemble and are made to behave like human beings and the human voice is always present as a part of the performance.

A basic question, then, is "What is acting?" We can approach that question by considering 1) the nature of acting in general; 2) the actor's task in rehearsal and performance; 3) the qualities required of an actor; and 4) the nature of an actor's training.

THE NATURE OF ACTING

Some of the meanings of the verb "to act" as given by *Webster's Seventh New Collegiate Dictionary* are "to represent or perform by action esp. on the stage, FEIGN, SIMULATE, IMPERSONATE; to play the part of, as in a play; to behave in a manner suitable to; to behave as if performing on the stage, PRETEND: to take action; to perform a specified function." All of these selected definitions have in common the idea of doing something. Thus, if we say "he acts stupid," we mean that he does certain things that appear to us to be stupid. The actor, then, is first of all a *doer*. Some contemporary theatre groups have argued that it is doing — performing tasks or actions — that is fundamental to acting. The dictionary definitions, however, suggest that something more is implied by the term as it is commonly used. That something more is *seeming, pretending, impersonating.* The actor has traditionally pretended to be someone else and to be performing certain imaginary actions. Thus, there is a very close link between acting and children's play; we recognize this link when we say that the actor plays a role. Children will often read or hear a story, watch a film or television drama, and then play it, taking the various roles and either following the basic plot or acting out their own variations upon it. Children usually do this for their own amusement rather than for an audience. As adults we continue this role playing; the politician pretends to be confident though the polls are running heavily against him, the criminal feigns innocence though the police "have the goods" on him, the student pretends to be interested though he is bored stiff. The actor extends and refines this daily role playing. Through highly developed skills and much hard work, he makes of it an art.

Though we say that the actor has traditionally pretended and impersonated, we must not conclude that every actor in every period of history and every culture pretends and impersonates in exactly the same way. Raised on the "realistic" theatre and the film, we tend to think of the good actor as being able to assume the identity of the character to the extent of making us temporarily believe that he *is* really that character. Many good actors, of course, are able to do this. Hal Holbrook, in both his stage and his television appearances as Mark Twain, so completely assumes the voice, gestures, and personality of the great American humorist that it is possible to forget that we are watching an actor playing Twain. It seems that we are seeing Twain himself. Dustin Hoffman's Benjamin, in *The Graduate,* and his Ratso Rizzo, in *Midnight Cowboy,* are two distinctly different characters yet each is equally believable as is Rod Steiger's pawnbroker, in the film of that name, and his Southern police chief, in *In the Heat of the Night.* Even within this realistic tradition, however, there are variations. Many film actors and stage actors as well essentially play themselves from one role to another. Audiences come to the theatre not so much to see a fully realized character as to see a John Wayne or a Jimmy Stewart or, on the legitimate stage, a Carol Channing or an Ethel Merman. This tendency to go to the theatre to see a favorite personality is probably more common in the musical comedy, though it is not necessarily absent from the straight play. But can we say that these "personality actors" are not as good as those who more completely submerge their own personalities in their roles? To define acting as the impersonation of another human being so that we temporarily believe that the actor is the character does not take into consideration much that has been called acting at other periods in theatre history and in other cultures even today.

We tend, in our contemporary theatre, to look for realism and identification between actor and character. We use make-up to enhance that identification, to help us to believe that Hal Holbrook is Mark Twain. In contrast, ancient Greek actors and actors in the Japanese *No* theatre today wear masks which identify them as the character but get in the way of our believing that they actually are the characters. Actors in the Japanese Kabuki and in some other Oriental forms use elaborate and stylized make-up to much the same end. In the Greek theatre, the Medieval theatre, the Elizabethan theatre, and in the Japanese traditional theatre of today, male actors played all the female roles. Make-up and costume can go a long way in creating the illusion that a man is actually a woman, but they cannot create the same effect as if the female roles were played by women.

Furthermore, in many theatres of the past and in the Oriental theatre of today, actors have not even attempted to perform in such a way as to resemble real life. The Greeks acted in outdoor amphitheatres that could seat approximately fourteen thousand people. The actor may have been as much as seventy-five feet away from the *nearest* spectator and from the top row of the theatre at Epidauros the actor must have appeared to be about three inches high. Historically we do not know a great deal about Greek acting but in such a huge theatre the subtleties of voice and movement which are visible in our theatres would be completely lost. Elizabethan actors performed before a noisy brawling crowd interspersed with beggars, pickpockets, prostitutes, and food and drink vendors and had constantly to compete with the rival appeals of bull and bear baiting and public executions. It is likely that their style of playing had to be a good deal bigger, more lively, and vigorous than life in order to attract and hold the attention of this disorderly crowd. The advice which Shakespeare has

Figure 3–1. A Kabuki actor in a Genroku *mie.* (From Masakatsu Gunji, *Kabuki,* John Bester, transl. New York: Kodanska International Ltd., 1969. Photo by Chiaki Yoshida.)

Hamlet give to the players suggests that it sometimes may have become too lively and vigorous for his taste. In Japan's *No* theatre the actor intones his lines slowly in a high-pitched, artificial voice and moves very slowly through a series of stylized and conventional gestures and poses, each of which has a symbolic meaning. The action in the Kabuki is a bit more lively and fast moving but it is still highly stylized and choreographed and the dialogue is also spoken in an artificial "theatrical" style. The high spot of a Kabuki actor's performance is the *mie,* a stationary, sculptural pose every aspect of which is prescribed by tradition. The mie can safely be altered only by the most renowned and highly praised actor. There is a whole repertory of such poses: the "stone throwing" *mie,* the "around a pillar" *mie,* the "standing upright" *mie,* the "close of the curtain" *mie,* etc. Here is how Earle Ernst, a well known scholar of the Kabuki describes one of them:

> In the Genroku *mie,* supposedly invented by Ichikawa Danjuro I for use in *aragoto* (NOTE: *a special class of Kabuki play*), the right arm is extended outward and upward, the right hand is clenched in a fist, the left hand is on the sword hilt and the feet are wide apart, the right leg bent and the left leg straight.[1]

Acting, therefore, does not have to be "realistic." What we can say is that the actor performs a series of actions or tasks, that he usually does them as someone else, and that he usually does them in an imaginary situation or context.

THE ACTOR'S TASK

Even though acting styles and conventions vary and have varied widely, it is still possible to suggest that all actors of whatever time and place have certain things in common. Actors probably have a twofold task: first they must discover the essence or core of the role and second, must find the means to project that essence to the audience. Differing styles and conventions in acting can be explained in part by the fact that different ages and different cultures have perceived that essence in different ways. In approaching a dramatic character today, especially in a serious play, we are apt to be interested in his uniqueness and in the many attitudes, personality traits, and ways of behaving that set him apart from all other persons. We are likely to be interested in the many influences from the character's personal experience, going all the way back to childhood, that have made him what he is. This approach to a dramatic character tends to reflect the way we approach people in real life, outside the theatre. We tend also to be interested in the individual's personal and private relationships — the relationship of a man or woman to a job, to husband, wife, or lover, to children or parents, etc. The ancient Greeks, by contrast, tended to be interested in people in their public role and in the personal, social, and moral consequences of the things that were done and the choices that were made. They were concerned also with the manner of their response to crises, and how they tolerated both good and ill fortune. The habitual choices of characters and the ways in which they usually respond will, of course, both result from and reveal the kind of person(s) they are, so it would be incorrect to conclude that the Greeks were not interested in psychology. The difference seems to be one of emphasis and direction; we tend to emphasize explanations and reason forward to the behavior while the Greeks probably emphasized the behavior and reasoned backward to the explanations. Aristotle's writings, not only the *Poetics* but also the *Ethics,* the *Rhetoric* and the *Politics,* suggest that the Greeks saw man as possessing intrinsic moral qualities—qualities associated, at least partially, with rank or status. Thus, goodness is more likely to be the property of a king, a prince or a member of an illustrious family than it is of a common man or a slave. In the Elizabethan theatre as well one rarely finds an upperclass person presented comically and never finds a "commoner" as the hero of tragedy. Looking at both of these theatres, then, we should not be surprised to find that the actor does not view his task so much as the natural re-creation of an individual human being with all his unique quirks, mannerisms and complexities, but more as the depiction of a type that is definable by rank and status and by his visible and audible actions and words—the way he behaves and the way he responds to situations. In the Japanese *No,* influenced primarily by Buddhist thought, even though the aim of the actor was said to be identity or "truthful imitation," he approaches his role differently than does the typical Western actor:

> The *No* actor does not seek naturalistic re-creation of one individual person or object in its entirety. He seeks, rather, an identification with the interior, essential traits of a universalized character or type, such as the old man, the warrior, the beautiful court lady, the monk.[2]

Our approach to human character, both in the theatre and outside it, is a product of a number of influences: democracy, the rise of the middle class, the Romantic movement in literature and the arts and especially of the work of Sigmund Freud and other depth psychologists around the turn of the century. It was given great impetus in the theatre by the work of Russian actor and director named Konstantin Stanislavski. Prompted by his own difficulties in acting and by the work of famous actors he had seen—especially the Italian, Tomasso Salvini—Stanislavski evolved a "system" to help the actor discover and portray the truth in his role. A large part of that system, probably the part that is best known, involved a method that the actor could employ in discovering the essence of his role. Though it is only one approach and probably works most effectively with the realistic play, it is useful to consider it as an aid to understanding this aspect of the actor's task.

Discovering the Essence of the Role

The first step for the actor is to study the script. Since the bulk of Western theatre, and probably all of the theatre with which Stanislavski was concerned, has been based upon the written script, this means that the actor reads the play. His first reading will be for the purpose of understanding the shape and direction of the total action and how his character functions within it. Having done that, he can then focus upon the primary motivating factor in his character's actions. What does he want? Why does he want it? What is he willing to do to get it? In many plays, especially those we label realistic, the character has a goal, something he is trying to achieve or to obtain through all of his actions. This single overriding goal is sometimes referred to as the character's "spine," sometimes as his "super-objective." Whatever it is called, it can usually be phrased as an infinitive with an active verb. The character wants "to" something. Thus, in Tennessee Williams' *The Glass Menagerie,* Amanda's spine might be "to hold my family together," while that of Tom and Laura might be "to escape from reality," though each attempts that latter spine in a different way. The spine must always be an action—something that can be done—since, as Stanislavsky argued, you cannot act an emotion or a state of being; you can only act actions that will lead the audience to certain conclusions about your condition or your emotions. Whatever spine the actor or actress comes up with must be discovered by a close reading of the play and be justifiable on the basis of suggestions within the text. This does not mean, however, that there is only one possible interpretation of a character. Two actresses playing Ibsen's Hedda Gabler, for instance, might discover two rather different spines—"to have power over another human being" and "to obtain my freedom"—and both can be justified from the text. Having discovered the spine the actor must then go back to the text and try to discover his character's goal or objective within each of the individual scenes in which he appears. These individual goals or objectives will be related to, but not necessarily identical with the spine. For example, in various scenes of *The Glass Menagerie* Amanda's specific objective is "to find a gentleman caller" for Laura. This is related to, but obviously not identical with, her spine, "to hold my family together." Now the actor can go back and reread the play attempting to discover the "why" of his character's objectives and behaviour. What details in the script might account for what the character wants, why he goes about seeking it the way he does, why he wants it. The actor may fill in the gaps left by the playwright with his own imagination, but it should be stressed

31

again that his imagination should always be based upon and stimulated by hints, however subtle, provided by the playwright. The following analysis of the character of Martha from Edward Albee's *Who's Afraid of Virginia Woolf?,* though done from a director's rather than an actor's standpoint, may help to clarify this process:

> SPINE: to punish George (for loving her? for failing to measure up to Daddy? for accepting? for all three?)
>
> From the very beginning of the play we see Martha on the attack. She seems intent on humiliating George, both when they are alone together and when others are present. It would be very easy to make her a bitch with no sympathetic qualities at all — which is dangerous. She is cruel, loud, crude, vulgar, aggressively sexy — but the crucial question is why? Has she always been that way or was she driven to it? What information can we derive from the script? Martha is the daughter of the president of the college. She and George have been married twenty-three years and she is six years older than he is. According to George she went to a convent school when she was a little girl but that may be one of his stories. According to her own testimony she subsequently went to "Miss Muff's Academy for Young Ladies" — she refers to it as a college but the name suggests a kind of finishing school. . . . While there she was briefly married to a gardener's boy but her father had the marriage anulled and had her removed from school. Apparently she didn't finish college unless she did so at home — but she says she just sort of "sat around." Martha does not mention her mother. George says Martha's mother died and her father remarried but later says maybe that isn't true. At any rate, Martha refers only to her father, whom she calls "Daddy." For a middle-aged (52) woman to refer to her father as Daddy seems slightly ludicrous and suggests a possible hang-up. She seems, most of the time, inordinately fond of Daddy and proud of him. "I was hostess for Daddy and I took care of him . . . and it was . . . nice. It was very nice." If Martha's mother died when she was a little girl and her father didn't remarry till she was grown, or the second wife also died when she was young (or alternatively, George's story is false and he never remarried), Martha grew up in a household where her father was the central figure. She "took care of him" — like a wife, perhaps. Martha didn't get married for real until she was at least twenty-nine. Why not? There are three possibilities:
>
> 1) She wasn't very attractive. Some of her lines suggest this. "I wasn't the albatross," "for (George) having seen me and said 'Yes, *this will do.*'"
> 2) Her father wouldn't allow her to marry anyone who didn't come up to his expectations. His action with the gardener's boy and his concern with picking an heir apparent might substantiate this.
> 3) She worshipped her father and compared every man she met with him. Again, there is a good deal in the text to substantiate this.[3]

Of course the actress who plays Martha may not write out such a formal analysis, but her thinking about the role is apt to proceed pretty much along these lines. Having done this much analysis the actor may go back to the script yet again and attempt to discover the "subtext," a term that can mean both the psychological/emotional motivations underlying a particular set of actions and the unspoken thoughts and feelings that are going through the character's mind while the lines of the text are being spoken.

What has been described thus far is preparatory work. All or most of it may be done by the actor in isolation long before rehearsals of the play begin. The process of discovery is not, however, necessarily completed in this preparatory stage. It goes on during rehearsal and is deepened and enriched by new insights achieved by the actor and by suggestions from the director and other actors.

There is a school of acting that would reject all or much of Stanislavski's approach. The external or "technique" school of acting would argue that it is only necessary that the actor intellectually understand what the character does and says in the play, that he understands the ways in which emotions are vocally and physically conveyed and that he possess the highly developed control of voice and body to be able effectively to project that behavior and emotion to the audience. Some directors, such as the late Tyrone Guthrie, have asserted that the "Method," as Stanislavski's approach came to be known in America, is useful primarily with the realistic play dealing with middle class characters, while to play the classics a firm command of technique is much more important.[4] It is probably true that Stanislavski's system works better with realistic plays than with other types and that for some plays—the typical Broadway farce, for example—such in-depth analysis is not even necessary. It is also true that in order effectively to portray the characters in Greek and Elizabethan classics, a command of vocal and physical technique is required which many American-trained "Method" actors lack. At the same time it is probably true that for most good plays, including the classics, some such analysis is helpful and that it should be combined with a solid grasp of the necessary techniques.

Projecting the Essence to the Audience

It is possible to discuss the actor's task of projecting the essence of his role to the audience in terms of three relationships: actor-character, actor-material and actor-audience. The nature of those relationships will again be determined by the conventions of the individual's theatre and historical period and also by the nature of the material—the play with which the actor is working. Each of these relationships is probably best thought of as a continuum between extremes at some point along which the actor is able to locate a particular method of projection.

At one end of the actor-character continuum, the actor can seek the closest possible identification with the character. It is impossible for an actor to literally *become* the character being portrayed, but he can seek to share to the greatest degree possible, the character's feelings, ways of thinking and reacting, and modes of behavior. The actor's aim is to make his own personality disappear within that of the character he is playing. Much of the preparatory work we have just described is aimed toward achieving that end. Once he completely understands the character, however, he still has the problem of how to bring about an identification between himself and that character. There is a great gap, for example, between an emotionally stable young college actress and the neurotic, middle-aged Martha. Again, Stanislavski had some suggestions to help the actor achieve this identification. Much of what the actor has discovered about the character through analysis can be called the "given circumstances" of the play. To this Stanislavski adds the element of "if" – in simple terms the actor asks himself, "what would I do *if* I were this character in these circumstances?" To further aid his identification, the actor may look to his own experience for situations comparable to those he is asked to play. Let us use a hypothetical example. Suppose that a young college actor is asked to play the role of an Irish peasant being abused by his English landlord. The character resents the abuse and hates the landlord but for his own safety he must conceal his resentment and hatred. The actor has obviously never been an Irish peasant but he may have experienced a similar relationship with a teacher, with a high school principal, with an employer or, if he has been in the military service, with a sergeant. Thus, the actor is able to employ both feelings and behavior in that situation as a kind of springboard to the situation in the play.

Farther along the continuum, the actor may stand slightly apart from his character. He does not seek close emotional identification but a degree of understanding and he may be more concerned with discovering the appropriate physical and vocal attributes of his character than with his psychological complexities. The famous British actor, Laurence Olivier, has been quoted as saying that he finds the key to his character as soon as he finds the right nose.[4] For another actor it may be the character's walk or a peculiarity of speech that provides the key. Standing still farther from the character, the actor may be concerned primarily with vocal and physical skills and with the effect to be produced. That is, there is less concern with identification or even with understanding which leads to the creation of a believable character than with striking the proper pose or employing the proper vocal inflection that will produce the thrill of horror or the burst of laughter from the audience. At the farthest extreme, perhaps, is the totally stylized performance such as one finds in the Kabuki or the No, where the actor is concerned with practicing and perfecting a set of conventional and traditional skills, gestures and poses. In the Western theatre this actor-character relationship may be present in the kind of mime practiced by Marcel Marceau or perhaps in grand opera.

We have discussed, perhaps somewhat vaguely, a series of different possible relationships between the actor and the character but we should offer two qualifications. First of all, no value judgments are intended about any of these relationships. That is, it should not be concluded that one is necessarily better than another. The value or usefulness of each may vary with the kind of material, the kind of theatre, even with the individual actor. Second, we are talking about comparatively subtle distinctions. The differences at the extreme ends of the scale may be quite obvious but within the continuum it may not be readily discernible to the audience whether the actor identifies completely or stands slightly apart, especially if the actors are skilled and the material similar.

A second set of relationships is that between the actor and his material, and this one can be discussed more easily. Does the actor wish to have his material taken for a representation of real life or does he wish it to be seen as spectacle or show? Does he himself take it seriously and expect his audience to do so or is he playing with it? Again we have a continuum and again the point along that continuum at which the actor chooses to operate may be partly governed by convention. At one extreme is the objective of causing the audience temporarily to believe that they are watching events from real life transpiring before their eyes. Somewhat further along the continuum, we may find the depiction of real emotions and situations but not the complete illusion of real life. The chorus in Greek tragedy, and the use of poetry in both Greek and Elizabethan drama serve to remind the spectator that he is not watching actual events but a play. The actor's mode of projecting character to audience will vary, then, with the point along this continuum at which his material falls. If the intent is to represent the illusion of real life, speech, body movements, gestures and facial expressions will all be aimed as much as possible at reproducing the behavior of real people in real situations. If, on the other hand, he is acting in a Greek or Elizabethan play, he may be concerned with conveying the real emotion but also with the poetry and the sense of vocal and physical grandeur that is present in drama of that type; he must move and speak in a different way. At the extreme again, if the vehicle is primarily show or spectacle, he may employ frankly unreal styles of speaking, moving and gesturing. Perhaps once again the traditional Oriental theatre serves as a good example here. Another dimension of this relationship, though perhaps a more subtle one, is the seriousness of the material. Playing comedy, even if it is cast in realistic form, probably always requires that the actor stand a little aside from the material and share the joke with the audience, and it always requires that the actor pay close attention to correct stressing and pacing of the line or gesture so as to get the desired laugh.

The third relationship is that between actor and audience and the extremes here are easy to discern. At the one extreme is the realistic play in which the actor essentially pretends that the audience is not there at all; at the other he plays directly to them. Between the two are various degrees of acknowledging the audience's presence and sharing with them. In comedy, for example, the actor not only "points" the line and gesture, as mentioned above, but he waits for the audience's laughter to subside before going on. The plays of Shakespeare provide the possibility both for ignoring the audience in dialogue scenes and for talking directly to them in soliloquies and asides, though even in the scenes where the audience is not directly played to it is probably never ignored as totally as it is in serious realistic drama. At the other extreme, some modern groups have not only talked directly to the audience and even argued with them, they have taken members of the audience into the playing area and made them part of the scene.

Obviously, these three relationships overlap. The actor who wishes as completely as possible to create the illusion of real life is likely to try to immerse himself completely in the character and to ignore the audience. The actor-character, actor-material, and actor-audience ratios influence one another. No matter what the exact degree of those relationships the actor on the stage must be concerned with projecting vocally and physically so that the entire audience can see, hear and understand what is going on. This might introduce a fourth relationship, actor-theatre. All stage acting probably requires a degree of heightening or exaggeration, the amount depending upon the size and shape of the theatre in which the play is done. Here is another significant difference between theatre and film. The tiniest change of facial expression can be picked up by the camera close-up and the most softly whispered sentence can be caught by the

Figure 3–2. Actors perform "presentationally" to audience. (*Godspell*, Slippery Rock State College, directed by Milton Carless, designed by Raymond Wallace. Company photographer Michael F. Sunderman.)

microphone suspended overhead. The stage actor must make sure that the audience sees and hears his performance and the acting that is perfectly acceptable in a large theatre might look ridiculously exaggerated on the screen. The problem for the actor is to determine exactly how much heightening is necessary for the type of play he is doing, for the desired relationship with the audience, and the size, shape and configuration of the theatre in which he is working.

To project the essence of his character to the audience the actor has two tools — his voice and his body. No matter how well he understands the role or how deeply he identifies with it, he will not be successful unless he has the necessary skill in the effective use of those tools to convey what he understands or feels to the audience. Many actors and directors insist, therefore, that the actor must keep a constant check on himself. He maintains a kind of dual personality, on one level portraying the character and on the other constantly listening for his cues, adjusting his timing, checking his body positions and his vocal tone and maintaining a readiness to adjust to an unexpected reaction from the audience or from his fellow actors. This is true even of the actor who attempts to immerse himself deeply in his character, though the proportion of actor-character duality obviously varies along that continuum. The actor who becomes so completely "carried away" that he forgets he is acting is probably not a very good one.

THE QUALITIES OF AN ACTOR

What, then, is required to be an actor? Are actors very special people endowed with a mysterious "talent" which the rest of us can only envy? It might be rash to say that anyone can be an actor, but there are probably more potential actors in the world than we suspect. This chapter began with an analogy between children's play and acting. Indeed, children at play seem to be natural actors. At least they seem to need little help or encouragement to enter totally into an imaginative situation, especially if they are not conscious of being watched by critical adults. The child has a free and active imagination, but as he grows older he is subjected to the sanctions and injunctions of society, first from his parents, then from his teachers, and even from his peers: "Don't show off!" "Don't act silly!" "Boys don't cry!" "Young ladies don't act like that!" etc., etc. By the time he is ready for junior high school he is equipped with a full-blown set of inhibitions so that, as one acting teacher put it, the first challenge in an acting class is to get the student to overcome all those forces in society that say to him, "Don't be an actor." This is not to say that all manners and societal restraints should be cast aside, but the unfortunate side effect of much social conditioning is the killing of the first requisite for an actor, or indeed a creative individual, the imagination. There is a delightful line in Dylan Thomas's *A Child's Christmas in Wales* which suggests how this inhibiting process affects the visual arts as well. In remembering his childhood Christmas presents, the adult narrator recalls, "a painting book in which I could make the grass, the trees, the sea and the animals any color I pleased, and still the dazzling sky-blue sheep are grazing in the red fields under the rainbow-billed and pea-green birds."[5]

If the first requisite of an actor is imagination, the second is sensitivity—the ability to feel into the situations of others. Once again, our society tends somewhat to discourage the overt display of emotion, so that to become too excited over anything, whether a sunset or an airplane crash, is regarded as unsophisticated or bad form. One is expected to keep both positive and negative emotions under some degree of control, though these sanctions are probably slightly less severe on women than they are on men. It may be, then, that not only our ability to express our emotions, but even our capacity to feel deeply about situations that do not directly affect us has tended somewhat to wither away. This effect may even be heightened by the constant diet of tragedy and horror with which we are bombarded through the mass media. The actor, however, must be able to feel not only those things which affect him directly but he must be able to enter imaginatively into the feelings of others. Another way of putting it might be to say that the actor must wear his emotions very close to the surface. This is not to say that all actors must constantly run around in a state of emotional excitement or hysteria. In their private lives they may be just as conventional as lawyers, plumbers, or members of any other occupational group. It does imply, however, that they are likely to be less rigid and more open to experience than most others.

The third quality which is necessary for anyone who wishes to be an actor is simply the willingness to work very hard. It is perhaps the most important quality. Many people are attracted by the supposed glamor of the theatre, by the fact that it looks like fun, or by the adulation and applause that actors seem to earn. Such people frequently drift away again when they learn that actors spend long hours rehearsing in dingy, poorly lighted, ill heated theatres and, after rehearsals are finished, have only energy enough to go home and flop into bed. Acting involves the same hard work and dedication as any other art or profession, perhaps more than some. Not only does the actor spend hours of rehearsal on a specific show, but if he is to be a truly accomplished actor he spends long years perfecting his skill with his instrument just as does, for example, a concert violinist. The tradition of thorough training for an actor has not been as strong in the United States as it has in Europe and the Orient. Stanislavski's actors, who spent a great deal of time using his system to develop their imagination and sensitivity, were also thoroughly trained in voice, speech, acrobatics, dancing and fencing. British actors, too, spend a great deal of time on these skills. The Japanese Kabuki actor, until recently, began his training as a child of five and was not considered to be a truly accomplished actor until around the age of fifty. That may be a bit extreme but the fact remains that any actor must be willing to work hard for years at perfecting his art. One who is not willing to devote that kind of dedication to his art should probably confine himself to dabbling in the theatre or should stay away from it altogether and seek his satisfaction, praise, and adulation elsewhere. He should certainly not think of becoming a professional actor. Stanislavski put it well when he told his actors, "Love the art in yourselves, not yourselves in the art."

THE ACTOR'S TRAINING

Actors' training programs have varied widely and continue to do so as the stress has shifted from feeling to technical skill, from psychological exploration to vocal and bodily control. There is now, however, almost universal agreement among acting teachers that, whatever the particular approach used, the actor needs a thorough program of training and that that training should include stress upon both his "inner state" and his vocal and physical skills. Such a program will typically involve development of the several phases of the actor's instrument and his craft: his imagination and sensitivity, his voice and speech, his body and movement and his ability to come to grips with, understand, and communicate a text.

In developing the actor's inner state — his imagination his sensitivity and his ability to use his emotions, a necessary first step is relaxation. The actor must learn to free himself of the tensions that he brings to the rehearsal or to the acting class from the outside world and he must get rid of the inhibitions that his society and upbringing have programmed into him. This is so vital because the actor is required by his art to do publicly and regularly things that our society has taught us to be reluctant to do. He puts himself on display, reveals his most private thoughts and feelings and engages in the most intimate of situations before hundreds or thousands of viewers. One of the currently most popular approaches to this problem is the "theatre games" method pioneered by Viola Spolin. It proceeds from the premise stated earlier that children are natural actors or "players" until societal pressures begin to stifle their creativity. According to teachers who follow this approach, the best way to develop the actor's creativity and imagination is to return him to a childlike state and this can best be done by having him do childlike things. To achieve such relaxation and freedom from inhibition a free atmosphere in the acting class is necessary and to create this atmosphere much depends upon the personality of the teacher. The student must feel that he is being helped, that his progress is being evaluated but that he himself is not being ridiculed or condemned, either by his teacher or by his fellow students.

There are a number of exercises which the student might do in order to develop this state of relaxation. He might begin, for example, by lying on his back on the floor, with his eyes closed going through a sequence of tensing and relaxing of individual muscles, beginning with the toes and working up to the face. He then might be asked to play "marionette" in which he imagines he is a puppet held up by strings attached to various parts of his body and then imagine each of the strings being relaxed or tightened. Having done this, he might be asked to move around the room in a circle letting himself flop like a rag doll. There are too many such exercises or variants of them to discuss them all. Whatever methods are used the actor must learn to attain a state of *creative* relaxation—not a lethargy but rather a condition of relaxation from which he can generate the required actions of the classroom exercises or of the role in a play with spontaneity and without strain.

Another aspect of the development of the inner state is observation. The actor must learn fully to use his senses, first with real and then with imagined stimuli and he must learn to concentrate fully on those senses and the stimuli which aroused them. A story is told that a young man once came to the great Norwegian playwright, Henrik Ibsen, and asked him what he had to do to become a writer. Ibsen casually asked the color of the wallpaper in the young man's room. When he couldn't reply Ibsen became furious and shouted at him in words to this general effect, "You want to be a writer and you can't describe your own room? To write is, first of all, to *see*." What Ibsen said to the would-be writer applies equally well to the prospective actor, though we should add that he must also be able to hear, to smell, to taste, and to feel. Again there are exercises which are designed to stimulate the senses. The student may be asked to lie on the floor with eyes closed and to catalogue all the sounds he hears. The effect of such an exercise is to make him aware of the fact that he usually does not hear most of the sounds around him because he selectively perceives—he eliminates all of those sounds which are not important to him. Similarly, he might be asked to look carefully at and describe his surroundings, a specific object, another person, perhaps a part of his own body. He may be asked to catalogue and identify smells, to identify and describe objects on the basis of touch, etc. From these exercises with real objects he can be led on to reacting to imaginary stimuli; he might, for example, be asked to listen to imaginary music or to react to the smell of an imaginary campfire.

The actor must also learn to trust and to interact with other people. One approach to this end, which can easily be combined with the sort of exercises we have been describing, has been borrowed from *gestalt* therapy, sensitivity training, and other recent developments in psychotherapy. A beginning exercise might be the trust circle, in which one person gets in the middle of a circle of five or six others, relaxes and lets himself fall. The others are to catch him and move him around the circle. The aim of this exercise, of course, is to lead the prospective actor to trust and rely upon his fellows. Many people are quite rigid and untrusting the first time they attempt it and if the aim is to be achieved it is vital that the members of the circle stay alert and do not allow the person in the middle to fall or to hurt himself. Later the class might progress to other sensitivity exercises in which the members are asked to look intently at each other or to explore each other by touch. Still later they might be asked to perform actions in conjunction with each other, perhaps merely patterned movement at first and later activities that involve imagination. Students might, for example, hold a tug of war without a rope or play a game of dodge ball with an imaginary ball. Obviously such exercises are cumulative because here the students must not only work together but must imagine and must recall the feel of the rope and the size and weight of the ball.

The preceding exercises have already led us toward the next step, which can be called "Let's Pretend." Playing children's games such as dodge ball can lead on to pantomiming imaginary activities — simple ones at first, such as washing a car, sorting the laundry, shining a pair of shoes. To these activities the teacher may add "given circumstances," a context or situation in which they are done, thus providing the student an opportunity to imagine not only a physical activity but an emotional state as well. A next logical step might be the development of improvisations in which the students take various roles in a situation or "mini-plot" and make up the dialogue as they go along. All of this is moving the student closer to the task of developing characters and situations from plays at the same time that it is developing imagination and sensitivity.

The actor's inner state is, however, only part of his equipment and a major complaint against American teachers of the Stanislavski system is that they have focused almost entirely on that part and ignored the others. A thorough training program must deal also with the actor's voice and body.

In the Western theatre at least, a good deal of the actor's time on stage is spent speaking lines. It stands to reason, therefore, that he should have a trained and flexible voice and good diction. A minimum requirement is being able to speak clearly and distinctly with sufficient volume to be heard, with no obvious and distracting regional accent, in a voice that is not harsh or unpleasant. The stage actor has the problem also of having to make himself heard and understood often in a large theatre and sometimes when the circumstances of the play indicate that he should be speaking in low tones or even in a whisper. In addition to these minimum requirements the actor may often have to employ a regional or a foreign dialect and thus, he needs to understand the sound system and intonation patterns not only of English, but of English spoken with a variety of dialects. He may also be called upon to alter the quality and timbre of his voice for age, hoarseness, ill health, or a variety of other factors, or may be called upon to sing, either reasonably well or deliberately badly. All of these skills are required for playing realistic drama. When he plays classic drama, such as Shakespeare, he should be able to use his voice as a musical instrument to convey not only the exact shadings of meaning but also the sound value of the poetry. For many years the American actor has been somewhat deficient in these respects, while British trained actors are usually superb.

To be able to do all these things requires a varied program of training. The actor must first of all learn to relax his vocal apparatus and free it of tension. He must then learn breath control, in much the same way as does a singer, not only so that he can project but in order to sustain his voice through a long line or a long speech. Singing lessons can be valuable here as can other disciplines such as Yoga. He must also master the sound system of his own language, studying phonetics and learning both to hear

Figure 3–3, 3–4, 3–5. Actor training exercises—from Robert Benedetti, *The Actor at Work* (Englewood Cliffs, N.J.: Prentice-Hall, Inc., 1970). Photos by R. Benedetti.

Figure 3–3

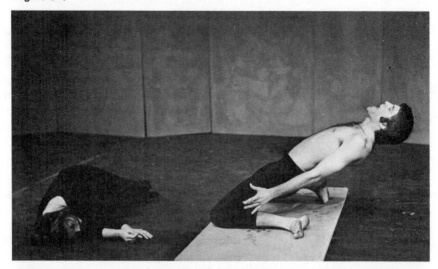

Figure 3–4

and to reproduce the precise differences between sounds. In order to be able to articulate clearly and rapidly he must drill constantly on pronouncing nonsense syllables, lists of words, phrases and sentences at varying rates of speed. He must also learn vocal control so that he can alter his pitch, volume, rate, and stress at will to convey subtle shades of meaning and to create specific emotional effects. Again this requires practice and drill under a variety of circumstances and often involves breaking down old speech patterns and replacing them with new ones.

But we communicate, as scholars are making us more aware, not only through words, but through a variety of nonverbal means. Professor Ray Birdwhistel and others have been doing research in an area called kinesics—the study of significant or communicative body movement. A popularized version of their studies has been reported in Julius Fast's book, *Body Language*. In a sense, of course, actors have known for years that the body and its use is an important part of their total instrument. We communicate a good deal about the kind of people we are by the way we stand, move, sit, gesture and handle objects. Watch, for example, the way people of different occupations, say a jeweler and a carpenter, handle their eating utensils. Notice the walk of a soldier, a freight handler, an athlete, a cowboy, a nurse. A. Conan Doyle's fictional detective, Sherlock Holmes, was able almost completely to characterize a person by the way he walked, stood, and gestured. Our movement can also reveal a great deal about our moods and about the way we react to persons, objects, or situations. A great deal of the actor's communication takes place through movement and therefore, he needs to be able to control and manipulate his own body.

Figure 3–5

Figure 3-6. Notice how facial expression and body position convey a message without words. *A Midsummer Night's Dream:* (Hilberry Theatre, Wayne State University, directed by Richard Spear, scenery by Russell Smith, costumes by Vic Leverett, and lighting by Gary M. Witt.)

Physical Training

In addition to its importance for communication, the actor's body needs to be trained for another reason. Many roles of the actor demand great stamina and endurance. This is obvious in the swashbuckling adventure films which were made by Errol Flynn or Douglas Fairbanks Jr., but it is probably even more true of the stage actor. In Albee's *Who's Afraid of Virginia Woolf?,* for example, the two leading characters are on stage almost constantly during approximately two hours and forty-five minutes of playing time. During much of that time they are involved in highly emotional scenes involving quite a bit of physical activity. Even though there are no acrobatics, no sword or fist fights and no swinging on ropes or leaping from buildings, the energy expended is considerable and the actors are likely to be exhausted by the time the final curtain closes. Similarly, in the "Interview" segment of Van Itallie's *America Hurrah!* the eight actors are in almost constant movement for approximately thirty-five minutes; they almost never sit or stand still. The film actor can shoot physically active scenes in bits and pieces or can employ a stunt man or stand-in; the stage actor must do the scenes himself and must sustain his energy for the length of the performance. It is obvious, then, that the actor needs physical conditioning just to sustain the demands placed upon him by the playing of the role.

44 In the past the development of the actor's body consisted chiefly of

training in dance, fencing, and perhaps acrobatics. These are valuable skills, for the actor may need to know how to dance, how to fight with a variety of weapons, and how to make leaps or take falls without getting hurt. Current actor training, however, is recognizing that those activities are somewhat limiting in themselves.

Teachers of acting today are becoming aware that any physical training program for the actor must not concentrate exclusively upon the development of the body. The human being is a totality not a separable body, a separable mind, a separable set of emotions. Contemporary actor training, then, tends to aim at developing in the actor a total control of his apparatus which involves both physical activity and complete mental concentration. Jack Clay, writing in *The Drama Review,* refers to this approach as "self-use," and defines it as " . . . preparation for expressive-use. It is a fundamental understanding of one's physical self in the here and now that makes possible intelligent work."[6] In theory it is similar to the concepts underlying Oriental physical practice such as Yoga or the martial arts.

The practice of the actor's physical training takes many forms and much of it is frankly experimental as teachers and their students work through a variety of systems or techniques to find one or a combination of several that seems to yield results. Many of the exercises described earlier for developing imagination and sensitivity involve physical activity. For a more systematic approach many acting teachers have turned to the East, employing Yoga, Oriental theatre techniques such as the Indian *Kathakali* dance forms, *Kung fu* and *Karate,* and a Chinese exercise form called *T'ai-chi-ch'uan.* This last seems particularly interesting since it involves a series of 108 forms which are performed very slowly and smoothly and blend subtly into one another. The aim of *T'ai-chi* is to produce not only physical stamina and flexibility but a kind of body-mind harmony which involves total concentration and calmness. In China it has been the basic exercise for centuries for boxers as well as for actors and dancers. Another direction, has been backward to the nineteenth century and the work of Francois Delsarte, a Frenchman who developed a system of codified gestures and movements to express specific emotions. Delsarte was extremely popular in his own time both with actors and with public speakers, but for much of this century he has tended to be scoffed at. Within the last few years, however, he has been rediscovered and reevaluated by actors and teachers. The specific gestures he emphasized may have become cliches – the folding of the hands for supplication or entreaty, for example – but the notion that there is an organic connection between our emotions and the way we move and gesture, and the idea that there are conventional patterns of movement that, within a particular culture, convey emotional states, are valid ones. The American, for instance, may scratch or shake his head to convey puzzlement; the Japanese will suck air in between his teeth. Professor Birdwhistel's studies in kinesics have shown that the attempt to discover and teach a set of conventional

Figure 3–7. Actors' warm-up exercises for *Godspell*. (Slippery Rock State College, Milton Carless director, designed by Raymond Wallace, company photographer Michael F. Sunderman.)

communicative gestures and postures may be a worthwhile enterprise. Still another approach is that of employing exercises from the dance, mime and gymnastics, but always blending them into sequences of movement that are best suited to the actor's purposes. Such a system is the *exercises plastiques* employed by Jerzey Grotowski in his Polish Laboratory Theatre. Whatever the specific approach, the aim of all such conditioning is to give the actor complete control over his/her total organism.

In addition to developing an inner state and his physical and vocal equipment the actor must know how to deal with the text, whether written or not. He must know how to discover the basic action and the sequence of smaller actions that comprise it. He must learn how to discover the rhythm of the script and, if he is dealing with a written text, the rhythm of the individual lines and speeches. He must learn how to analyze character and how to "read between the lines" to discover possible unspoken meanings. Since an actor may be called upon to perform it he must understand the structure of poetic drama and how the poetic qualities of the written line are translated into speech. Here the best training approach is probably to work with a variety of texts, analyzing and taking them apart to a much greater degree than by studying them as literature and then putting them back together and playing them, always under the guidance of a skillfull teacher.[7]

What we have considered in the preceding discussion is not so much a real or perhaps even a typical actor training program, but rather the major areas of concern upon which such a program should focus and some of the ways in which it has been or might be done. As with any other subject or skill, no two teachers will approach their task in quite the same way, but all acting teachers should be aiming at the same goals and concerning themselves with the same phases of the actor's art. Obviously such a thorough training program takes a great deal of time, but there is no reason to believe that an actor should be able to master his art any more easily or quickly than can a singer, a dancer, or an instrumentalist.

Acting is central to the theatre because without it the theatre would not exist. It is, of course, only one element of the theatre's language. The actor must act something, he must act in some place, and he usually does so in some kind of scenery under some kind of light, employs some kind of costume and make-up, uses some sort of properties and perhaps sound effects. The aim of the actor, together with all the other elements of the theatre, is to create on the stage a vision of human life, though that need not imply a literal realism. Acting is difficult to judge and evaluate for two reasons. First of all, the actor employs, most obviously in realistic drama, the same tools we employ in everyday life — voice and body, speech and movement. It may, therefore, be difficult to distinguish between the actor as creator of a character and the personality who always plays himself or plays a particular type to which he is suited. Second, like dancing, pole vaulting or many other activities, when acting is well done it looks easy. We have seen that there is a great deal involved in acting. It demands dedication, study, hard work and a set of highly developed skills. To see fine acting in the live theatre is a great thrill, all the more so when we know what has gone into developing the actor and the performance we are witnessing.

Figure 3–8. Student actors rehearse Arthur Miller's *The Crucible.* (Eastern Montana College.)

Notes

[1] Earle Ernst, *The Kabuki Theatre* (New York: Grove Press, 1956), p. 179.

[2] Benito Ortolani, "Zeami's Aesthetics of the No and Audience Participation," *Educational Theatre Journal,* 24 (May, 1972): 111.

[3] The above is an expert from a director's analysis of the character done for a production at Slippery Rock State College. It continues at considerably more length but space considerations preclude the inclusion of the whole analysis.

[4] Sir Tyrone Guthrie, "Is There Madness in the Method?" *In Various Directions* (New York: McGraw-Hill, 1965), pp. 165–72.

[5] Dylan Thomas, "A Child's Christmas in Wales," *Quite Early One Morning* (New York: New Directions, 1954), p. 26.

[6] Jack Clay, "Self-Use in Actor Training," *The Drama Review,* 16 (March, 1972): 18.

[7] For some books which deal in more detail with various aspects of the kind of training program outlined here, see the list of supplementary readings at the end of the chapter. Benedetti and Spolin are particularly useful.

Suggested Readings

The literature on acting is extremely vast. The following represents only a selected list of sources to which the interested student might be referred.

BENEDETTI, ROBERT. *The Actor at Work* (Englewood Cliffs, N.J.: Prentice-Hall, 1971).

BENTLEY, ERIC. "Enactment" in *The Life of the Drama* (New York: Athenaeum, 1967).

BOLESLAVSKY, RICHARD. *Acting: The First Six Lessons* (New York: Theatre Arts Books, 1969).

DUERR, EDWIN. *The Length and Depth of Acting* (New York: Holt, Rinehart & Winston, 1962).

GROTOWSKI, JERZEY. *Toward a Poor Theatre* (New York: Simon & Schuster, 1968).

SCHECHNER, RICHARD. "Performer" in *Environmental Theater* (New York: Hawthorn Books, Inc., 1973).

SPOLIN, VIOLA. *Improvisation for the Theatre: A Handbook of Teaching and Directing Techniques* (Evanston, Ill.: Northwestern University Press, 1963).

STANISLAVSKI, CONSTANTIN. *An Actor Prepares* (New York: Theatre Arts Books, 1963). (Note: This book deals largely with the development of the actor's inner state. Stanislavski's two other books, *Building a Character* and *Creating a Role* deal with other aspects of actor training.)

The Drama Review, 16 (T-53) (March, 1972).

4

THE PLAY

SOME THEATRE PEOPLE, wishing to make clear that their art is not merely a branch of literature, define the play as "what happens in the theatre" — the performance. In order to make this meaning clearer they may refer to the basis for or vehicle of the performance as the script. Thus, a script can be either a book containing the actors' dialogue and the stage directions or it can be a set of improvised or preplanned actions. Either one serves as the pattern of development or the organizing principle of the performance. In everyday usage, however, the term "play" refers both to the basis for performance and to the performance itself. We may read a play or we may go to see one. An analogy with music may be useful here. In everyday usage "music" can refer both to the written notations and to the sounds made by the orchestra in performance. When we discuss "the play" in this chapter, then, we shall be abiding by that everyday usage and talking primarily about the basis for performance, though we should always remember that, as with music, a play is never fully realized until it is performed. The greatest part of theatre as we know it is based upon the written script. Consequently the greatest part of our discussion will deal with such scripts, though there is no reason that much of it cannot apply to nonwritten ones as well.

A BASIC DEFINITION

To say that a play is a volume of dialogue or a sequence of events meant to be performed by actors is only to state the obvious. If we are to go beyond that and understand how theatre works we must ask what kind of events and what sort of dialogue make up a play.

The Play As Action

Over two thousand years ago Aristotle, in the *Poetics,* defined drama as "the imitation of an action." An immediate difficulty arises here, however, for when we use the word "action" we tend to use it to mean something done, some kind of physical activity such as batting a ball, climbing a mountain, or raking the yard. Consequently, when we speak of a play or a film as having or not having action we are apt to be thinking of such things as battles, fights, chases and so on. Looked at in that way, many plays, even of the suspense or melodramatic variety, have little or no action. One answer to this problem, of course, is to observe that all action is not physical; it may also be intellectual, emotional, and verbal. A mathematician struggling with a difficult problem, a wife trying to decide whether or not to leave her husband, a lawyer arguing a case before a judge and jury are all acting, though each may involve only limited overt physical activity. Each of these situations, depending upon the amount of stress present, may be equally as physically exhausting as running a race or working eight hours a day as a carpenter. There is, furthermore, a close relationship between intellectual, emotional, verbal, and physical action. Physical action usually results from intellectual or emotional activity and verbal action. Talking is often the mediating link between the two. In a violent argument, for example, there is clearly a great deal of "inner" action which precedes or accompanies the talk. The argument is a kind of verbal combat from which the additional step to physical combat is often, thought not always, a short one. It is actually this kind of prephysical action that makes up the stuff of most plays and one explanation for our interest in such material may be the *expectation* of physical action arising from it.

We have still, however, not disposed of all difficulties with the term "action" as Aristotle used it. A tragedy—the kind of play with which he was primarily concerned—is an imitation of *an* action. Obviously any play can contain a number of the intellectual, emotional or physical actions we discussed above but in using the singular form Aristotle seemed to mean that a play is not merely the imitation of people doing a variety of things. Common sense reinforces that argument; a play is not merely a random series of events performed by actors. Aristotle emphasizes that the action should have a beginning, a middle, and an end. Thus, when he speaks of *an* action he seems to mean a series of events which are linked or unified in some manner and which lead to a conclusion. An action, viewed in this way, can contain many of the individual actions we discussed above. Let us use Sophocles' *Oedipus the King* as a brief example. In the beginning of that play the city of Thebes is being ravaged by a plague which has caused the fields, the animals, and the people all to be barren. Oedipus' decision to find and remove the cause of that plague sets off the action. Early in the play he learns that the cause of the plague is the fact that the killer of the old king, Laius, is still unpunished so, like a modern detective, Oedipus sets out to discover and punish that killer. In the course of his investigation he has several arguments, questions several witnesses and learns a bit more of the truth each time until at last the investigation is complete and he learns that he himself is the killer he is seeking. Each interview, each argument, each additional revelation of the truth is *an* action in the sense that we first used the term. The search for and discovery of the murderer is *the* action in the sense that Aristotle used it. It gives unity to or connects all the individual actions.

The Play as Patterns of Events

One recent book on dramatic theory defines the fundamental structural principle of a play as a "Basic Pattern of Events." This seems to be essentially what Aristotle meant by an action. Life, of course, contains many patterns or sequences of events, but not all of them can serve as the bases for plays. Our work or school days are patterned as we go to the same classes or repeat the same sequences of tasks from day to day. The day itself is patterned by the apparent movement of the sun, as is the year by the change of seasons. Our lives are patterned by the growth cycle — birth, childhood, adolescence, maturity, old age, death. Many such patterns, however, are not very interesting except to the people who experience them, and not always to them. To be the basis for a play, therefore, the pattern must be of a special type — "a pattern which seems to the people who accept it to illustrate a significant aspect of human life in time."[1] A beginning definition of a play, then, might be that it is *a representation through action of a pattern or sequence of events that seems significant to its viewers.*

There are several patterns in human experience that strike us as significant, either in themselves or because they are so universally encountered. One such is a pattern that involves transformation or change, especially one in which the status of an individual is significantly altered. We said in a previous chapter that primitive societies often construct rituals around important changes in the life of an individual and we observe many such rituals in our own society — confirmations, *Bar-Mitzvahs,* initiations, weddings, graduations, etc. Such a change seems even more significant if it is brought about by the intervention of some outside influence or crisis which forces the change. Consider, for example, how many stories, plays or films are based upon the pattern that we can label the boy's initiation into manhood. Both *The Last Picture Show* and *The Summer of '42* are based on such a pattern. Stories such as Stephen Crane's *The Red Badge of Courage* and William Faulkner's *The Bear* also exhibit it, differing only in using war and the hunt rather than sex as the occasion that brings about the change. In the theatre one of many plays that exhibits such a pattern is Eugene O'Neill's *Ah Wilderness* which also served as the basis for a musical called *Take Me Along.* The play is set in 1904. The central character is a rebellious fifteen-year-old boy who gets into trouble with the father of his girl friend because of some "lurid" poetry that he has sent her. When she fails to keep an appointment with him he assumes that she has rejected him and decides that he will "show" her and the community. He goes to a local bar, gets drunk, almost becomes involved with a prostitute and, of course, becomes very sick as a result of the escapade. Because the play is a comedy everything turns out well. The boy and girl are reconciled but young Richard Miller is not the same person that he was when the play began. He has ventured into the world of adulthood and has a little better understanding of himself, his parents, and other people than he had before the crisis.

The initiatory pattern in the examples we have just cited is just one type of the general pattern of change. Another type, which may also involve change of status, is a pattern of learning. Actually, the two overlap considerably, but the learning pattern does not need to involve the initiation of youth into adulthood. *Oedipus the King* is again a classic example. More important than the simple story of crime detection which we have already discussed is the fact that Oedipus learns who and what he is. He begins the play taking great pride in himself and in his achievements and criticizing others for their weaknesses and supposed misdeeds; he finishes it by learning that he is himself guilty of two loathsome crimes, the murder of his father and marriage with his mother. His status changes from that of the powerful and self-confident king to that of the blinded and banished criminal. Often the learning pattern involves the testing of an individual by extreme pressures, in the course of which he learns who he is and of what he is capable, either by successfully meeting the crisis or by collapsing in the face of it. Such patterns are of interest to us not only because most of us have probably experienced them, but because we seem naturally to be interested in how people respond to extreme crises.

Another kind of pattern of change is the rise to or fall from power or a combination of the two. We seem to be interested in the "success story" and the "failure story," perhaps because, once again, the desire for success, status and power and/or the fear of losing them seem to be natural motivations in man. Success and status may, of course, be differently defined by different individuals but most of us seem to be interested in the gaining and losing of them. The pattern of rise to and fall from power forms the basis of both *Macbeth* and *Richard III*. Though the details of the two plays differ both deal with the gaining of the throne by unlawful means and the subsequent loss of it. A number of plays have dealt with the rise to prestige and status after a series of struggles and trials, while Shakespeare's *Othello* is a good example of a play representing the decline and fall pattern.

Another common pattern in drama, as well as other forms of fiction, is the struggle against evil. That evil may be external as represented frequently, for example, by the villain, the criminal or the enemy, or it may be internal—some character trait in the individual that has a destructive and poisonous effect upon him. The most obvious example of such a pattern, of course, is the crime melodrama in which the private detective or the police hunt down and destroy or bring to justice the representatives of evil. A good example of the struggle against internal evil may be Albee's *Who's Afraid of Virginia Woolf?* The marriage of George and Martha is clearly poisoned by some evil influence which causes their eternal battling. In the course of one night their ordinary marital warfare rises to new heights of savagery, apparently provoked by the presence of Nick and Honey, who may represent George and Martha when younger. During the night's fighting they expose a number of their failures and frustrations but the chief source of the evil seems to be the imaginary child about whom Martha had spoken in spite of George's warning. Thus, George decides that he must "kill" the child and does so in the third act, after which both couples appear to have changed. The titles Albee has given each act support this argument. The first act is called "Fun and Games," the second, during which the battling becomes extremely vicious, "Walpurgis Night" — the witches' sabbath — and the third act in which the child is destroyed, "The Exorcism." This is not, of course, to say that everything will now go smoothly for George and Martha nor is the struggle against an evil force the only thing that the play is about, but it does seem to represent the basic pattern which underlies it. In the typical melodrama the struggle against evil is usually successful though that is not the case with all plays.

Our discussion of Basic Patterns has certainly not exhausted all possible ones but it does provide us with some initial insights into how a play works and perhaps into why plays appeal to us. The theatre not only provides us with the opportunity to reexperience significant and familiar patterns from our own lives but also with the chance to try out other patterns without the risks that would be involved if we experienced them in real life. It should be obvious also that several patterns may overlap in the same play. *Oedipus the King* involves both the attempt to discover and remove evil and the pattern of learning. *Hamlet* involves both the struggle against evil — "something is rotten in the state of Denmark" — and a testing of the central character when faced with the obligation of revenge. However, although patterns may overlap, one pattern should be dominant within a single play. To return for a moment to our discussion of acting, once we have discovered the central character's spine or super-objective we may be well on the way to discovering the Basic Pattern of the play or, conversely, the discovery of the Basic Pattern may help the actor to discover the spine.

In the discussion of Basic Patterns we have frequently mentioned or alluded to crises, pressures, or tension. Such crises or pressures frequently involve conflict and conflict has been the major element of many if not of most plays. Human beings seem naturally to be interested in conflict as the widespread enthusiasm for competitive sports indicates. People flock to see football games, hockey games and boxing matches and the sports which appear to be most popular are those in which the conflict is most obvious and intense. The motivation for going to see such contests is both to observe the skill of the players and to see how the game will come out. In the theatre the same two motivations frequently operate. We go both to watch skilled performers and to see how the events turn out.

Conflict can be broken down into three basic types, with the last one containing several subtypes. First and most obvious is the conflict of *man vs. man*. Here we have two individuals pitted against one another in what may be either a physical contest, a mental contest, or a contest of wills. The physical contest is probably most apparent in the western or crime show; the final showdown between marshall and badman or between police and criminals is the logical and necessary conclusion of that conflict. The mental conflict is exemplified in the crime or espionage play in which detective and criminal or the spies of opposing nations try to outwit one another. At the time of this writing such a conflict is probably best illustrated by a very popular TV show called *Columbo* in which the title character disguises a very shrewd mind behind a mask of clumsiness and stupidity. The contest of wills can be seen in an excellent example drawn from the theatre. The play is Sophocles' tragedy, *Antigone*. Prior to the beginning of the play Antigone's brother Polyneices, had led an army against his native city and his brother, Eteocles, who was the king. The two brothers had met in single combat and killed each other. The new king, Creon, has decreed that as an object lesson to other would-be traitors Polyneices' body will lie unburied and rot. Antigone, however, is convinced that family duty and the laws of the gods command that she bury her brother, even though the King has declared the penalty of death for anyone who does so. When Antigone is caught Creon is willing to conceal the whole business if she will agree to give up her plan. Antigone, however, will not relent. Two strong wills are locked in conflict and the result is the death of Antigone and the destruction of Creon and his family. Behind the conflict of individual wills, of course, is a conflict of principles—the laws of man and the state vs. the laws of the gods.

A second type of conflict is *man vs. himself*. Such a conflict can be between two aspects of a person's character—greed and morality or love and ambition, for example—or it can be between an obligation and a human feeling. The classic example of this form of conflict in Western theatre is *Hamlet*. Volumes have been written about the play and the character, attempting to explain why Hamlet vacillates. Whatever the explanation, the fact remains that Hamlet is faced with an obligation—avenging his father's murder—that he cannot or does not wish to assume. The major part of the play is the story of Hamlet's internal conflict.

A third kind of conflict is *man vs. outside forces* These forces can include society, the environment, nature, God, or the supernatural, destiny, or fate. The point is that the opposing force is bigger and more powerful than the individual. An excellent example of this type of conflict in which the outside force is society is to be found in Henrik Ibsen's *An Enemy of the People*. The central character, Dr. Stockman, is the medical officer of a small town in Norway which is preparing to open a set of medicinal baths. As a part of his duties Dr. Stockman has sent in a sample of the water for anlysis. Shortly after the play begins he receives the report and learns that the water is dangerously polluted. When he communicates this fact to his brother, the mayor, he is urged to keep it quiet; it will be bad for business. The mayor's political opponents, however, are happy to hear about it and promise to run the story in the opposition newspaper— until they learn that they too may be financially hurt by it. At that point they turn on the Doctor and try to hush him up. When he insists upon speaking out anyway and attacks his home town for its moral cowardice he is declared an "enemy of the people," is abused on the streets, his sons are beaten up on the school playground, his daughter loses her teaching job, and rocks are thrown through the window of his house. The Doctor had dared to take on the whole community and stands alone or almost alone against them.

These three types of conflict may overlap in one play. In *Hamlet* and in *An Enemy of the People* we find conflicts of man vs. man, though the basic conflict of each play is something else. The play which involves conflict, of course, also generates suspense, since a crucial question with many such plays is "how will things turn out?"

DRAMATIC STRUCTURE

We have thus far said that a play is a pattern of events that seem significant, that such patterns frequently involve crises and change, and that conflict is an important part of many of them. We need now to go a little more deeply into the question of dramatic structure. We should be aware, however, that any generalization about play structure is very risky. Almost as soon as one makes any kind of statement about the "typical" structure of a play one can think of a dozen plays that do not fit that pattern.

With that caution in mind, then, let us consider some fairly common aspects of structure, without, however, making any claim for their being typical. The Greek dramatists and Aristotle structured plays in terms of cause and effect. As applied to drama this cause-effect structure required that event A bring about event B which in turn would bring about event C and so on, so that the conclusion of the play could be seen as the result of events that had occurred at its beginning or even before it began. One method of heightening interest in such a play was to construct it in such a way that the audience could see the results of an action some time before the characters were able to. Thus, in *Oedipus the King,* we know what Oedipus is going to find out about himself before he does. This may act to set up in the audience a conflict between what they know will happen and what they hope will not. It also makes it possible for the playwright to trick our expectations—to lead us to believe that one consequence will result from an action and then show us something else.

Crisis, conflict, suspense and cause-effect ordering also make possible a type of structure that is fairly common in Western plays. Simply described it involves the mounting of the crisis, the intensifying of the conflict, the increasing of the suspense until a high point or climax is reached, after which the crisis diminishes, the conflict is brought to a close and suspense is released. A nineteenth-century German critic named Gustave Freytag noted this pattern and analyzed it closely. He began by recognizing two parts of the play which he called rising and falling action and then subdivided the play into five parts. The first segment of the play Freytag labelled *exposition.* It is that part of the play that tells us what we need to know to understand the events that follow. Any play must start somewhere in time and wherever it starts something has happened before that bears upon the events of the play and that the audience must therefore know about. This is especially important in a play structured on a cause-effect pattern, for the basic premise of such plays is that effects follow from causes and that we can better understand the effect if we know the cause. In *Oedipus the King,* for example, we need to know that Oedipus is King of Thebes, that he came from another place shortly after the old king had been killed, that he saved the city from the Sphinx and was rewarded with the kingship and marriage with the widowed queen. The exposition can be handled in various ways; a prologue or set speech was one method but since the nineteenth century the most common way has probably been through dialogue — a conversation between characters. Obviously, exposition must be handled quite skilfully and economically so that it does not take up too much time, delay the action, and bore the audience.

At some point in the exposition an event occurs that sets off the action. This *inciting action* is not really a segment of the play but it is an important point in its development, for it begins the next phase, a series of *complications.* In *Oedipus* the inciting action is the return of Creon from Delphi with the news that the plague is ravaging the city because Laius' killer is still unpunished. It is this bit of information which sets off Oedipus' investigation with its ultimately tragic results.

The complications are a series of events that make the hero's fate uncertain. In plays involving intense conflict the complications constitute stages in the battle: the hero seems to be winning, he encounters a setback, overcomes it, encounters another, etc. Typically these complications mount and become more intense causing the audience's interest and involvement also to mount until a point is reached at which the situation must be resolved and the tension must be released.

This high point of tension and audience interest is called the *climax.* Here an event occurs which ends the complications; the hero's fate is decided and even though all the details may not yet be worked out it should be clear at this point whether he is going to win or lose his struggle. The climax often involves a confrontation and final conflict between the opposing forces as in the Western or the suspense melodrama. In *Oedipus* the climax comes at the point where Oedipus learns the final truth about his guilt.

The climax is followed then by the *resolution* during which the complications are worked out and leads to the *conclusion* at which point the action of this particular play has ended. Once Oedipus has learned the full extent of his guilt he puts out his eyes and imposes banishment upon himself. There is a brief scene of leavetaking from Creon and his children and he then goes off, an outcast, to beg on the highways. This obviously does not mean that Oedipus' life story has ended but the pattern that makes up the action of this play has been concluded.

This type of structure can be illustrated by a diagram representing a pyramid (see Figure 4–1). One side of this pyramid would involve the rising action (exposition, complications) the climax would be at the peak and the other side would represent falling action (resolution and conclusion).

This diagram, however, is deceptive in that it implies that approximately the same amount of time is devoted to rising and falling action. In many plays, especially those of the suspense type, the climax is held off till very near the end and the resolution and conclusion come very swiftly. Thus, a more accurate diagram for many plays would be one in which the line representing rising action is quite long and that representing falling action very short (Fig. 4–2).

The kind of structure we have been discussing here lends itself easily to an act division in which the first act is taken up mostly with exposition but includes the inciting action and the initial complication, the second act includes the mounting complications and the third act is comprised of the climax, resolution, and conclusion. Some critics have ar-

Figure 4–1.

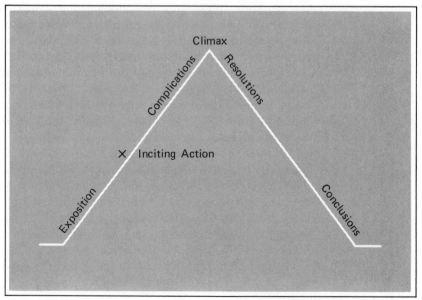

gued also that the structure of each act and of each scene within an act ought to repeat the structure of the entire play. That is, each act and each scene should have its own pattern of rising and falling action and its own climax.

The Freytag formula and the type of structure just presented are useful for analyzing many plays provided that we do not insist on it too strongly. It seems to apply reasonably well, for example, to many Greek tragedies but it does not apply to Greek Old Comedy such as the plays of Aristophanes. It applies fairly well to *Oedipus the King* but not to Euripides' *The Trojan Women*. In the latter play even the element of conflict is minimal; it is primarily a series of catastrophes that occur to the women of the title and to their queen, Hecuba. In fact, the rising action-climax-falling action pattern fits most neatly a type of drama that was developed in the nineteenth century, chiefly by Eugene Scribe, and was called the "well made" play, and to those realistic plays that were influenced at least in part by it.

The attempt to find a universal structure which will describe all plays is probably futile because of the fact that artistic conventions change as artists perceive reality in different ways and as artists search for new forms through which to express new perceptions. The cause-effect pattern, for instance, implies a world that is orderly, that makes sense, one in which there are perceivable relationships between actions and their consequences. If, however, a playwright is convinced that the world is not orderly and does not make sense, he is unlikely to express that belief through a cause-effect structure. Similarly, the pattern of change implies that things do change and the pattern of learning implies that people are capable of learning. If a playwright questions either or both of those assumptions he must find an alternate structure to express that perception. Perhaps the best way to deal with this whole problem is to consider some

Figure 4–2.

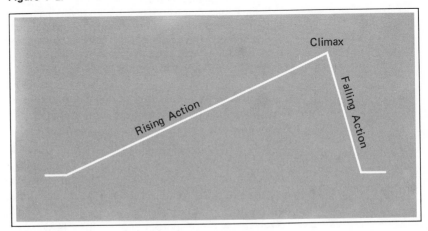

possible alternate structures using one or more plays to illustrate each one.

The cause-effect structure is linear. That is, it has a beginning point, a middle, and a clear conclusion. Much of our thinking about reality tends also to be linear and this is revealed by the way we organize many aspects of our lives. Education, for example, "begins" in the first grade and "ends" with graduation from high school, college or, perhaps, with a graduate degree. In fact, we start learning long before we begin school and continue long after we graduate. The linear organization, therefore, is just one way of looking at reality. Another may be circular; that is we may see existence not as a straight line between two terminal points, but as a pattern that repeats itself like the pattern of day-night-day or the pattern of the seasons. A play which may be familiar to many readers is Thornton Wilder's *Our Town*. If we examine it carefully we will find no conflict, no suspense, no rising and falling action, no real cause-effect sequencing. What we do find is a series of events that represent the pattern of living in a small town. Each act covers roughly the course of a day, beginning in the morning and ending in the evening or night. The first act begins just before dawn and the last act ends at bedtime. The total play covers a span of nine years and depicts a typical day in Grover's Corners, New Hampshire, the marriage of George Gibbs and Emily Webb, and Emily's funeral; in other words, the central events of the play are the ordinary events of everyday life which repeat themselves with each new generation. There is change, of course, but the rate of change is slow and tends to reflect a kind of eternal rhythm. There are constant references to the movement of the sun, to the stars, and to Grover's Corners' past. One of the Stage Manager's speeches, introducing Act Two, emphasizes this cyclical nature of reality and change:

> Yes, the sun's come up over a thousand times.
> Summers and winters have cracked the mountains a little bit more and the rains have brought down some of the dirt.
> Some babies that weren't even born before have begun talking regular sentences already; and a number of people who thought they were right young and spry have noticed that they can't bound up a flight of stairs like they used to, without their heart fluttering a little.
> All that can happen in a thousand days.[2]

The form of Wilder's play is not completely circular in that it does not come back exactly to where it began, but each act repeats the pattern of the previous one and the entire play creates a cyclical feeling in keeping with its subject which is the life cycle. The circular pattern does not deny change but rather asserts that change is only a part of a great circle or eternal recurrence—a notion which is typically more common to Oriental thinking than to ours. Wilder's play was, in fact, influenced both in form and content by his stay in China.

Another way of perceiving reality, however, might be to deny change altogether and the dramatic structure through which this perception is communicated might be a static one. As an example we can look at Samuel Beckett's play, *Waiting for Godot*. Two tramps are sitting by a roadside in a barren landscape which is marked only by a single leafless tree. They are waiting for a certain Mr. Godot, though they do not really know why. They talk, they argue, they encounter another character named Pozzo and his slave, Lucky, and spend some time talking with them. They consider leaving but do not do so. At the end of the first act a boy comes to tell them that Godot cannot come today but that he will surely come tomorrow. The second act begins in almost exactly the same way as the first; again the tramps are by the roadside waiting for Godot. Only two things have changed. The tree now has a few leaves and when Pozzo reappears he is blind. The act is filled with much the same kind of talk as was the first. Again a boy appears; Godot cannot come today but he will surely come tomorrow. The play ends. It has been almost completely static. Nothing has happened, the changes have been insignificant ones, all the conversation has revealed nothing and led nowhere. The second act repeats the first and in production they could probably be switched around without making much apparent difference. Underneath this static structure, however, we can recognize a Basic Pattern that we are not unfamiliar with from life. The pattern is that of waiting for someone or something that will bring us happiness of satisfaction, whether it is graduation, a degree, the right job, the right boy or girl, retirement or any of the other things for which people wait. We shall return to Beckett, his view of life, and the play-writing movement of which he is a part, in a later chapter. For the moment, though, we can say that *Waiting for Godot* seems to suggest that whatever we wait for will never come; that, indeed, there may not be anything to wait for.

The events of a play may also be organized in an episodic structure. In such a structure we are presented with a series of events having no cause-effect connection. Each of them, in fact, could probably stand alone but they are tied together by a common theme. During the early years of World War II, Bertholt Brecht wrote a play called *The Private Life of the Master Race*. It consists of a series of scenes, each depicting some aspect of life in Nazi Germany, interspersed with songs. Each of these scenes could be taken out of context and be done as a one-act play. In fact several of them have been, especially the segments entitled "The Jewish Wife" and "The Informer." They are held together only by the theme, "Life in Nazi Germany." Another play of Brecht's, *Mother Courage,* is slightly more traditional but still episodic. Mother Courage is a traveling peddlar, selling a variety of goods to both sides in the Thirty Years' War during the sixteenth century. She has two sons and a daughter. In a series of encounters with one or the other army all three of her children are killed. She loses the horses that draw her wagon. At the end of the play she is alone, pulling the wagon herself, still searching for business. Again, each episode could almost stand by itself; it is the movement of Mother

Courage and her wagon that holds them together. Under the episodic
structure of this play is yet another Basic Pattern—that of carrying on in
the face of misfortune.

Obviously, then, there is no universal structure that can be applied
to all plays. The problem is perhaps made even more complex in modern
times as playwrights search for new forms to communicate new perceptions of reality. We can say only that underlying every play is a basic
pattern of events which seems significant to those who see it. The Basic
Pattern may seem significant because of its familiarity or because it appears to touch upon some profound aspect of experience. Often such patterns involve conflict, crisis, and change and many of them, though by no
means all, may exhibit a pattern of rising action-climax-falling action. Specific structures may vary, however, according to the playwright's insight
and purpose.

THE ELEMENTS OF DRAMA

Aristotle, from whom we derive our concept of the play as an imitation of
an action, also argued that a play was made up of six basic elements—
that, indeed, a play was made up of only these six things. They are: plot,
character, thought, diction, music, and spectacle. A consideration of these
six elements—though we may give some of them meanings slightly different from those intended by Aristotle—should help to provide a better understanding of the nature of a play.

Plot is defined as the arrangement of the incidents and Aristotle con-
siders it the most basic of the elements. Aristotle's use of the term plot is
similar to our use of the term "structure." There is, however, a distinction. We have seen that the same Basic Pattern can underlie several
plays. Both *Richard III* and *Macbeth,* for example, deal with the gaining
and losing of power. Obviously too any number of different plays could be
built upon the various structures we have discussed—the linear, rising
and falling action; the circular; the episodic and so on. Yet in spite of
being built on similar patterns or structures they are not all the same play,
for the specific details of the action differ. The term plot is commonly used
to refer to the specific events of one play. Aristotle placed plot first for the
simple reason that without it there is no play. In spite of what we said
about *Waiting for Godot* a play cannot exist without some action. Indeed,
many things are said and done in that play; the point is they lead nowhere
and it is for that reason that we call it static.

Aristotle does assert, however, that it is possible to have a play without character—that, indeed, the plays of his time were characterless. He
clearly does not mean that we can have a play without people for if action
is to be performed it must be performed by someone. There seem to be
two basic ways of approaching the people in a play, from the playright's
point of view. One is to regard them merely as the objects or tools neces-

sary to carry out an action or to illustrate a point. A mystery, for example, merely requires a detective, a victim, and a group of suspects, one of whom is the killer. They need not be any more fully developed than is necessary to carry out the required action of investigation and discovery of the killer. Indeed, in many mysteries the characters almost seem interchangeable from one to another. The same is true of a good many situation comedies. Such plays Aristotle would call characterless. The other way is to create fully developed and individualized characters, face them with a problem or put them into a set of circumstances and let the action grow out of the kind of people they are. Both approaches can obviously yield a play, but the play that can be said to include character is likely to produce the better and more satisfying play and the one that strikes us as being more true and more real.

Thought, Aristotle's third-mentioned element, is present in every play in the sense that a play deals with ideas. The ideas dealt with in a play need not always be profound ones; indeed, they may often be trivial or stupid, but in so far as it depicts human beings in action and employs dialogue a play can not help but deal with ideas. In contemporary terminology, a related term might be theme. Some teachers of drama and some critics who write on the subject have suggested that a play has a single theme which frequently can be condensed into a one sentence statement. To say that a play has a single theme, however, is an unfortunate oversimplification. First of all, it implies that the play exists to illustrate a moral—a statement such as "Crime does not pay" or "Winning isn't everything." While it is true that some playwrights have deliberately set out to illustrate a moral in this fashion, many have not and perhaps the best plays are those in which a number of different themes or ideas can be found. It would be a mistake to conclude that every playwright is or wants to be a philosopher, but every play must present an interpretation of life. The serious playwright, furthermore, thinks about and reacts to existence, to the reality around him and transforms that thought into a work of art which is his play.

Another word for diction, as Aristotle uses it, is language or speech. In Western plays, especially, the action has been carried on largely through speech. Listening to well expressed thoughts and feelings is one of the pleasures to be derived from the theatre. Here is yet another difference between the live theatre and the film. Although film may be almost entirely visual and though we do have a wordless form of theatrical art in mime, it is doubtful that a play can be entirely visual. In the plays of Shakespeare and in other poetic drama, language is one of the chief elements and it is important that the actor know how to speak it well. In the realistic plays and films with which we are most familiar today, the language appears to be that of everyday life. Yet if we listen to an ordinary conversation and then listen to a dialogue scene from a realistic play we are likely to notice some distinct differences. First of all, everyday conversation is apt to wander, to repeat itself, to be interrupted, and at times to be unclear, while the section of dialogue is likely to be tighter, more condensed, more to the point. Second, we will probably find that in realistic prose thoughts and feelings are frequently better expressed than they are in ordinary conversation. Indeed, the dialogue may occasionally come close to the quality of poetry. Consider, for example, the following few lines from Tom Wingfield's opening speech to the audience in *The Glass Menagerie:*

> Yes—I have things up my sleeve. I have tricks in my pockets. But I am the opposite of the stage magician. He gives you illusion disguised as reality. I give you truth in the pleasant disguise of illusion. To begin, I turn back time. I turn it back now to the quaint period, the thirties, when the huge middle class of America was matriculating in a school for the blind.[3]

Aristotle's fifth-mentioned element of a play is music. There has been some debate over what Aristotle meant by the Greek word that is usually translated as "music." It is a good possibility that he meant quite literally music, for there is evidence that some of the choral speeches in the Greek tragedy of which he was speaking were sung to the accompaniment of flutes and drums. Music as such is not necessarily present in every play, though many of them have made use of either instrumental or vocal music to enhance the mood or in some cases to lighten it. We are all familiar with the musical comedy in which the story often seems merely to be an excuse for stringing together a group of songs and dances. Even if we are not talking about actual music, however, every play has a kind of rhythm, involving the rising, dropping, speeding up and slowing down of the action as well as the contrasting sounds of actors' voices and the use of poetic or near poetic dialogue.

Aristotle placed spectacle at the end of his list and considered it the "least artistic" of the elements. It is nonetheless of considerable importance in the theatre. We said earlier that a play probably cannot be entirely visual, yet neither is it merely a collection of people talking. It should provide the audience with something exciting and interesting to look at. The plays of Shakespeare and other plays of past historical periods frequently employed a good deal of pageantry—processions, royal entries, court scenes, battles, etc.—which, if effectively staged, can keep them visually alive and exciting. Perhaps one of the disadvantages of realism and the play set in the ordinary living room is that it provides relatively little spectacle. Throughout the twentieth century, however, many individuals and theatre groups have attempted to restore visual excitement to the theatre and that trend continues with some of the modern experimental groups and imaginative directors. A part of Aristotle's reason for considering spectacle the least artistic of the elements was the fact that he was approaching the drama mostly from the point of view of the writer and argued that spectacle had more to do with the stage machinist. In a sense, he was correct. The designer of scenery, costumes and properties, the lighting designer and the director, in the way in which he arranges people on the stage, all contribute a great deal to the spectacle of a performance. Nevertheless, the playwright can construct his plays to include spectacle and to provide an opportunity for these other artists to realize it on the stage.

THE TASK OF THE PLAYWRIGHT

We have had a great deal to say about the structure of plays but so far we have said nothing about how a play comes into being. In this section, then, we will consider in general terms what a playwright is, how a play gets written or made, and the special responsibilities of the playwright.

Many people argue that a playwright is less a writer than a maker of plays. To support their argument they point to the last syllable of the word, "wright," the same one as in shipwright, wheelwright, etc. They also argue that the playwright needs to be directly involved with a theatre company and that he does not so much write a play as develop it in cooperation with a group of actors. This argument can be defended, both historically and in terms of some current practice. Both Shakespeare and Moliere, for example, had lifelong involvements with theatre companies and both worked as actors. It is possible, then, though we do not have any evidence to prove it, that scenes, characters and effects in both men's plays originated from suggestions made by the actors they worked with. In both cases, however, the unity of the written style suggests that the plays were put into final shape by the playwrights, wherever the ideas may have come from. We know also that in the Broadway theatre plays are often rewritten, sometimes extensively, during the rehearsal period and in response to suggestions and reactions by actors and director.

On the other hand a number of playwrights have had little or no connection with the theatre during much of their careers. Ibsen, for example, directed or aided in the direction at the Norwegian National Theatres in Bergen and Oslo for ten years and wrote some of his early plays while so employed. After he left that position, however, he had no formal connection with a theatre group and in fact rarely went to see his plays staged. Yet during those later years he wrote such plays as *Peer Gynt, A Doll's House, Hedda Gabler,* and *The Master Builder,* among others. It is probably true that a playwright needs some acquaintance with the theatre, at least to the extent that he understands what is effective there, but that does not necessarily involve a lifelong active involvement with a producing group.

Ideas for plays can come from a variety of sources. A play may develop out of a general theme or idea with which the playwright is concerned, it may arise from a character or a situation that he finds interesting, it may be a response to an event in public life, it may be stimulated by some aspect of the playwright's private life, or it may be an attempt to deal with a personal problem.

The notes for Ibsen's *A Doll's House* suggest that that play may have been stimulated by a general idea—there are different laws for men and for women—though at the time some critics felt that the situation had been inspired by that of Ibsen's mother-in-law and another female acquaintance insisted that she was the model for Nora Helmer. *An Enemy of the People,* however, seems to have come out of Ibsen's anger at the critical reception of *A Doll's House* and *Ghosts* and to some extent he seems to have identified with Dr. Stockman who is viciously attacked merely for telling the truth. Strindberg's *Miss Julie* is reported to have been inspired by a newspaper account of an aristocratic young lady committing suicide because she had allowed herself to be seduced by a family servant. In this incident Strindberg saw the opportunity to develop two of his favorite themes, the struggle between man and woman and the struggle between social classes. Others of his plays, such as *The Father,* in which a wife drives her husband mad, seem to have been inspired by his own marital problems. Euripides' *The Trojan Women* was, as we have said, inspired by his city's unprovoked slaughter of the inhabitants of the island of Melos. Brecht's *The Caucasian Chalk Circle* was based on a traditional Chinese play, which he retold to convey a contemporary moral. Eugene O'Neill's *Long Day's Journey Into Night* is an almost literal retelling of a portion of his life with his parents. In short, plays can come from a variety of sources. Anything that catches the playwright's fancy and stimulates his imagination has the potential of becoming a play.

Playwrights' methods of working vary almost as much as the sources of plays. Some go through a lengthy period of preparation, outlining, writing, and rewriting. Others may work very quickly and produce only one draft. Ibsen seems most often to have begun by making extensive notes and writing as many as three or four different drafts. The ideas in the preliminary notes are often considerably changed in the final draft. Often character's names will change from one draft to another or some planned characters disappear only to turn up in a later play. Some playwrights work by carefully preparing a scene by scene story outline before they ever set down a word of dialogue while others jump directly into the writing, letting the action develop as they work. The time spent in the writing process also varies. Ibsen typically brought out a new play every two years; Noel Coward has been known to produce one in a few days. Brecht is reported to have originally written his *Galileo* in 1938 and continued to revise it almost to the time of his death in 1956. In many cases plays are rewritten and revised during rehearsal. In some instances they are even extensively rewritten after the playwright has seen a production.

The playwright has special responsibilities that are not shared by other writers—except perhaps by television and screen writers. The beginning playwright especially may not know whether he has fulfilled these responsibilities until his work has been tried in the theatre. Written scripts can be read and enjoyed but if the script is truly a play it must be capable of being acted.

First of all, whatever the playwright sets out to communicate must be largely communicable through action. A novelist may go on for pages with subtle and elaborate explorations of his characters' states of mind, limited only by the necessity of not boring the reader. Whatever insights the playwright wishes to convey, however, must be conveyed through what his characters do and say and through what others say about them. Furthermore, any psychological analyses the characters do either of themselves or others must be done in such a way that they advance or at least do not slow the action. The same is, of course, true of social or political analysis. The novelist also can set the scene by lengthy descriptions of the environment within which the action takes place. Whatever the playwright wishes to convey about the surroundings of the action must be realizable in the theatre by the actors and scenic artists.

Second, the conditions of the enacted play more closely resemble those of public speech than those of written work. The spectator in the theatre cannot go back and reread. If he misses a crucial line or a bit of action, if it is confused or unclear, he does not have a chance to see or hear it again or to pore over it until he understands it. Although it is possible to go back and see a play a second and even a third time, we are less likely to do so than we are to reread a portion of a book. Material chosen for inclusion in a play—the words spoken and the actions performed—must be selected and arranged with great care. Even a play which seems formless and disorganized is likely, if it is a good one, to be carefully organized, though perhaps not in the way we expect it to be. And like the public speaker, the playwright must place great emphasis upon sharpness, clarity, repetition and a variety of stimuli to retain the audience's interest.

Third, the playwright must be aware of the demands, both physical and mental, that he is making upon actor and audience. The actor must be able to do and say the things that the playwright asks of him. More importantly perhaps, the audience must not be strained beyond its limit of attention and endurance. The reading of a large novel can be interrupted and resumed over a period of several days or even weeks; a theatrical performance, on the other hand, is usually confined to a single evening and there are outer limits, depending upon convention, to the amount of time an audience is willing to spend watching the play. Japanese audiences are willing to spend up to six hours at a performance of the Kabuki, though there are frequent and long intermissions. In our culture three to three and one-half hours is probably as long as most audiences wish to spend at a single performance.

The original artist often breaks or alters the conventions of his art and sometimes is far ahead of the rest of the world. The playwright, however, can probably not afford to be as far ahead of his audiences as can other artists, at least if he wants his play to be produced. The painter or the poet works in isolation and can put his revolutionary work aside and wait for it to be discovered. The playwright must work with other people, first actors, technicians, and a director and then an audience. The very nature of theatre demands that the play be performed. In a theatre such as ours where the playwright's income is largely based upon his ability to sell his play, he is especially dependent upon finding a large enough audience with which he can communicate. This does not, of course, mean that he must pander to the audience or give them what they want but it does mean that his liberty to be original or experimental is probably more restricted than is that of many other artists.

At base, then, the play is a sequence of events, a pattern of human action that carries the audience forward with it and perhaps suggests some wider significance beyond the events themselves. Suzanne Langer says that the primary illusion of drama is "virtual destiny"—a present that is filled with its own future.[4] That is to say, in watching a play we are aware of the development of events, of a future coming into being. In our everyday lives and experiences we do not, perhaps, have that sense of impending or developing future, but when life is at its most intense—in moments of great joy, expectation, crisis or uncertainty—we do. Those moments are, in fact, likely to be called "dramatic." What the play usually presents us with, then, is an impression of life lived at a higher than normal intensity, a sequence of events in time in which every word and every action seems significant. The playwright envisions it, the actors and scenic artists give it life, and its effect is modified or enhanced by the physical relationship between the actor and audience.

Notes

[1]Jackson G. Barry. *Dramatic Structure: The Shaping of Experience* (Berkeley: University of California Press, 1970), pp. 25–30.

[2]Thornton Wilder, *Three Plays* (New York: Harper & Row, 1957), p. 46.

[3]*The Glass Menagerie,* copyright 1945 by Tennessee Williams and Edwina D. Williams. Quoted by permission of Random House Inc.

[4]Susanne Langer, *Feeling and Form: A Theory of Art* (New York: Scribner, 1953), pp. 306–325.

Suggested Readings

BARRY, JACKSON G. *Dramatic Structure: The Shaping of Experience* Berkeley: University of California Press, 1970.

SMILEY, SAM. *Playwriting: The Structure of Action.* Englewood Cliffs, N.J.: Prentice-Hall, 1971.

WHITMAN, ROBERT. *The Play Reader's Handbook.* New York: Bobbs-Merrill, 1966.

5

THEATRE
SPACE

ART COMMUNICATES SOMETHING about human experience. Each art has its own language made up of the elements it employs and the way in which they are arranged to convey its "message." The theatre's language may be broken down into actor, play or script, theatre space, technical elements, and director. Perhaps a better way of looking at it is to suggest that as a communicative act, a performance can be seen in terms of the elements of a communication model. There is, therefore a sender, a receiver, a message encoded into a certain set of symbols, a channel, and feedback or response from the receiver. The generalized message of the theatre is an impression of human life though the message of any given play is more specific. The receiver is obviously the audience. The identity of the sender may be open to debate, and strong claims have been advanced for the playwright, the actor, or the director as the primary communicator or the major artist. We have argued that the actor is central simply because the mode or channel of theatre is enactment. In practice, however, the actor's contribution cannot be so easily separated from that of the other theatre artists. What the audience encounters in the theatre is a total experience in which the contributions of the individual artists are fused.

The communicative act takes place in a *matrix* or field – that is, in a situation located in space and time. The performance of a play occurs somewhere at some time and involves a particular relationship between play, actor, and audience. The matrix, in other words, is the physical situation that surrounds the performance and the time at which it takes place. It is a physical relationship, which in turn affects the psychological relationship and thus influences what is communicated. Kenneth Burke, in speaking of symbolic or communicative acts in general borrowed a term from the theatre and referred to this time and space dimension as the *scene*.[1] Matrix, or scene in this sense, involves the theatre building, the time and condition of performance, and the scenery (as the term is conventionally used). Scenery, including the other technical elements, is, in fact, almost impossible to separate from the theatre building, for the space in which a performance takes place tends in large part to dictate the kind of scenery, lighting, costumes, make-up and sound-effects that are used. In spite of the difficulty of that separation, however, this chapter will deal with the theatre building and to some extent with the time dimension of the performance, while the next will deal with the technical elements.

THE PROSCENIUM THEATRE

When we hear the word "theatre" most of us conjure up a fairly consistent mental picture. We see a large hall with a raised stage, separated from the auditorium by a curtain; we see rows of seats with one or more aisles to permit access to them, and perhaps a balcony. When the play is on the curtain is open, the stage is brightly lighted, and the auditorium is dark. We conjure up such a picture because that is the kind of theatre with which we are most likely to be familiar. If we have seen a play at all the odds are at least eight to one that we have seen it in the kind of surroundings just described. Indeed, that type of theatre and that type of stage — the proscenium stage — have tended to dominate theatre architecture for nearly three centuries. Furthermore, when the film became a significant form of entertainment in the early years of this century, it adopted the proscenium design to its own use with only minimal changes.

The proscenium theatre design creates a certain kind of physical and psychological relationship between the play and the audience. The actors and the audience inhabit two separate spatial domains; in a sense they are in two different rooms. The stage, together with the scenery, the properties, etc., belongs to the actors; the audience occupies the auditorium. The actors are the doers, the audience the watchers. Thus, in the typical play on the proscenium stage, especially the one we label realistic, we pretend to be eavesdropping upon real conversations and spying upon

Figure 5–1. Whiting Proscenium Theatre, Rarig Center, University of Minnesota, Courtesy of University of Minnesota Theatre and University of Minnesota Photographic Laboratories.

real events. The actors enter into the pretense by going about their business as though we were not there at all. Normally we do not acknowledge each other's presence except by our applause and laughter at the appropriate places and by the actors' bows at the end of the play. In the proscenium theatre the stage represents one place presented in its completeness. If the location of the action changes, that place is followed by another place, usually requiring a change of scenery. In the proscenium theatre, then, we seem to be looking through a transparent fourth wall into someone's house, apartment, or place of business. Such a theatre and stage may be ideally suited for the kind of situation in which the actor wishes to identify deeply with his character, create the illusion of real events in a real place, and ignore the presence of the audience. In short, it tends to force a separation between play and audience, casting them in the role of passive observers and restricting their participation in the play to an intellectual, or emotional and largely internal type of involvement.

The design of the typical proscenium theatre resembles that of the lecture hall. The seats are in rows and the focus of the audience is directly or almost directly to the front. Now, the major purpose of the lecture hall is that of imparting information and that task is made easier by the front focus which minimizes interaction among the members of the audience. Every symbolic act, including the theatrical performance, conveys *some* information. In all plays there is something that the audience needs to know in order to appreciate and understand the action, and in the linearally structured play discussed in the previous chapter there is probably a good deal. We should not, however, assume that the main purpose of a play is to convey information in the form of facts or data. We do not go to see *Macbeth* to learn about the history of medieval Scotland nor to see *A Doll's House* to find out what life was like in nineteenth-century Norway, though we may gain some such information as a kind of byproduct of the play. Though any broad generalization is risky it is probably correct to say that the main purpose of most plays is to create a *shared experience*. The degree of sharing versus the degree of separateness may, of course, vary with the kind of play presented and the theatrical conventions at work. Many people would argue that the proscenium convention, by forcing a separation between stage and audience and by minimizing interaction among the members of the audience, actually works against the main purpose of theatre.

There have been three principal objections to the proscenium stage and to the kind of relationship it creates. In the first place, the concept of the stage as representing one localized place or a succession of such places creates serious problems in staging plays such as those of Shakespeare in which there are a great many changes of scene. To represent these scenes realistically, to try to recreate a literally different place in each one, is difficult and time consuming; it extends the playing time of the show and forces the audience to wait while scene changes are made.

Directors frequently avoid this by playing Shakespeare on a set consisting of platforms, levels and ramps which represent no place in particular. The British director, Sir Tyrone Guthrie, who spent much of his life staging Shakespeare, argues that that is an unsatisfactory compromise and that we need other kinds of stages upon which to present not only Shakespeare but other plays as well:

> The proscenium stage is certainly not out of date. It probably never will go out of date. But it cannot any longer be regarded as the only kind of stage upon which a professional production can satisfactorily be presented. For certain kinds of plays — almost all those written since about 1640 — it is suitable, because it is the sort of stage which their authors had in mind when they were writing. But quite a number of plays, and indeed quite a number of interesting and important plays, were written before 1640; and it by no means follows that, either in theory or in practice, the proscenium arch theatre is the best mechanism for their production.[2]

A second argument is that the ability of the proscenium stage to represent the illusion of reality has been diminished by the appearance of a new art form that can do it better — the film. If a film maker wants to represent a street in Harlem, a castle on the Rhine, or a square in Venice he can simply take his cameras there and film the scene in its actual locale. Indeed, as the costs of materials and the wages of stage carpenters and technicians have risen in Hollywood, it has become cheaper to film in the actual locations even if they are halfway around the world. Scene designers and technicians in the live theatre can often produce some amazingly realistic effects but they cannot compete in realism with the actual place.

The one thing the theatre has that the film does not is the living presence of actor and spectator in the same space and time. There is a unique interaction made possible by this presence. The third objection to the proscenium theatre is that the separation of actor and audience in the proscenium theatre fails to take advantage of the one element that is unique to theatre. This has been the argument underlying some of the most radical modern experiments with theatre space and we shall return to it shortly.

ALTERNATIVES TO THE PROSCENIUM THEATRE

These objections to the proscenium stage have given rise over the last half-century to the development of several new kinds of theatre space, some of which are related both to historical theatres of the past and to the ways that people tend naturally to arrange themselves to watch an event. Suppose, for example, that a fight breaks out on a crowded city street. If people stop to watch, as many will, they tend to group themselves in a circle around the fighters. If the event is a performance of some kind, for example a juggler or a streetcorner musician, the performer is likely to wish to focus outward toward the watchers and will play against a backdrop of some kind, perhaps a wall. The spectators, then, are apt to group themselves in a half or three-quarter circle. The full or the partial circle makes possible a close contact with the performer and promotes interaction among the members of the audience. In such real life situations complete strangers who might otherwise have ignored each other are likely to begin to interact. We see here the rudiments of a different theatrical space — the performer in the middle of a circle of spectators or in front of a background and partially surrounded. The problem with such a spontaneous arrangement, however, is that if the crowd gets too large the people in the back will be unable to see and hear. In the theatre the audience can be raised, as on bleachers, so that those in the back are looking down on the action, or the performer can be raised by placing him on a platform, or both performer and audience can be raised. In these natural arrangements we have the prototypes of at least two historical theatres, the Greek and the Elizabethan.

The Greek actor first performed in a large circle and eventually against some form of building as a backdrop. The spectators sat in roughly a three-quarter circle arrangement on a hillside, probably first on the ground, later on wooden benches and still later on stone. Historians still argue about how early the backdrop building was introduced and about whether or not the actor performed on the ground or on a raised platform. These Greek theatres tended to be very large with some of them seating as many as fourteen thousand spectators. The Elizabethan outdoor theatre in which Shakespeare's plays were originally performed was much smaller but the principle was similar. The actors performed on a platform

Figure 5–2. The Greek Theatre at Epidauros. The people in the orchestra circle give an idea of its size. The spotlights and set are for a production by the Greek National Theatre. (Photo taken in the summer of 1973 by Orley I. Holtan.)

thrust out into a courtyard or pit. Spectators who payed the lowest admission prices stood in the pit almost surrounding the stage. The roofless building in which the stage was housed contained galleries of perhaps three or four levels for the higher paying spectators. Thus, some of the audience looked up at the action, others down upon it. Again historians argue about the specifics of the Elizabethan theatre and whether all theatres were alike, but it is clear that all of the spectators must have been quite close to the action of the play.[3] The arrangement of both theatres probably forced the actors to play outward toward the spectators much of the time thus keeping the spectators constantly aware of the fact that they were watching a play rather than spying upon real events. Furthermore, the playing areas, rather than representing a specific locale, tended to be a kind of neutral space that could be any place the playwright wished it to be.[4]

The two most common modern versions of this natural arrangement are the arena stage—sometimes called theatre-in-the-round—and the "thrust" stage. Arena staging, as the name suggests, typically involves the spectators completely surrounding the action. Shapes may vary, circular, square or rectangular, but in all cases the action is in the middle and the audience watches from outside. Arena theatres can be of almost any size but typically they tend to be fairly small. This means that not only does the audience see the actor in three dimensions, unlike the flat picture effect of the proscenium stage, but typically actor and audience are brought quite close together. Consequently the acting can frequently be very subtle and need not involve the exaggeration necessary to get to the last row of the balcony in a proscenium theatre. The actor in the arena must, of course, play to his entire audience and this usually requires more move-

Figure 5–3. Arena Theatre, Rarig Center, University of Minnesota. (Courtesy of University of Minnesota Theatre and University of Minnesota Photographic Laboratories.)

ment and movement in circular rather than straight line patterns. Realistic scenery can obviously not be used because it would block the view for part of the audience, but almost any kind of play can be done in the arena, the only exceptions being those in which the action is somehow dependent upon a piece of scenery. One great advantage of arena staging is that it can be done in almost any room that is large enough to hold actors and audience and that provides some sort of means of lighting the acting area. Thus, a high school, college, or community group need not feel that it is prevented from doing theatre because it has no stage and has only limited funds for scenery.

The thrust stage consists of a platform which extends out from a background and is about three-quarters surrounded by audience. It is really a very slight adaptation of the Elizabethan outdoor theatre. The two earliest examples of the thrust stage on this continent are the Stratford Ontario Festival Theatre and the Tyrone Guthrie Theatre in Minneapolis, Minnesota. Both of them resulted from Guthrie's effort to find a better way of staging Shakespeare and the classics. Another example is the Stoll Thrust in the Rarig Center at the University of Minnesota. The thrust stage has many of the advantages of arena staging. In the Guthrie Theatre, for example, though the seating capacity is large, no spectator is more than fifty feet from the stage. This means that everyone can see and hear clearly. It is also a very flexible stage which, like Shakespeare's, is a neutral space on which one scene can follow another with great fluidity. Yet, despite its lack of scenery in the conventional sense, it is not limited to the production of classic or Elizabethan plays. The company at the Guthrie has successfully presented such "realistic" plays as Chekhov's *The Cherry Orchard,* Ibsen's *The Master Builder,* Miller's *Death of a Salesman* and Williams' *The Glass Menagerie.* None of them suffered from the lack of a conventional set.

Figure 5–4. The Elmer Edgar Stoll Thrust Theatre, Rarig Center, University of Minnesota, seating capacity, 487. (Courtesy of University of Minnesota Theatre and University of Minnesota Photographic Laboratories.)

In both arena and thrust staging members of the audience are able to see each other and the separation of actor and audience into two separate rooms found in the proscenium stage is at least partially broken down. There remains, however, an element of separation between spectators and playing area which is frequently reinforced by different levels of lighting. The relationship of active performer and passive spectator also tends to continue. A number of people have argued, therefore, that a still more drastic breakdown of traditional theatre space is necessary. Probably one of the most interesting and important experiments in discovering new physical and psychological relationships in the theatre is that carried on chiefly by Richard Schechner and the Performance Group. Schechner describes what he is trying to do in his book, *Environmental Theater:*

> The fullness of space, the endless ways space can be transformed, articulated, animated — that is the basis of environmental theater design. It is also the source of environmental theater performer training. If the audience is one medium in which the performance takes place, the living space is another. The living space includes all the space in the theater, not just what is called the stage . . . .
>
> The first scenic principle of environmental theater is to create and use whole spaces. Literally spheres of spaces, spaces within spaces, spaces which contain, or envelope, or relate, or touch all the areas where the audience is and/or the performers perform. All the spaces are actively involved in all the aspects of the performance. If some spaces are just used for performing, this is not due to a predetermination of convention or architecture but because the particular production being worked on needs

Figure 5–5. Experimental Theatre, Rarig Center, University of Minnesota. (Courtesy of University of Minnesota Theatre and University of Minnesota Photographic Laboratories.)

space organized that way. And the theater itself is part of larger environments outside the theater. These larger out-of-the-theater spaces are the life of the city; and also temporal-historical spaces — modalities of time/space.[5]

The aim of environmental theatre is to find new ways of relating among the performers, the play, and the audience — the specific ways depending upon the nature and purpose of the play being done. The Performance Group typically does not do conventional plays but either drastically restructures classic scripts or works with original pieces. They work in the Performing Garage, literally an abandoned garage in New York. It is a fifty by thirty-five foot space which can be arranged or transformed in various ways to suit the needs of the play being worked upon. The audience may sometimes be a part of the play or sometimes be separated from it. Also, at times, the audience may be divided with part of the audience separated from the action and some in the middle of it. Schechner emphasizes that it is the performance, the director, the performers, and audience all interacting together that determine how the space is used in a particular case. Nevertheless, he offers a "standard environmental design" which takes into account a number of different ways in which this interaction can take place:

> A theater ought to offer to each spectator the chance to find his own place. There ought to be *jumping off places* where spectators can physically enter the performance; there ought to be *regular places* where spectators can arrange themselves more or less as they would in an orthodox theater. . . . there ought to be *vantage points* where people can get out of the way of the main action and look at it with detachment; there ought to be *pinnacles, dens, and hutches:* extreme places far up, far back and deep down where spectators can dangle, or burrow, or vanish. At most levels there ought to be places where people can be alone, be together with one or two others, or be with a fairly large group. Spaces ought to be open enough so that in most of them people can stand, sit, lean, or lie down as the mood directs. Spaces ought to be open to each other so that spectators can see each other and move from one place to another. The overall feel of a theater ought to be of a place where choices can be made.[6]

All this takes us some way from the traditional proscenium theatre and is even a considerable break with the arena and the thrust stage. It creates a situation in which the play is much more of a communal event than a thing merely to be watched, though Schechner emphasizes that the audience has a choice as to whether they wish to be spectators or participants.

There is still another aspect of theatre space, however, that should be considered. The traditional proscenium theatre, the arena stage, the thrust stage, even the Performing Garage are places to which the audience *goes* to experience theatre. That is, spectators must take themselves physically from where they are to some place that is designated as a theatre. The first three, furthermore, are usually specifically designed to be theatres and nothing else. The practice of theatre-going also frequently involves "dressing up," making reservations in advance, and often spending a considerable amount of money on tickets. Often, too, the theatre is located in a special area or neighborhood, sometimes, as with the Guthrie Theatre or Lincoln Center in New York as a part of a "cultural center." The argument has been advanced that the conditions described above tend to restrict the potential audience to the relatively affluent middle class that can afford to dress up, to pay the price of the ticket, to travel sometimes a considerable distance. They also feel comfortable in the surroundings of a cultural center. (Ironically, Walter Kerr, the New York critic, has argued that affluent middle-class audiences today feel uncomfortable about passing through an area where pornography shops, "adult movie" houses, drugs addicts, and derelicts abound in order to go to the Broadway theatres.) A more important philosophical argument is that if theatre is essentially a relationship between actors and audience gathered in the same space, it is not necessary to single out and designate any specific place as a theatre. Out of these conditions and this philosophical argument have come some additional approaches to theatre space the most important of which are probably the concepts of "street theatre" and "found space."

If the traditional theatre operates on the formula of the audience going to the theatre, street theatre reverses that formula. It brings the theatre to the audience. There are two approaches here that can both be designated as street theatre. The more formal and traditional one is to provide some kind of mobile performing facility that can be brought into the neighborhoods. The Shakespeare in the Streets Company in Minneapolis performs from the back of a flatbed truck specially designed to fold out and operate as a stage. Performances are held in various parks or street-corner locations around the Twin Cities. As the name suggests the group performs traditional and classic plays though not all of them are by Shakespeare. The aim is to take the play out into the neighborhood and thus reach people to whom it might not occur to go across town to a theatre. A somewhat similar effort is carried on by the San Francisco Mime Troupe which performs on a platform attached to the back of a van and again goes to the various parks in the city. The Mime Troupe, however, usually does original plays with political or social themes. One such play presented in the summer of 1972, for example, dealt with an alleged relationship between the CIA and the drug traffic among American soldiers in Viet Nam. Another production that same summmer dealt with problems of urban renewal in San Francisco—a concern of the people there at that time. A more radical version of street theatre is simply to use the streets themselves either with no performance facility or as extentions of an existing facility. Thus, during performance of Brecht's *A Man's a Man* at the Firehouse Theatre in Minneapolis, part of the action was taken out of the old firehouse that served as the groups' performance facility and was played in the street. A similar "exploding" of the theatrical space occurred at a performance of *Dionysus in 69* by the Performance Group when the action spilled out of the Garage and onto Wooster Street.[7] Sometimes such street theatre events are spontaneous or semispontaneous. For example, in 1970, just a few days after the shootings at Kent State University, a group of young people in New York's Greenwich Village reenacted the event in the streets. Some participants, representing the National Guard, were dressed in parts of army uniforms and carried toy guns while others, dressed in their ordinary clothing represented the student demonstrators who were fired upon. Some street theatre is clearly political in its purposes; some of it is more traditionally "artistic." In either case the major aim is to bring theatre into the community and allow the audience to experience it in their natural surroundings.

This second type of street theatre brings us very close to the concept of "found space." The philosophy behind it is similar to that involved in "found art." Traditionally we think of art as something made by an artist. It is possible, however, simply to find and pick up some object — a piece of driftwood, a glass bottle, an automobile part, etc. — that, because of its form, texture, or color appeals to the finder. This then can be mounted or displayed in a particular way and becomes a piece of "found art." "Found space," therefore, is any space that appeals to a group of performers and holds interesting possibilities for a performance of either an original work or a traditional play. Such space can be anywhere that provides a place for actors to work and spectators to watch — a playground, the steps of a public building, a railroad coach, a junkyard, etc. The important point is that the space is not created for the performance, but rather the performance takes advantage and makes use of space which already exists.

All of these more radical experiments with theatre space have two essential purposes. One of them is to create a closer relationship between audience and play than is possible in the proscenium theatre or even in the arena or the thrust stage. Another is to overcome the attitude that theatre going is a kind of special, formal event. Behind both is the desire to increase the scope of theatre and to make of it more of a community event and less one that is participated in by a "cultured" few. A great deal of contemporary thinking about the theatre is in a state of flux and there is probably no way of saying at this time whether any of these experiments point the direction toward future organizations of theatre space. It is worth noting, however, that several of them have been in existence for eight to ten years at the time of this writing and that they are still much talked and written about among theatre people.

THE AUDIENCE

Sir Tyrone Guthrie argues that the audience's experience in the theatre is very much affected not only by its closeness to the performer but by its closeness to one another. It is much better he feels to have many people in a small space than a few people in a large space. One proof of his argument is that at a comic play or even at a film if the audience is small and scattered throughout the theatre the laughs are likely also to be small. There is something about laughter that is infectious and when a group of people are gathered in a small space all laughing, it is difficult not to join in. In a more subtle way the same thing is true for the more serious emotions; there is an atmosphere created by a large number of people, close together, deeply involved in a serious play. Thus, Guthrie argues that theatres should provide a maximum number of seats in a small space, bringing the audience not only close to the performance but as close to each other as possible. Some of the giant theatres and concert halls of England and Canada, he feels make the audience at a play much too conscious of the empty space around them.[8] The same might be said of many of the "multi-purpose" auditoriums in American high schools and on college campuses.

The atmosphere of the theatre building is created not only by the type of stage or playing area and by the size of the auditorium but also by the decor of the building. Many of the Baroque theatres of seventeenth- and early eighteenth-century Europe were elaborately decorated and contained a great deal of gold and red velvet. Many of these theatres were attached to royal courts and were designed to present lavish spectacles for aristocratic audiences, but they influenced the building and decoration of public theatres as late as the Victorian era. The question is whether elaborately decorated theatres are suitable for plays which are not dependent upon lavish spectacle and whether they provide a comfortable atmosphere for the ordinary nonaristocratic audience. Trends in modern theatre construction, beginning in Europe in the late nineteenth century, have been toward a greater simplicity in theatre decor so that the focus of the audience is on the play rather than on the theatre building. Similarly, theatres tended, beginning with the Italian Renaissance, to separate audiences socially or financially, by providing certain sections of the auditorium for those who paid higher admissions and another section, usually farther from the stage, for those who paid the lower prices. This trend continues in most commercial theatres today, though attempts were made to get away from it as early as the mid-nineteenth century. Again, the modern experiments have attempted to eliminate all such social distinctions as well as to provide a theatrical atmosphere in which the working man, the poor, and the young will all be comfortable. The atmosphere of the Performing Garage, for example, is deliberately simple.

Another variation of theatre space is the cabaret or dinner theatre. Here the playing area may be either a proscenium stage or some form of open stage—arena or thrust, but the audience does not sit in typical theatre seats. They sit at tables and are able to eat, drink, and smoke either before the performance, during it, or at intermissions. Cabaret theatre has had a long history in Germany where the material presented was often political or social satire. In the United States the material at the dinner theatre is usually of a light sort, comedy or musical, and the situation probably lends itself particularly well to such light entertainment. There is no reason, however, why more serious material could not also be presented in the context of a restaurant or cabaret.

The physical surroundings in which the performance takes place are a part of the experience of theatre going. A number of people, Tyrone Guthrie among them, have concerned themselves with the relationship between the play and the type of stage upon which it is produced. Comparatively few, however, have explored the various psychological effects of different physical relationships between actors and audience. Consequently, much of what can be said about that relationship is pure theory. In this chapter we have tried to consider some of the different ways in which audience and performer have been physically related to each other. The proscenium stage with which we began has been severely criticized in recent years but, as Guthrie said, it is probably not out of date. The truth seems to be that no single arrangement of theatre space is the best or most suitable one for all plays and all occasions. A variety of arrangements are possible and all of them are theatre. Depending upon the play and the purposes of actors, director, and playwright, we may wish to cast the audience as silent observers from a fixed point-of-view or we may wish them to be able to see the action from a variety of points of view and in three dimensions. We may wish them to surround the performance or we may at times wish to make the performance surround them. We may sometimes wish to make them active participants in the action. The theatre can take and has taken many forms in different cultures and different periods of history. An interesting and exciting aspect of today's theatre is the fact that many of these forms coexist and therefore provide us with a considerable variety of theatre experiences.

Notes

[1]In talking about communication of all types Kenneth Burke uses what he calls the "dramatistic metaphor." The other four terms are act i.e. what is done, actor, who does it, agency, by what means, and purpose, with what end. These correspond fairly closely to the terms, sender, receiver, message, channel, etc. that are used in communication theory.

[2]Tyrone Guthrie, *A Life in the Theatre* (New York: McGraw-Hill, 1959), pp. 202–3. For an extended and perceptive critique of the proscenium theatre the student would do well to read the entire chapter, entitled, "The Picture Frame."

[3]For the general line of this discussion I am indebted to an article by Richard Southern entitled "Unusual Forms of Stage," in Stephen Joseph (ed.), *Actor and Architect* (Toronto: University of Toronto Press, 1964), pp. 48–56.

[4]In *most* of the Greek plays, though not all, the stage or playing area represented one place and the scene did not change. In the Elizabethan theatre the scene changed freely and frequently and the stage was truly a neutral space that could represent anything.

⁵Richard Schechner, *Environmental Theater* (New York: Hawthorn Books, Inc., 1973), pp. 1–2.

⁶*Ibid.,* p. 30.

⁷A photograph of this event is to be found in Schechner, *op. cit.,* p. 34.

⁸Tyrone Guthrie, "Theatre at Minneapolis," in Joseph, *op. cit.,* pp. 32–33.

Suggested Readings

BRACKETT, OSCAR G. *History of the Theatre*. Boston: Allyn & Bacon, 1974. (An excellent source of information and illustrations.)

GUTHRIE, TYRONE. *A Life in the Theatre*. New York: McGraw-Hill, 1959.

JOSEPH, STEPHEN, ed. *Actor and Architect*. Toronto: University of Toronto Press, 1964.

NICOLL, ALLARDYCE. *The Development of the Theatre*. New York: Harcourt, Brace Jovanovich, 1966. (A standard work dealing with the design of theatres in earlier times.)

SCHECHNER, RICHARD. *Environmental Theater*. New York: Hawthorn Books Inc., 1973.

The Drama Review. New York University: New York, N.Y. Nos. T39 and T58.

THE TECHNICAL ELEMENTS

IN THE BEGINNING of the previous chapter we discussed the production of a play as a communicative act and suggested that it involves sender(s), receiver(s), message, channel, feedback, and matrix. The matrix we defined as the physical and temporal location of the event consisting of the theatre building or the location in which the production occurs, the time and circumstances in which it occurs, and the technical elements of the theatre, the scenery, lights, costumes, make-up, properties, and sound. In any communicative act, however, the matrix is more than the surroundings of the act; it becomes part of the act itself and contributes to its meaning. For example, consider the following sentence spoken in two different situations: "It's a beautiful day, isn't it?" In the first case the sun is shining, the birds are singing and the air is pleasantly warm; in the second it is dark and cloudy, there is a chilly wind blowing and a cold mist in the air. The meaning of the sentence obviously shifts from one situation to the other. In the first it means what it says while in the second the meaning is exactly the opposite of what the words seem to be saying. The situation or matrix has become a part of the meaning of the act. In the same way a play produced in the arena or on a thrust stage becomes a different experience than one produced on a proscenium stage. Extending the argument to the technical arts of the theatre, it is clear that they are not merely window dressing or background but a part of the total theatrical experience.

Our habit of thinking of the play first as a piece of literature — as lines written by a playwright which are in turn memorized and spoken by actors — often leads us to think of the technical arts as "extras." Among theatre people themselves there is sometimes a tendency to think of the playwright, the director, and the actors as the true artists and to regard those who design and build the scenery, make the costumes and properties, design and run the lights as theatrical second-class citizens. Even Aristotle fell into that trap when he said that spectacle was the "least artistic" of the six elements of drama because it belonged more to the work of the scenic technician than to that of the playwright. It is true, as we have said earlier in this book, that the actor is the one irreducible element in the theatre. Without actors the art of the theatre would not exist. It is true, also, that a play can be staged in a bare room, in a park, on the hillsides or in the streets and that the actors can wear elaborate costumes, faded blue jeans or nothing at all. Yet in all of these situations there is something to look at, there is a location that affects the performance, and there is some kind of lighting, if only the natural light of the sun. In each case also the location of the performance, the clothing worn, and the kind of light available were deliberately chosen by the performers. While we might be tempted to say that in several of the situations described above there were no technical elements, it would probably be more correct to say that scenery, costume and lighting in some form at least are present in *every* play.

The experience of a play is created partially by what we hear — the lines memorized and spoken by the actors — but it is created also by what we see. Part of what we see is, of course, the actors' bodies, their movement, gestures and facial expression. A large part of it, however, consists of the technical elements of the theatre, the scenery, the costumes, the make-up, the lighting, the properties. Each of these technical elements has its own function or group of functions in creating the total theatrical experience and the people who work with them are as much artists as are the actors and the director.

SCENERY DESIGN

Mordecai Gorelik, who was very active as a professional scene designer in the American theatre of the 1930s and 1940s, has said that scenery has four functions in the theatre:

> As *documentation* the setting records the geography and history of the locale.
> As *environment* the setting represents a place that has been made by human beings, or that has an effect on human lives, or both.
> As *machine for the theatre* the setting answers to the sightlines of the auditorium and the physical limitations of the machinery of the stage; it serves the actors who in turn act upon it.
> As the *scenic metaphor* . . . the stage design is most nearly related to the script. It seems to me that a setting can have no greater usefulness or distinction than to be poetically right for a given play.[1]

The first of these functions can be described simply as the giving of information. The curtain opens and we see a Victorian drawing room with plush furniture, wood paneling, heavy drapes, paintings on the wall, etc. and we know that we are probably going to see some aspect of the life of the upper classes, probably in England and taking place around the turn of the century. Suppose that we look more closely, however, and we see that the arms of the chairs are worn threadbare, that the upholstery is soiled, the wood paneling is splintered, there is an electrical outlet in the wall and a radio set on the table. Now what we know both about the time in which the play takes place and the people who are likely to live in that room has changed. In either case, however, we have received quite a bit of information before a single line of dialogue is spoken.

Probably the most common method of such documentation is what we usually call realism. The scenic artist can try to create as completely as possible the illusion of a real place, either by using the actual materials that would be present in such a place or by cleverly counterfeiting them. David Belasco, an American director of the turn of the century, is reported on one occasion to have actually bought a tenement room from a building that was being torn down and had it carefully reassembled on the stage. Few designers or directors would go that far to achieve realism but the attempt to create the illusion of an actual place is still commonly practiced. Frequently this results in the so-called box set, in which the audience sees three walls of a room which completely fill the proscenium opening and is asked to believe that it is looking through an invisible fourth wall. One can document time and place, however, without going to those extremes. An analogy may be helpful here. A sort of code with which children used to amuse themselves consisted of leaving out lines from printed letters as in the following example:

$$\text{ΟΟΞΝΞℛ}$$

You can actually draw in the missing lines, but if you know the English alphabet you can fill in the gaps mentally and get the message. Similarly, in a stage set a partial wall may give you information about the room just as well as will the complete wall. In some instances a single element is enough to locate the play; the Eiffel Tower, for example may be quite sufficient to identify Paris. In the accompanying illustration from the Abbey Theatre production of *Borstal Boy* stools used in an earlier classroom scene are turned upside down and placed around the stage. When the boys enter with hoes in their hands we know that they are in a garden,

Figure 6–1. A typical box set for *Hedda Gabler*. (Slippery Rock State College, designed by Raymond Wallace.)

even though the overturned stools do not look like real plants. In short, documentation and realism are not necessarily the same thing. The imagination of the spectator added to the suggestions provided by the designer can often be as effective as a completely realistic set.

Environment and documentation may overlap somewhat but they are not synonymous. Documentation is primarily concerned with locating the place of the action and the time period in which it occurs—the battlements at Elsinore, midnight, or a New York apartment in the upper sixties, late afternoon. It can also concern itself with providing information about the people who live in that place and time. Environment, however, is time and place plus a set of circumstances that surrounds one's life—physical, economic, political, social, religious and so on. Environments may be natural or they may be created by human beings, but whichever they are, they are affected by the people in them and in turn the people are affected by environments. On a fairly simple level we can readily observe this in daily life. The bustle, crowds, and noise of New York City produce a different kind of person than do the deserts and mountains of New Mexico. The student from the state college and the student from the Ivy League university are likely to be quite different people, even though they also have a great deal in common. Environment consists of such things as climate, terrain, the architecture of buildings and the furnishing of rooms, one's work and the conditions surrounding it, even the other people in one's vicinity. We, as individuals, are affected by all of these things and we affect some of them. In creating environment, then, the scene designer is doing more than giving us information; in a sense he is making the scenery an actor in the play an active presence that affects and is affected by what goes on there.

Figure 6–2. A bed and a partial wall are sufficient to create the illusion of a room. (Abbey Theatre Production of *Borstal Boy.* Photograph by the late Dermot Barry, reproduced by courtesy of Mrs. M. Barry.)

Figure 6–3. Hoes carried by the actors turn classroom stools into garden plants in this Abbey Theatre production of *Borstal Boy*. (Photograph by the late Dermot Barry, reproduced by courtesy of Mrs. M. Barry.)

Not all settings document or provide environment but all of them function as machines for the theatre. A simple way of defining this function is to say that the set provides a place for the actors to act where they can do what is required of them while clearly visible to the audience. More importantly, the good scenic design organizes, arranges, and dic-

Figure 6–4. The set as "machine" for actors. Arthur Kopit's *Indians.* (Hilberry Theatre, Wayne State University, directed by Don Blakely, setting designed by Russell Paquette, costumes designed by Vic Leverett, and lighting by Gary M. Witt.)

tates the movement of the actors and does so in a way that is at once efficient, in keeping with the director's and the playwright's intent, and interesting to watch. Lee Simonson, another designer and roughly a
contemporary of Gorelik's, expresses it this way:

> Scenic design is related to architecture, not because it reproduces
> architectural forms but because it is based on architectural plan and like the
> plan of a building directs whatever human activity it shelters.
>
> The design of a stage setting is analogous to the design of a building. Its
> plan, unseen by the audience, controls the pattern of movement made by a
> group of players; its facade expresses the prevailing emotions of the players
> as they move through this pattern.[2]

When Gorelik employs the term, "machine for the theatre" he is
saying metaphorically that a set should be designed so as to fit in with the
nature and limitations of the theatre space and to aid the actors in communicating the play through action. It is not merely something to act on or in
front of, but something to *use* and something which facilitates the action.
Even the realistic box set functions as a machine, for the placement of the
walls, of entrances and exits, staircases, fireplaces and furniture clearly
dictates the patterns of movement that can take place in it. In other instances the set may be deliberately designed to function primarily as a machine. That is, the designer is not chiefly concerned with documenting the
locale of the play nor with creating an environment but with providing a
set on which the actors can move in interesting patterns and arrange
themselves in attractive groupings. Such a set might, for example, make
use of platforms of various heights, ramps, and steps or it might make use
of such things as springboards, trampolines, ladders, trapezes, and jungle
gyms. The point in settings of this type is simply to provide something
for actors and director to use in order to create a theatrical experience.

When Gorelik talks about the scene design functioning as metaphor
he is talking about it as a significant and integral part of the play's meaning, message, or impact. While functioning in this way the setting may also
document, provide environment, and serve as a machine for the theatre.
Gorelik states:

> The designer must have in mind a definite scenic image, a creative, poetic
> thought which transfigures the historic and geographic documentation of the
> setting. This imagery must affect the audience subtly; it must never be
> obvious.[3]

Jo Mielziner's set for Arthur Miller's *Death of a Salesman,* for example,
shows Willie Loman's house surrounded and closed in by large high-rise
apartment buildings and thus the set reinforces at least one of the major
themes of the play, that of a man trapped in and overwhelmed by a world
that is too much for him. Willie Loman, one of his sons says, doesn't belong in a city and has no business being a salesman; he should work in the

Figure 6–5(a) & 6–5(b). Notice how the apartment houses figuratively smother Willie's home, in Jo Mielziner's designs for *Death of a Salesman*. (Peter A. Juley & Son).

The diagonal leaning lines of the apartment house drop (fig. 6–5b) suggest the way Willie sees the apartment houses. (See discussion of Expressionism in chap. 10.)

open air as a farmer or a carpenter. Much of what we learn of his character through the dialogue and action bears this out. Thus, as Willie Loman is smothered and destroyed by the city and the business world, the apartment buildings in Mielziner's design stifle and suffocate his house. They become both environment and metaphor for the play's meaning. To find this metaphor the designer must study the script carefully in a manner similar to that used by the actor. He must determine what the play means to him and then consult carefully and frequently with the director to be sure that the two of them understand the play in the same way. The scenery then becomes more than an environment or locale or even a machine for the actors. It becomes an integral part of the statement which the play makes about human experience.

The designer's work consists of several steps. As we said above he must first study the script intensively and consult with the director. Second, he must do whatever historical research is necessary to familiarize himself with the architectural details, furnishings, materials, etc., that were characteristic of the period in which the play takes place and also to understand as much as possible about the life of the people in that period. He then prepares a floor plan and a water color perspective sketch or a three dimensional model of the set. At this time the director and the designer confer again so that the director has the opportunity to approve, disapprove, or suggest changes. The designer then proceeds to make working drawings and elevations which detail the construction for those who are to do it. In many educational and community theatres the designer is also the technical director—that is, he supervises the construction and all the technical details of the show.

The designer of theatre scenery needs to be a person of many talents. First of all, he must be an artist as sensitive to the potential of color, line, mass and texture as any easel painter. Second, he must be a person of imagination, capable of perceiving the visual possibilities within a script. Third, he must be a theatre person; he must be familiar with its potential and its problems, with what will work and what will not work. Fourth, he needs to have a good deal of specialized knowledge about architecture, interior decor, furnishings and building materials from many different periods of history and he must know the resource material so that he can find information that he does not have at his fingertips. Fifth, he needs to know costume and lighting, even if he does not do those things himself, for he must be aware of how his scenery will be affected by the light thrown upon it and how the costumes will blend in and coordinate with his set. Sixth, he must be a draftsman so that he can lay out the plans for what he wants built in such a way that the builders can read and follow them. Finally, he must be familiar with building materials and construction techniques for he must not design something that cannot be built and in many cases he must supervise the work himself. In order to become a member of the professional scene designers' union he must pass rigorous examinations in all or most of these areas. It is no wonder that that union is one of the most difficult to join of all theatre unions.

LIGHTING

For most of the theatre's history the main function of lighting has been illumination; that is, its purpose was primarily to enable the audience to see what was going on on the stage. Actually, for many centuries lighting was not a real problem for, from the time of the ancient Greeks to the Renaissance, most plays were performed outdoors in daylight. It was only after the theatre moved indoors that something had to be done to enable the audience to see. Early theatre lighting was comparatively primitive, as was the lighting used in homes and in public buildings. It depended primarily upon candles or oil lamps. The artists of the Renaissance in Italy did develop methods of coloring light, of reflecting it off polished surfaces and even of dimming it, but the possibilities of what could be done with candles was obviously very limited. With the development of gas lighting in the early nineteenth-century theatre lighting became more dependable, brighter, safer, and more controllable. Gaslight was introduced into London theatres in about 1818 and was quickly adopted. By the 1840s its use was general throughout Europe and America. Toward the end of that same century, however, with the invention of the incandescent bulb by Thomas Alvah Edison, theatre lighting took a great stride forward. Electricity is more controllable and infinitely safer than any kind of light which employs open flame. The development of the incandescent bulb together with increasingly sophisticated dimming systems created the modern art of theatre lighting and made it possible for lighting to be used for other purposes beside sheer visibility.

At about the time that Edison was developing his bulb a Swiss designer named Adolph Appia laid the theoretical groundwork for modern theatre lighting. Appia was principally concerned with staging the operas of an earlier German composer and theorist named Richard Wagner. Wagner, in planning his operas, had envisioned a *Gesamtkunstwerk* — a united work of art in which music and all the arts of the theatre would blend into one harmonious whole. While most theatre historians today would probably agree that Wagner's operas fell short of that goal, his thinking and his practical work at Bayreuth had enormous influence on theatre theory and practice.

As Appia looked at stage productions he saw four elements: perpendicular painted scenery, the horizontal floor, the moving actor, and the lighted space within which he moved. The question was, how to unify and bring all these elements together. Appia saw the art of stage lighting as the great unifier. Following his lead, theatre people soon began to speak of

93 lighting as having five functions: to provide visibility, to aid in the por-

trayal of time and place, to create mood, to model actors and scenery in three dimensions, and to direct attention. His formula for doing this was essentially the one we use today. It involved, first of all, a combination of lighting for general illumination and lighting which could be focused on selected areas, achieved through the use of spot, flood, and striplights. Second, it involved controlling the amount, color, direction, and intensity of the light. That is, lights could be dimmed or brightened, colored in warm or cool colors to create the illusion of sunlight, moonlight, firelight, etc., to suggest time of day and year, and to create somber or happy moods. It could, furthermore, be directed upon the actor not only from the front, but from the back and sides to give him three dimensional quality. Third, that area to which the audience was supposed to pay primary attention could be lit more brightly while other areas could be dimmed. We have refined and developed the equipment greatly since Appia's day; we are now able to do things with light that would perhaps astound him. However, the theoretical basis of contemporary lighting is essentially the same as that which he outlined.

It would be beyond our purposes here to go deeply into the technicalities of lighting. Because it is a little more complex than the other technical aspects of the theatre, however, it might be well to consider it briefly. Lighting systems are divided fundamentally into two components, a source of illumination and a system of control. The first of these can be further subdivided into types of instruments used for different purposes. The one we think of most readily is the spotlight. It is used for lighting specific areas and exists in various shapes and sizes. Essentially, a spotlight consists of a hood, a lamp, a reflector, and a lens. On most spotlights, also, one finds a color frame—a square of metal that is mounted just ahead of the lens into which can be inserted a square of colored gelatine or, more frequently today, colored plastic. As the light passes through this material it takes on its color. Thus, to create the illusion of night we would use a preponderance of blue color media, while for sunlight we would employ colors in the yellow-amber range. Spots range in size from tiny 250 watt "babies" to 2500 watt ellipsoidals which are used where the lights must be mounted a long way from the area upon which they are focused. Spots of this latter type are said to have a "long throw."

The second type of light is the flood. The easiest way to visualize it is to think of a large bowl with a highly polished interior to serve as a reflecting surface for the lamp. Floods do not have lenses and are usually not used for lighting specific areas.

The third type is the striplight. Here we have a series of lamps mounted in a trough and usually wired in three or more circuits so as to allow for the use of three or more colors. The lamps themselves may be colored, they may have colored gel, or plastic or glass roundels in front of them. These lights are placed upon the stage floor, hung above the stage or recessed in a trough in front of the stage—the footlight position. One of their main purposes, along with floodlights, is to blend and tone the acting area. That is, spotlights, because they have a lens, will throw a circle of light onto the stage floor or the back wall. In most instances the director and lighting designer do not want those clearly defined pools to be visible, so they add lights of these last two types to soften or wipe out the edges. Furthermore, scenery, properties, and actors when lit from the front will throw shadows which are sometimes distracting to the audience and destructive of the illusion. Another use of floods and strips is to wipe out these shadows. Floods and strips can be used for a variety of other purposes. One such is to create the illusion of natural light, such as sunlight streaming through a window, or a natural effect such as a sunrise or a sunset. Striplights are commonly used to light the "sky cyclorama," a pale blue backdrop which when properly lighted can create a very effective illusion of sky. Of course all three types of instruments are usually used together and supplement and reinforce one another.

Control systems are designed to allow the technician to control the amount, direction, color and intensity of the light that is on the stage and to blend smoothly from one scene to another—as one lighting designer puts it, to literally paint with light. The first true dimming or control system was probably the gas table, developed in about 1850, as a central location from which all of the gas jets could be controlled. Since the advent of electricity, however, they have become increasingly efficient and compact. Some of the earliest systems consisted of rheostat dimmers which had huge handles, required a great deal of muscular effort to manipulate and, unless they were carboned regularly, squeaked loudly. With systems of this sort a complicated light change often took three people. Today's dimmers have been reduced to a size that can be managed with a finger and it is even possible to preset all of the individual dimmer readings so that the change can be made merely by pressing a button. In a few of the most modern theatres all of the light changes for a show can be pro-

Figure 6–6. A student technician works on a portable light control system. (Eastern Montana College.)

grammed onto a set of computer cards, so that a lighting technician becomes almost unnecessary.

For an ordinary straight play which does not require a lot of complicated area lighting or special effects, the average educational or community theatre uses about ten to fifteen spots. Typically the stage is divided into five areas, two upstage and three down with two or three lights focused on each, usually at angles of at least forty-five degrees. The two upstage areas are lit from the "first pipe" — a rod or batten hung directly behind the front curtain. The downstage areas are lit from the "bridge," "beam," or "balcony" position. The latter term comes from the fact that in many older theatres these lights are mounted on the front of the balcony, so that the spectator seated in the first row of the balcony can study the lighting instruments as well as watch the show. There may also be a trough in the ceiling about a third of the way back in the auditorium in which these lights are mounted. Depending upon the size of the theatre and the stage the first pipe instruments may be quite small, while those in the "bridge" position may need to be ellipsoidals with a long throw. In addition to this basic lighting floods and striplights are placed where the director and the designer feel they are needed. The commercial theatre uses essentially the same system and the same hanging positions but typically uses many more instruments.

COSTUMING

The functions of costume in the theatre are very similar to those of scenery. Costumes are able to:

1. document time and place
2. aid in the portrayal of character
3. assist the actor in playing his role
4. function metaphorically to help convey the basic theme or mood of the play
5. add color and spectacle.

To add color and spectacle has always been a function of costume and through a large part of the theatre's history costumes have helped the actor to portray character and to play his role. The use of costumes for documentation or as metaphors for the theme is probably of much more recent origin. There is a good deal that we do not know about costuming in the ancient theatre and much of what we think we know is based upon educated guesswork. We do know that from the time of Shakespeare to the middle of the nineteenth century most actors made little or no effort to costume the characters they played with historical accuracy. Shakespeare's Romans in *Julius Caesar,* for example, probably wore Elizabethan street dress with only occasional touches to suggest that they were Romans. They did not, of course, wear their everyday street clothes but tried to find more elegant costumes that would add a touch of color and spectacle to the show. It seems to have been a fairly common practice for actors to approach the widows of recently deceased prosperous gentlemen and buy their clothes for stage costumes. Each actor, furthermore, was responsible for providing his own costumes and this practice continued until well into the nineteenth century. A few actors, such as the Englishmen, Charles Macklin in the eighteenth century and W. C. Macready in the nineteenth, made attempts at historical costuming, but the most important figure in the evolution of modern costuming practices was a German nobleman and amateur theatre director, the Duke of Saxe-Meiningen. In his company, which was a significant one from the mid-nineteenth century until the beginning of the twentieth, he insisted upon costumes that were completely accurate for the historical period, geographical locale, and social status of the characters in the play. Furthermore he often insisted on the real costume rather than accepting something that looked like it. Grube, in his history of the Duke's company, tells of the unhappiness of two visiting actors when they learned that they had to wear real Roman togas, which were yards longer and much heavier than the imitations to which they had been accustomed. Following the Duke's lead it is common practice today to carefully research a period and try to recreate as accurately as possible the dress of the characters.

Anyone even remotely familiar with the history of fashion knows how important costume can be in documenting time and place. Just in the period since World War II we have had a half dozen different "looks" and we can quite precisely identify the historical period of a character wearing one of them. In the early 1950s, for example, rebellious male teen-agers adopted a uniform of blue jeans, white t-shirts, leather jackets, and motorcycle boots in imitation of a famous actor of the period, James Dean. By the late 1960s that look had changed considerably in emulation of the Beatles and other rock stars. By the same token the business executive of the 1950s would probably have worn a gray flannel suit, a white or pale blue button-down shirt, and probably a crew-cut. By the late 1960s he might wear an Edwardian style suit and a brightly colored shirt and his hair, while not shoulder length, would be considerably longer than that of his 1950s counterpart. If these differences are so prominent between roughly 1957 and 1967, how much more obvious are they between 1967 and 1867.

Clothing, however, tells us much more than time and place. It tells us about social class, economic status, and personal habits and thus aids in character portrayal. Clothing can become a badge to identify a member of a group. The insurance salesman, the service station attendant, the truckdriver, the cowboy, the college professor, can all to some degree be identified by the clothing they wear. Not long ago, at the time of this writing, very short skirts, knee-high boots and a short fake fur jacket was a standard uniform for prostitutes on the streets of New York and a girl who innocently wore such a costume could easily find herself mistaken for something she was not. An experienced and skilled headwaiter in an expensive restaurant can very quickly assess the value of the clothes you are wearing, and is likely to treat you accordingly. If clothing functions this way in life then costume on the stage can clearly tell us a good deal about the people in the play.

An important aspect of costume is that it often helps the actor, especially the inexperienced one, *feel* like the character he is portraying. In period costumes or very specialized costumes this may only be because the costume forces the actor to move and stand and sit like the character. One moves differently in cowboy boots, for example, than one does in flat heeled shoes and the tight blue jeans, the snugly cut shirt, and the big hat are likely to add to this different movement. Military uniforms are often designed with exactly this idea in mind; their purpose is not only to make one look like, but also to feel like a soldier. This suggests that our usual theatrical practice of putting off dress rehearsals until a few days before the show opens may be a mistake. Perhaps we should get the actor into costume, provided it is significantly different from his everyday dress, as soon as lines are learned and the real work on the show begins.

It is more difficult to discuss how costume functions metaphorically for that function is often very subtle. In essence the designer makes use of the symbolism of color, shape, texture, etc. to help convey the meaning or mood of the play. Suppose, for example, that we have a play in which there are two warring factions, one of which is costumed primarily in blues, the other in greens. Now suppose that in the course of the play the central character makes a gradual change of allegiance from the blue group to the green group. In the beginning, his costume is blue but as the play progresses his new costumes begin to take on more of a green tone, so that by the end of the play, when he has made his change of loyalties, his costume has changed completely to green. This, of course, must be done subtly, so subtly that the audience may not even be aware of the change until it has been completed. This is only one way in which costume might function as metaphor. In another instance the play might wish to suggest that all of modern life is being mechanized and dehumanized. The designer and the director might decide to use costumes of a very similar cut material and color so that in the course of the play the characters become more and more alike and more and more like robots. Thus, costume, in cooperation with scenery and lighting, reinforces the message of the play developed through the script, the directing, and the acting.

Aristotle listed spectacle as one of his six elements of drama and that the theatre should have something to delight the eye as well as the ear. Costume plays an important part in spectacle and the large crowd scenes of period plays and many musical comedies in which all of the characters are dressed in colorful costumes adds a great deal of visual stimulation to the theatrical experience.

It is clear, then, that the costume designer has to know fashion and its history, how clothes should fit, what different cuts and drapes will do for the figure of the actor, and what clothes reveal about historical period, social position, and character. He needs also to know how to make the costumes and what kinds of materials can be substituted for the actual ones used during the period. The real material—silk, brocade, velvet, fur, etc.—is often not only uncomfortable to wear under hot stage lights but also prohibitively expensive. Very often the costume that looks so elegant from the audience is rather shabby when we see it close up. That, however, is part of the magic of the theatre.

Probably almost anyone who knows basic research skills can study a period and discover what people wore. The creative costume designer will know not only *what* people wore, but *why*—what those clothes reveal about the life style of the period, the way people thought, how they saw themselves. The history of fashion is also social history. The way people dress reflects the way they live and relate to each other. A student admiring the females' costumes for Wilde's *The Importance of Being Earnest,* remarked that it would take those women all day to dress. That, of course, is precisely the point about that society. The women of that class and that period had little else to do but dress themselves and the men than to think up fashionable and frivolous amusements. Certain lines from the play make that quite clear as in the following exchange from the first act:

> LADY BRACKNELL:
>   Do you smoke?
> JACK:
>   Yes, I must admit, I do smoke.
> LADY BRACKNELL:
>   I am glad to hear it. A man should always have an occupation of some kind . . .

The play is, of course, comedy and these lines are an exaggeration, but they are an exaggeration of a very real social attitude which is revealed in large part by the clothes that people wore. This relationship between fashion and life style is equally true of our own day. The short skirts and pants suits worn by women today indicate that they are a good deal more active and free and do not see themselves as much as objects of admiration as they did in Wilde's day. The costumer who is sensitive to these relationships between clothing and the social, psychological, and physical lives of the characters is likely to be more creative and successful than the one who merely knows how to make clothing.

MAKE-UP

Make-up may be the oldest of the technical elements. One legend, at least, has it that Thespis, who is credited with being the world's first actor, coated his face with white lead for one of his early performances. The Greeks eventually, however, came to use masks and they continued to be used through the Roman period at least. Even in the Italian Renaissance

Figure 6–7. A stylized make-up for a mime production. Jeffrey Walker, Slippery Rock State College student.

the Commedia players used partial masks and masks are still used today in the Japanese No theatre. The difficulty with the mask, though, is that it is much less flexible than the actor's own face. Eventually, make-up came to be used again and today it may have several functions.

One function of make-up is simply to enhance the actor's own natural features. The principle is the same as that behind regular street make-up but on the proscenium stage especially this is a very important function. The actor works under much brighter light than we normally employ anywhere outside the theatre and on the proscenium stage a great deal of that light strikes him from the front. Consequently it has a tendency to wash out his own natural features and his coloring to the point that, without make-up, the face might look like a pale lump of dough. It is important, therefore, that the actor be colored, that his eyes and mouth be highlighted and that such features as eyebrows, especially if they are very thin, be made heavier. This type of make-up, which is also used by people such as television newscasters who work under intense front lighting, is called "straight" make-up.

A second function of make-up is to aid in character portrayal or, perhaps, to document certain information about the dramatic character. Often it may be necessary to change the actor's natural features, to make him older, sicklier, healthier, uglier, etc., than he is in real life. In the commercial theatre, where older actors are available, older roles are usually cast with people approximately the same age as the character. In the educational theatre, however, the seventy-year-old may have to be played by a college junior and thus make-up becomes especially important. Also, for some roles the actor may wish to alter the shape of his nose, cheeks, eyes or ears, to have a scar, a mole, a bruise or some other marking that is revealing of the character he plays. Make-up of this type is, as you might guess, called character make-up.

Like costume, character make-up can help the actor feel the role. When the young actor looks at himself in the mirror after a skillfull old-age make-up has been done on him he is likely to start to feel older. There is probably no way of proving this except by recourse to personal experience. We noted before that the famous British actor, Laurence Olivier, has said that he finds the key to his character once he determines the shape of the nose.

Lastly, make-up can function metaphorically. When Marcel Marceau does his mime performance, for example, he uses a stylized masklike make-up that is designed not so much to create a particular character as to create a universal one—perhaps man as clown. Other examples can be found in the stylized *kumadori* make-up of the Japanese Kabuki actor or in the mosaic or stained glass make-ups employed by the Everyman Players at Pineville, Kentucky, in their production of *The Book of Job*.

The basic techniques of make-up are relatively simple but they require great skill and a fine touch in application, especially if the audience is to be close. The first step is usually the application of a base, often grease paint, though for television and some small theatres ordinary street pancake may be used. This is put on the face sparingly and blended with the fingertips so that it is not greasy and the actor's entire face and neck is covered. A color is selected which suits the actor's natural complexion as well as the state of his character's health, age, national or racial origin, occupation, and other activities. Following the application of the base the eyes may be outlined, usually by drawing a dark line along the edges of the upper and lower lids. The application of a little rouge to the cheeks and lips and the touching up of the eyebrows completes a straight make-up. For a character make-up—for example, old middle-age—an additional step is necessary. The actor must first locate the wrinkles in his own face. The young actor may have problems here but by tightening up his facial muscles he can discover where he is likely to have lines in the future. Lines in the face are created when the skin begins to lose its tautness and to fall into folds which create hollows and shadows. Consequently, the actor does not simply paint lines on his face. The trick is to create natural

Figure 6-8. A Kabuki actor applies *Kumadori* make-up. (From Masakatsu Gunji, *Kabuki*, John Bester, transl. New York: Kodanska International Ltd., 1969. Photo by Cheaki Yoshida.)

looking shadows by drawing a thin line with a dark color blending and feathering it with the finger tips and then adding a lighter color above and sometimes below the dark area, also blended so as not to be too obvious. This technique is known as lowlighting and highlighting and the skillful make-up artist can create astonishingly realistic effects, even when seen from only a few feet away. The same technique can be used to create jowls and sunken cheeks, to widen or narrow the bridge of the nose, and for a variety of other effects. The actor must always start with his own face and make as much use as possible of his natural features. To what has already been done the actor can add false hair, false whiskers, nose putty, collodion, wax, etc., to further alter his natural features.

The technique that has just been described is standard for most stage and even a good deal of film work, but there are other methods that yield very realistic effects for the kind of extreme close-up work that is common in films, television and in arena theatre. To obtain a very good old-age effect the actor tightens up his facial muscles and holds the tension while his face is painted with a coat of liquid latex. When the latex has set he relaxes his face and the latex falls into folds and wrinkles where they will naturally appear when the actor ages. Usually three or four coats are necessary and it is a tedious and somewhat painful process but the effect even from only three or four feet away is so realistic as to make it worthwhile. A modification of this technique was employed to make a reusable latex mask which was used to make up Dustin Hoffman as the ancient Jack Crabbe in the film, *Little Big Man*.

PROPERTIES

Properties also play an important part in the total production, especially in documenting time and place and in creating environment. Properties, or "props" as they are usually abbreviated in theatre parlance, can be divided into three classes: set props which stand on the set—furniture, lamps and even such things as rocks and tree stumps in an outdoor scene; trim props which hang on the set or stand on other props—pictures, drapes, vases, knick-knacks of various types; and hand props which the actors carry—cigarettes, cigars, pipes, lighters, weapons, money, etc. All of these serve to tell us something about when and where the play takes place and the nature of the people who own and use them. Finding the appropriate prop for a given play can be a challenge. Even such a simple thing as a newspaper can be a problem, for if the audience can see it clearly and the play takes place in Berlin in 1936 it cannot be last week's *Pittsburgh Press* or *Minneapolis Tribune*. Furniture, paintings, vases, cigarettes, etc. must all be appropriate to the period and to the people who live in the surroundings. A glance at the properties on the set of the currently popular television show, *All In The Family,* reveals much about the Archie Bunker family. Properties, however, not only create environment

Figure 6–9. Properties help to document and create environment in *Ceremonies in Dark Old Men*. (Bonstelle Theatre, Wayne State University. Directed by Martin Molson, scenery designed by Jim Seemann, costumes by Sharon Larkey, and lighting by Bill Drake.)

and document time and place but also reveal character and help the actor. As with scenery and costume, once the actor is surrounded by properties that are appropriate he begins to feel the reality of the play and the character more strongly. For amateur actors, also, they can help to dispel nervousness by providing something to manipulate.

The property man or woman on a particular show has two basic ways to acquire what he needs; he can either search for the props or he can make them. In an area where there are a lot of antique shops, used furniture stores, or old homes he can by diligent search buy or borrow what he needs. Many established theatres have properties in storage and when they acquire something new for a show they put it into storage for future use. If the period of the play is too far removed in time, however, the likelihood of finding the right piece is very small and so it must usually be built. The prop person must do research to develop a model for the thing that he needs. Often too, much like the costume designer, he must counterfeit the actual material that would have been used. Real plate armor such as that used by the Spanish conquistadores would be much too heavy for an actor to wear through a play, but very realistic looking armor can now be made out of a plastic material. Another material commonly used for counterfeiting all sorts of things is surgical plaster—the medium that is used for making orthopedic casts. Once good props are made they again are stored for future use. Properties is perhaps one of the most difficult technical jobs in the theatre but it is also one of the most challenging, for it can be great fun to see what can be made out of ordinary contemporary materials. It takes fully as much artistry and craftsmanship as any of the other technical arts.

Figure 6–10. A student prop man makes an antique lantern for *The Crucible.* (Eastern Montana College.)

SOUND EFFECTS

Sound also contributes greatly to documentation, to creating environment and mood. It consists of any noise, including music, that is a part of the action of the play or serves as background for it — city traffic, gunfire, telephone bells, locomotive whistles, crickets in the grass, rushing winds, thunder, hoofbeats.

Sounds that are readily identifiable can be used to document. European train whistles, for example, have a very distinctive sound which identify the locale immediately as Europe. The booming of Big Ben's bell identify the scene as London. An air raid siren identifies the time period as World War II.

How sound can be used to create both environment and mood is best seen in the old radio drama. Through the chattering of monkeys, the screeching of parrots, and the cough of a distant leopard the radio show could immediately transport the listener to Africa. The creaking door that opened and closed the horror program, *Inner Sanctum Mysteries,* could send chills up the spine. Many of these old shows are available commercially today on records and if a contemporary listener can imaginatively put himself in a pretelevision frame of mind he should be very aware of the power of sound alone to create environment and mood. Of course sound does not usually play this predominant a part in the live theatre but it is important.

There have been many ingenious methods of producing sound effects throughout the theatre's history. One of the earliest sound-effect "machines" that we know of may have been used in ancient Greece to produce the sound of thunder. It consisted of shaking a large clay vase in such a way that pebbles inside it rolled around to make a rumbling sound. Until quite recently a device called a thunder sheet was used for the same

104

purpose. The thunder sheet was a long sheet of light guage flexible iron that was hung from a batten. When pulled from the bottom it produced a rumbling sound. Today the majority of sound effects except for such things as door and phone bells, door slams, or gun shots are on tape or records which makes the job of the sound technician enormously easier provided that he has good equipment and that it is working correctly.

THE TECHNICAL VOCABULARY

All of the visual aspects of the theatre employ certain basic elements which we can call the technical or visual vocabulary. They are quite similar to the elements employed in the other visual arts but the theatre has both special advantages and special problems in their use. Unlike the easel painter the theatre artist is not confined to a flat two-dimensional surface though he may occasionally have to create the illusion of depth where there is none or of rough texture where the surface is actually smooth. The theatre artist has the advantage too of being able to manipulate the light which falls on his work. He can also prevent the audience from seeing it up close. At the same time he is limited by the fact that his work is a part of the whole and must not be so interesting and attractive as to completely overpower the acting that must take place in it, on it, or in front of it.

The basic elements of the visual vocabulary of the theatre are movement, line, mass, texture, and color. Although movement involves the actors and is really the province of the director, the way in which the set and costumes are designed clearly affects the patterns and kinds of movement the director can employ. The other four elements, however, are very much the province of the technical artists. Before we begin a discussion of how they affect the audience we must remember that there is likely to be a good deal of disagreement about those effects. Some psychological testing has been done to determine the effects of line, mass, texture and color on the viewer but many of the conclusions we are about to present must be classified as "rules of thumb"—things which seem to continue to work though we may not be able completely to prove the cause-effect relationship.

Lines are, first of all, either curved or straight. Straight lines may be either horizontal, vertical, or diagonal. Curved lines may be either slow and gentle or quick. Horizontal lines suggest the horizon, something lying down or resting; they tend to suggest tranquility and quiet. The sense of peace and serenity that one experiences on the prairie may result from the long almost unbroken horizontal line and a similar psychological effect might be present on a calm day at the seashore. The vertical line is a line of strength. One sees it in towers, in trees, in smokestacks, in people standing. In an interior a long vertical line leading to a high ceiling may suggest a kind of grandeur as in some of the cathedrals of Europe. Things in action, such as a man or a horse running, driving rain, a group of people pushing against an object, make diagonal lines. Thus, the diagonal is an active line. Diagonals which intersect at sharp angles forming jagged lines suggest violence, struggle, nervousness, etc. They tend to be harsh and unsettling. In a style of drama known as expressionism, which will be discussed in more detail in a later chapter, the aim was often to depict the central character's inner turmoil, uneasiness, or insanity and that of the world in which he lived. Expressionist sets were often full of jagged and irregular lines.

Curved lines are also active but in general they tend to be pleasant and attractive. An immediate example is the curve of an attractive vase or bowl or of a gently sloping row of hills. The sharper or quicker curves are still attractive but express more action as in the curving lines of a powerful sport or racing car, which make it seem to be moving even when standing still. Because of this pleasant and active quality of curved lines they are often used in sets for light and frivolous comedy.

Mass is the quality of size, volume, or heaviness. Heavy masses — stone walls, large buildings, massive furniture, fireplaces, etc. — may suggest solidity, security or somberness and threat, depending upon how they are combined with other elements. Objects that are light, slender, airy, suggest pleasantness, insubstantiality, perhaps frivolity. The set for a tragedy may call for heavy, large, solid masses, while that for a comedy might seem to suggest something light, delicate, and insubstantial.

Texture involves the sense of touch initially, but we are usually able to evaluate textures also by the eye. Smooth, sleek textures, such as that of satin or silk for example, often suggest elegance, sophistication, sensuality. This is readily apparent in a good deal of women's fashion and in our own experience in wearing silk or satin materials. Rough textures, such as those found in Scottish tweeds or Icelandic sweaters, suggest both ruggedness and warmth. In interior decor a smooth surface painted white often seems cold, while a rougher one in a pink seems warmer. Rough textures can, of course, also be unpleasant in so far as they suggest abrasiveness. Texture is very important in scenery in giving the illusion of solidity and depth and there are a number of techniques of stage painting that are designed to counterfeit texture on a flat surface. The scenic artist and the costumer work with texture as well as with mass and line to create an effect on the audience that is appropriate for the particular play.[4]

Color is perhaps one of the most studied of the visual elements. Attempts to account for the effect of color go back at least as far as Goethe in the eighteenth century and several books written in this century report medical and psychological experiments designed to determine the effects of color on such things as pulse rate, blood pressure, and breathing. Some of these studies suggest a fairly clear relationship between, for example, accelerated pulse rate and colors in the red and yellow range, but others seem to be inconclusive. Be that as it may there are certain fairly univer-

Figure 6–11. Notice the use of curved lines in this set for the comedy, *A Flea in Her Ear.* (Hilberry Theatre Repertory Company, Wayne State University, directed by Richard Spear, settings designed by William Rowe, costumes designed by Stephanie Schoelzel, and lighting by Gary M. Witt.)

sal connections between color and mood which, even if not scientifically verifiable seem to be so common as to be useful to the theatre artist.

A good beginning point in the discussion of color is the relationship between light and dark. Dark and light have been treated as antagonistic powers, the one suggesting evil, the other good, in the mythologies of China, Persia, the Middle-East, the American Indian, and in our own Bible. The reason for this symbolism may be very deeply rooted in the human mind or it may be as simple as the fact that at night we cannot clearly see in order to protect ourselves from potential dangers. Some animals as well as human beings become extremely uneasy in the dark. Rudolf Arnheim admirably sums up the way in which dark and light and their suggestive powers can be of use to the scenic artist, especially the lighting technician:

> Particularly when the shadow is so deep that it provides a foil of black nothingness, the beholder receives the compelling impression of things emerging from a state of non-being and likely to return to it. Instead of presenting a static world with a constant inventory the artist shows life as a process of appearing and disappearing. . . . In the film, *The Third Man,* the mysterious protagonist stands unseen in a doorway. Only the tips of his shoes reflect a street light, and a cat discovers the invisible stranger and sniffs at what the audience cannot see. The frightening existence of things that are beyond the reach of our senses and that yet exercise their power upon us is represented by means of darkness.[5]

The effectiveness of Arnheim's example is probably clear even if one has not seen the film that he is talking about. The implications for the theatre artist are also clear. Sets for plays involving crime, murder, tragedy, horror are often dark in color and dimly lit, while those which are happy, comic, frivolous, or optimistic may employ light colors and be brightly lit.

The color spectrum may also be divided into "warm" and "cool" colors. Those colors in the yellow, red, orange range are typically thought of as warm while those in the green, blue range are cool. The natural explanation for this effect is probably the fact that things such as sunlight, flames, coals, metal when heated are yellow, orange, and red whereas things that are cool or cold—water, ice, sky, shade trees, etc.—are in the blue-green range. One student of color argues that a photograph or a painting may be made to represent a cold or a warm day simply by shifting the dominant color scheme toward blue or yellow respectively.[6] This phenomenon probably accounts for the fact that in Northern climates some bright, sunny days in winter "look" cold. Both in color of scenery and of lighting the technical artist can make use of this warm-cool split to create a desired affect. For years it has been a kind of "rule of thumb" in the theatre to color sets and lights for tragedy cool and for comedy warm, though like all rules of thumb it is not universally followed. In the same way the color of a costume can suggest something about the character or personality of the individual wearing it.

Certain colors tend to have fairly specific emotional associations. Some of these may be universal and others confined to a particular culture. In our culture, for example, black is the color of mourning and solemnity. We wear black or dark colors at funerals, while the Koreans would wear white. A number of experiments which were designed to discover the emotional suggestiveness of color have been reported. Few of them are reported in detail and often the scientific control is not very rigid but the results do tend to agree. In a book published in the 1930s Matthew Luckiesh reports one instance in which the observer analyzed the effects of various colors on himself. He found that the reds and oranges suggest passion, blood, rage, excitement, irritation; the oranges, yellows and greens suggest joy, merriment, warmth, liveliness; the greens and blues suggest peace, coolness, tranquility; and the violets and purples suggest seriousness, sternness, melancholy, stateliness, pomposity.[7] Another experiment is somewhat sketchily reported in a lighting textbook written in 1958 by Rollo Gillespie Williams. Using a color-lighted background on a movie screen he came up with the following color associations:

Red—*danger*
Orange—*warmth and excitement*
Sun colors—*contentment*
Pale green—*kindness*
Green—*macabre*
Peacock blue—*sinister*
Blue—*quiet depth of feeling*

Violet — *delicate emotion*
Cerise — *deep affection*
Lavender — *wistfulness*[8]

There are contradictions in many of these color experiments, particularly as applied to the effect of a specific color, but there is enough agreement to establish two things (1) that colors do seem to have psychological or emotional effect and (2) that those effects are sufficiently standardized so that the theatre artist can make use of color to try to achieve particular emotional responses.

All or several of these elements of the technical vocabulary are, of course, used together. Line, mass, texture, and color complement and reinforce each other and the best scenic artists, lighting and costume designers use them quite consciously to coincide with and reinforce the effect and meaning of the play that the playwright, the director, and the actors are attempting to convey.

The technical arts of the theatre, then, are not mere "window-dressing;" they are an inherent part of the theatrical experience or the statement made by the play. Even where they may *seem* not to be present they still play a part, for the chances are that the place of performance, the background, the things used, the actors' clothes, even the conditions of light, were chosen with some care. The scene designer, the lighting designer, the costumer, and the technicians are artists of the theatre as much as are the playwright, the director, and the actors. A theatrical production is a collective art in which all contributions fuse into one total experience for the audience.

Notes

[1]Mordecai Gorelik, "Metaphorically Speaking" in Orville Larson ed. *Scene Design for Stage and Screen* (East Lansing: Michigan State University Press, 1961), p. 100.

[2]Lee Simonson, *The Stage is Set* (Copyright 1963, by Theatre Arts Books, New York). Reprinted by permission of the Publisher.

[3]Gorelik, *op. cit.,* p. 100.

[4]A more detailed discussion of line, mass, color etc. in the visual arts is to be found in Louise Dudley and Austin Faricy, *The Humanities: Applied Aesthetics* (New York: McGraw-Hill, 1967), and of course in other introduction to art texts.

[5]Rudolf Arnheim, *Art and Visual Perception: A Psychology of the Creative Eye* (Berkely and Los Angeles: University of California Press, 1954), p. 263.

[6]Ralph M. Evans, *An Introduction to Color* (New York: John Wiley & Sons, 1948), p. 180.

[7]Matthew Luckiesh, *The Language of Color* (New York: Dodd, Mead and Company, 1930), pp. 197–98.

[8]Rollo Gillespie Williams, *The Techniques of Stage Lighting* (New York: The Pitman Publishing Corporation, 1958), p. 191.

Suggested Readings

BARTON, LUCY. *Historic Costume for the Stage*. Boston: Walter H. Baker Company, 1938.

CORSON, RICHARD. *Stage Makeup*. New York: Appleton-Century-Crofts, 1967.

GILLETTE, ARNOLD S. *Stage Scenery: Its Construction and Rigging*. New York: Harper & Row, 1972.

JONES, ROBERT EDMOND. *The Dramatic Imagination*. New York: Theatre Arts Books, 1941.

LARSON, ORVILLE (ed.) *Scene Design for Stage and Screen* East Lansing: Michigan State University Press, 1961. (Probably the best collection of theoretical writings on scene design.)

MCCANDLESS, STANLEY. *A Method of Lighting the Stage*. New York: Theatre Arts Books, 1958.

MIELZINER, JO. *Designing for the Theatre: A Memoir and a Portfolio*. New York: Atheneum, 1965.

WELKER, DAVID. *Theatrical Set Design: The Basic Techniques*. Boston: Allyn and Bacon, 1969.

7

THE DIRECTOR

THUS FAR WE HAVE TALKED in terms of the elements or units of the theatre's language or of the components in a communicative act. We have discussed the actor, the script, the theatre space, and the technical arts individually. In order for theatre to take place, however, all of these elements have to be pulled together into a coherent statement. That statement is the production and it becomes a theatrical experience when production and audience are brought together. The person in the modern theatre who unites all these elements and makes of them a coherent statement is the director. The director as we think of him today, though, is a comparatively recent addition to the theatre and before considering what it is he does it would be well to look briefly at his history.

THE DEVELOPMENT OF THE DIRECTOR

As long as we have had theatre there has had to be someone to organize things so that the play could get on. In ancient Greece that task was apparently performed by the playwright who trained his own chorus and sometimes acted in his own play. In the medieval theatre, at least on the continent, there was a personage called the *metteur du jeu*—literally "master of the game"—who seems to have done some directing and organizing. Some old woodcuts show him standing in front of the performers with a baton. We know very little, however, about what he actually did. From Shakespeare's time until about the latter third of the nineteenth century the person chiefly in charge of the production was the actor-manager. For various reasons, though, the actor-manager did not function in the same way as does the modern director. First of all, since he was usually the leading actor of the company it stands to reason that he would be most concerned with his own role. Second, it was customary through the eighteenth and nineteenth centuries to employ actors for "lines of business." That is they always played particular types of roles for which they were especially suited or in which they were particularly skilled. Each actor was, then, a specialist in his line and might well resent suggestions from another actor about how he should play his part. Third, because of poor illumination in the days of candlelight and oil lamps it was customary for actors to gather in a semicircle well downstage or on the forestage so that

112

they could be clearly seen. Consequently there was little "blocking" or arranging of the actors' positions to be done. The actor-manager, then, was chiefly concerned with getting all of the actors to the theatre in time for the performance in a sufficiently sober state so that they could perform, making sure that they knew their lines, and arranging financial matters.

To do these actor-managers justice, there were several among them who recognized that something needed to be done in order to create a greater unity in the production and some of them tried. The real breakthrough did not come, however, until approximately 1870 when the Duke of the relatively small German state of Saxe-Meiningen set to work to make his state theatre the best and most artistically successful in Europe. In this enterprise he had the help of a former comedy actor, Ludwig Chronegk, and of his wife, the actress, Ellen Franz. The Duke can be said to have made four major contributions to the art of theatre:

1. He insisted upon extreme accuracy of design, materials and construction of costumes, sets and properties. To encourage this he did extensive research into the society and the historical period being depicted.
2. He strove for greater unity and more effective illusion in scene design. He introduced many three-dimensional elements into his scenery rather than depending upon two-dimensional painted ones. He also made the stage floor and the ceiling a part of the overall design.
3. He required all his actors to play smaller parts when they were not being used in large ones. Thus, his entire cast seemed to be very good and his crowd scenes are particularly famous.
4. He insisted upon thorough and meticulous rehearsal. The Duke would not release a play for performance until he thought it was ready.

In these respects, then, Saxe-Meiningen can be said to be the father of the modern director.[1] The Duke's concern for a polished production achieved through great attention to detail, a thoroughly understood common goal, and careful rehearsal influenced a great many people in the European theatre and as a result the director as the person completely in charge of all of the artistic aspects of the production came into the theatre.

The modern director is ultimately responsible for everything that goes on the stage. Though he may have colleagues who do the actual designing, construction, and so forth he is finally in charge and the produced play represents his artistic conception, his statement, his interpretation of the script. Since sets, costumes, lights, properties, and sound effects as well as acting contribute to that statement or conception the director must supervise them, if necessary, to the last detail. Since each of these arts typically involves several people, he must also keep a large and frequently temperamental organization together and functioning. Third, having decided what kind of artistic statement he wishes to make with the production, he must find the means of inspiring his actors to get it or to come as close to it as they possibly can. Last, in the educational theatre especially, the director is frequently, throughout the rehearsal period, an acting teacher. The director, then, is an artist, a diplomat, an organizer and a teacher.

THE DIRECTOR AS ORGANIZER

A simple diagram of the organizational structure of most productions will serve to emphasize the importance of the director's organizing function. The director, as the diagram on page 115 indicates, is in ultimate charge of the designer or designers, the technical director, and the crews who work under him, the stage manager, the actors, and the crews that actually run the show. In many noncommercial theatres he must also concern himself with such things as publicity, the operation of the box office, the designing of programs and the comfort and convenience of the audience. Not all theatre organizations of course, are exactly like this one. The functions of scene, costume, and lighting design may, for example, all be performed by the same person. In many theatres the designer or one of the designers functions as technical director — that is he supervises the actual construction of scenery, costumes, properties, the hanging and focusing of lights etc. In the American commercial theatre, largely because of the union situation, the role of the technical director does not exist. Whatever the specific shape of the organization, however, the director's decisions largely determine what we see on the stage. The number of people with whom the director must deal in his organizing capacity can, in a straight play, run to a hundred or more. In a musical he must deal also with a choreographer, a vocal coach, a musical director, singers, dancers, and orchestra, making the number even larger. Many of these people are artists in their own right and are men and women of strong feelings and ideas. The director can, of course, *demand* that his ideas be followed and some great directors have been complete autocrats, but a production will frequently suffer if there is open conflict in the ranks. Consequently the director needs to be a sufficiently skilled diplomat to get what he wants most of the time without having to assert his final authority. The individual who cannot work with and handle people is not likely to become a successful director.

THE DIRECTOR AS ARTIST

The director's artistic work can be divided into two phases. The first of these is preparation and consists of selecting the script, analyzing the script, and selecting the actors. The second phase is the actual work with the actors — the rehearsal process — and its success depends largely on how well the earlier phase has been performed.

In educational and community theatre and in many resident professional companies such as the American Conservatory Theatre in San

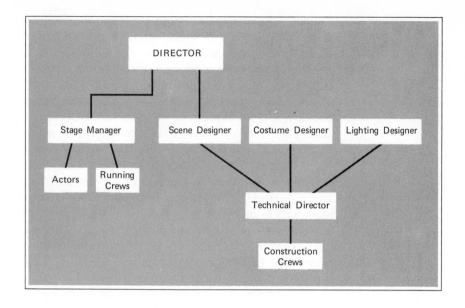

Francisco or the Minnesota Theatre Company in Minneapolis, the director's first task is to select the script. In doing so he takes several things into consideration. First, it must be a script that he likes and believes in — one that makes an artistic statement that coincides with his way of looking at the world or at least deals with a dimension of experience that he feels is important for his audience to consider. Second, he must take into account the total season of his theatre. Normally a theatre which produces a series of plays within a year attempts to balance its offerings so it does not present within one season all Greek tragedies, all light farces, or all modern experimental works. This will vary somewhat, of course, with the nature and function of the theatre, but directors usually try to achieve balance and variety within a single season and over the years. Third, he must consider the role his theatre fulfills in the community and the needs of his particular audience. Many community and summer stock theatres exist simply to provide entertainment of a light and undemanding sort. In such a situation the director might choose to do primarily musicals or former Broadway hits, now and then producing a classic in order to please his whole audience. On the college or university campus, however, the theatre also has an educational mission. It does not exist solely for the purpose of providing entertainment but to provide students, both participants and audiences with a variety of theatrical experiences. In those circumstances the director must consider what contribution will be made to the education of students and the cultural atmosphere of the campus by the play he chooses. Last, he must take into account his available facilities; theatre building, stage space, technical facilities and equipment, budget, time available for rehearsals, and the potential actors available. For example, the director will not try to do a show with twelve complicated scene changes if he has a stage with little depth, little height, and no wing space for the storage of scenery, nor will he try to do the most recent Broadway smash musical if he has a budget of five hundred dollars. In considering potential actors the director does not precast the show but in a college or community theatre where females outnumber males five to one he would be taking a considerable risk in deciding to do a play such as *What Price Glory* which has a cast of roughly fifteen men and one woman.

Having selected the play the director now turns to study and analysis. Assuming that he is working with a written script, he must read it carefully to determine its theme, its basic pattern, the rhythm or tempo at which it should be played, and even how it ought to look when it is finally mounted. At this stage he also consults frequently with the technical artists, getting their insights and giving them his, so that they will all be working toward the same end. He must study the characters trying to understand what kind of people they are, what makes them tick, why they do the things they do. He may also consider how he wants them to look and sound. The director, of course, cannot control the physical appearance of the people who audition for his production, but he can have general physical types in mind and he can consider how, once the show is cast, he wants his actors to move, stand, and sit. The necessary amount of such analysis may vary a great deal depending upon the kind of play chosen. The typical Broadway farce may require very little analysis; *Who's Afraid of Virginia Woolf?* may require a great deal.

In doing this analysis, particularly as it relates to the play's meaning or theme and the interpretation of characters, the director must depend largely upon his own understanding. Some people have argued that the director is the playwright's servant and must attempt to communicate what the playwright "really means." The difficulty with that argument is the fact that it is often impossible to know what the playwright really means. Unless the playwright is there to advise him or has written extensively about his own work the director can only determine the playwrights meaning or intent from the play itself. He can, of course, get some help from reading the playwright's other work. Many playwrights—Ibsen, Strindberg, Eugene O'Neill, Tennessee Williams—return again and again to similar themes and problems. But the director must depend on his own interpretation of those other plays also. Turning to scholars for help is often useless, for volumes of differing opinions have been written on many great plays. There have been, for example, attempts to explain the "real meaning" of *Hamlet* in Christian, Marxist, and Freudian terms as well as a great many others. The director does have a moral obligation to read the play as carefully and as often as necessary and to spend a good deal of time thinking about it. He must try to avoid imposing on it something that is completely contrary to what the playwright seems to have wished, but in most cases it is probably impossible to be certain that he understands the play *exactly* as the playwright meant it to be understood.

When the director has finished his analysis he turns to casting the roles. This may be done in a variety of ways. In the American commercial theatre the leading roles are usually cast by direct contact. Playwright, producer, and director decide that they want a particular actor for the role and contact him through his agent. After reading the script the actor may either accept or reject it. The reason for this practice is essentially economic. A great deal of money is involved in the production of a Broadway show and those involved naturally wish it to show a profit. One way of attempting to guarantee this result is to cast one or more "stars" whose names on the marquee will bring people into the theatre.

In the community and educational theatre casting is usually done by "open call." Auditions are publicized, scripts are made available for study, and at the audition all the potential candidates read scenes from the play so that the director can see, hear, and evaluate them. In these circumstances the director's first concern is to find actors who can do justice to the roles but there are a number of other things he must keep in mind as well. He must, for example, keep in mind how the members of the cast will look together, how well they are likely to work with him and with each other, and how dedicated and reliable they are. In the educational and community theatres, where actors are not paid for their services, this last consideration is a very important one. In the educational theatre the director must also keep in mind the educational value to the student of playing this particular role at this time. A director in a professional repertory company — one in which the same group of actors works together over a fairly long period of time on a number of productions — may also be concerned with developing young actors in their art and must, therefore, consider what the actor will learn from playing a specific role. Having heard all the potential candidates, preferably more than once, the director weighs all these considerations, compares his written notes and his recollections, and makes his choices. The artistic choices the director makes at this point — his selecting actor A over actor B for a particular role — is very important to the shape of the final production. Unlike the painter or the sculptor the director does not work with inert materials that he can shape in any way he chooses. Each actor is an individual, each has his own set of skills and aptitudes, and each has his own personal and artistic needs. The director must work with each individual in keeping with those skills, aptitudes, and needs, and the role as it is finally played necessarily becomes a compromise between the director's initial conception of it, the actor's conception, and the actor's ability. Occasionally a sensitive actor will, in the course of rehearsal, reveal to the director dimensions of the role that he has not seen before.

All of what has been done so far can be considered preparation. The prerehearsal work which has just been described is very important in laying the groundwork for what is to follow. The rehearsal procedure can be broken up into several phases: (1) read-through and discussion (2) blocking (3) line learning (4) working or polishing (5) run-throughs (6) technical rehearsals and (7) dress rehearsals. It may stretch over a period which can vary from three weeks to several months. The length of the rehearsal period is dependent upon the nature of the play, the experience of the actors, the other responsibilities of actors and directors, and the time available. Four to five weeks is a fairly common schedule. In the commercial theatre the actors may rehearse six to eight hours a day, occasionally more. In the educational and community theatres, however, the actors are usually students, housewives, businessmen, doctors, etc. and have other duties and responsibilities beside the play. Even the director usually has courses to teach or another job to perform. Consequently, in educational and community theatres the usual practice is to rehearse for three to four hours in the evening, five or six days a week.

The length of the read-through and discussion period varies with the nature of the play. The serious, complex psychological drama may take a good deal of discussion; the simple Broadway comedy or mystery melodrama will take much less. The necessary amount of discussion may also be affected by the experience and maturity of the actors. Middle-aged actors in the community theatre who have had considerable experience with marriage may understand the interrelationships of *Who's Afraid of Virginia Woolf?* more readily than will young college actors who have never been married. Usually at least one session in which either the cast members read the play through from beginning to end or the director reads it to them, is useful, if only to give all the actors a feeling for the shape of the entire play. This may be followed by one or several hours of discussion, dependent upon the factors mentioned above. Discussion of the play and the characters, of course, does not stop with these initial rehearsals. With a complex play it is likely to continue throughout the rehearsal period, but once a preliminary understanding has been gained there is other work that must be done.

Blocking rehearsals are those in which the director and the actors work out the general patterns of movement in the play. This may be done in at least two different ways. Actors with a good deal of experience may, especially if there is a lot of time for rehearsal, work out their own movements. In that case the director will guide, adjust and make suggestions so that the final movement pattern is a compromise between the movements worked out by the actors and the director's corrections and adjustments. It is probably far more common for the director to work out the movements ahead of time, making notations or diagrams in the margin of the script which indicate when and where the actors are to move. In rehearsal, then, he gives the actors those movements and they perform them. This can be done very meticulously down to the exact number of steps and the precise body positions or it may be done in more general terms allowing the actors leeway to modify and adjust. Usually the blocking is completed in three or four rehearsals, doing an act or a smaller segment of the play at each one. Of course, blocking too may be adjusted or changed in later rehearsals if it seems awkward or if the actor cannot do it easily and correctly, but these later changes are usually few and minor.

Line rehearsals are those in which the actors attempt to go through their lines from memory without using the script. These too are usually done in segments, with each rehearsal devoted to working on a portion of the play. For these rehearsals a prompter is used to help the actors when they forget. If the director is lucky enough to have actors who are "quick studies"—i.e. good memorizers—these rehearsals can go quite rapidly and he can even begin some work on characterization, rhythm, line readings and other concerns. If he is not, line rehearsals can be very tedious and line problems can even persist into dress rehearsals. The actual learning of lines must, of course, be done by the actor on his own time.

Once lines are committed the really serious work on the play can begin. At the same time that the actor learns his lines he should also think about his character, about how he is to be played and about the play as a whole. In working and polishing rehearsals the director guides the actors toward fully realizing all the potential dramatic values within the script. This may involve delving further into the character, guiding the actor toward a correct reading and stressing of a line, adjusting the tempo of a scene, suggesting physical activity or "business" for the actor, and a good many other things. Often, in these rehearsals, a scene or short segment of the play is run, stopped, critiqued and rerun several times until it begins to approximate what the director thinks it should be. If there are disagreements between the director and an actor concerning the interpretation of a character or the way in which a scene should be played they are resolved at this point. By the end of the polishing rehearsals the play should be beginning to take on its final shape, so that the remaining rehearsals can be devoted to fixing it and making it automatic and to dealing with other, non-acting, problems.

Figure 7–1. Actors rehearse movement while still carrying books in *Godspell.* (Slippery Rock State College.)

Run-throughs are simply a series of rehearsals in which the entire play is run from beginning to end. Their purpose is to give the actors the feeling of the shape, rhythm and continuity of the entire play. Some of the sort of work done in polishing rehearsals goes on in this stage, but the number of problems should be decreasing and becoming less serious. Typically the director will run an act at a time, critique it at the end, and repeat it only if something has gone drastically wrong.

Technical rehearsals are devoted to making sure that the scenery is right, that the scene shifts, properties set-ups, light changes, and sound-effects are all working correctly. During these rehearsals, especially if the show is a technically complicated one, the director can pay little attention to acting problems and for that reason most of them should be solved before "techs" begin. Anything in the technical aspect of the production that does not work correctly must be made right at this point. Many directors prefer to repeat a scene shift or a light change as many as a dozen times until it works correctly and can be done in the required time. Naturally such rehearsals are often long, tedious, and extremely taxing to the patience but they pay off in a much more smoothly running production.

The dress rehearsals are the last chance for smoothing out problems before the show opens. Here the actors are given their costumes and use make-up. Everything in dress rehearsal is usually run under performance conditions but there is still a chance for changes and adjustments to be made if necessary. The primary purpose of dress rehearsals, of course, is to get the actors accustomed to their costumes and to allow the costume crew a chance to make any changes that they or the director might wish. The number of such rehearsals varies; if the costumes are extremely different from the kind of clothing the actors are accustomed to wearing there should be several of them. If they are contemporary clothing two or three are enough.

The stage manager has usually taken charge of the running of the show backstage at the first technical rehearsal. Once the play opens he is in complete charge and the director normally stays out front. In the commercial theatre he is usually off salary after opening night and may go on to another show, only coming back if something has gone drastically wrong and needs to be fixed. In the educational or community theatre the director usually attends all or most performances and his words of encouragement before the show, like the athletic coach's "pep talk" are appreciated by the actors.

THE DIRECTOR'S TOOLS

The director works with certain elements in bringing the play visually and audibly to life. Starting from the meaning, theme, or message of the play and the nature of the characters in it, he employs movement, picturization, rhythm, tempo, key, and sound to create the final theatrical effect.

Each of these elements is discussed at length in textbooks and theoretical books on directing, some of which are listed at the end of this chapter. A brief discussion of them here, however, will help you to identify the director's contribution when you see a play.

All of the elements we have mentioned above will overlap within a given performance. In using them the director must take several factors into account—motivation, the theme, meaning, or emotional effect of the play and aesthetic considerations. As he moves his characters about the stage, as he arranges groupings or stage pictures, as he decides whether a given scene should play fast or slowly, violently or quietly, he must keep in mind why the characters do what they do, what this will convey to the audience and what it will look or sound like.

A certain amount of movement in almost any play is dictated by the script—i.e. the action of the play requires that certain things be done. If a phone rings a character must answer it, if the doorbell rings somebody must go to the door and someone must usually come in, characters must fight in a battle scene, etc. Movement of this kind is relatively simple for the director, but he must nonetheless decide where the character is to be in relation to the phone when it rings, how far he must walk to answer the door and where the door is to be located or exactly how much of the stage the fighting is going to cover. This is one area, obviously, where close consultation with the scene designer is necessary for, as discussed in the previous chapter, the way in which the set is designed affects the way in which the director plans movement. Other kinds of movement are required for practical reasons. If, for example, a character is going to come through a door other characters must be moved away from in front of it, first so that he can get through and second so that the audience can see his entrance. Other kinds of movement function to help tell the story, to make clear the character relationships, to reinforce the theme of the play, and to reveal something about the characters individually. As the director looks at a scene on paper in which no or a limited number of necessary movements are indicated, he must decide whether he wishes to keep the characters static or to move them. If the latter is the case, he must decide when to move them, in what direction to move them, how fast and how far to move them, and why they move. Suppose, for example, a husband and wife are seated across the room from each other and they are having an argument. The director must decide at what point in that argument emotions might get strong enough to cause one of the characters to get up and move. He must then decide whether he wants character A to move toward character B, which might suggest attack, or away which might suggest rejection. If he chooses the former, he needs to decide whether that movement should be slow and threatening or fast and violent. The exact nature of the movement should arise from the situation and from the specific line. Even while considering motivation—what makes the character move—he must also consider what the movement will tell us about the character and what it will tell us about the theme of the play. Suppose that the wife is a normally quiet and long-suffering person. A strong violent movement at this point might signify that she has now had all she can take, that she has reached a breaking point, that the "worm has turned." If the general theme of the play deals with resistance to tyranny — in this case, within the household, then the long-suffering wife's sudden strong movement might also mark a kind of turning point within the overall action — the point at which the meaning of the play begins to be fully realized. Of course, movement may operate even more subtly to make a dramatic point. In Ibsen's *Hedda Gabler,* Judge Brack has been trying to induce Hedda to enter into an adulterous relationship with him. She has successfully evaded him until the last act. In that act, however, he has learned that she gave one of her late father's pistols to another man, the pistol with which that man has just killed himself. The pistol could establish a link between Hedda and this man, who has an unsavory reputation, thus causing a great scandal in the community. The Judge uses this knowledge to blackmail Hedda. He reveals his knowledge to her through a kind of cross-examination in which he traps her into revealing that she had given the man the pistol. In one production Hedda was seated on the coach, while the Judge paced back and forth and around it, metaphorically suggesting two things — a prosecutor conducting a cross-examination and a tiger circling his prey. A the conclusion of the scene the Judge was standing directly behind Hedda, leaning on the back of the couch, telling her that she is safe so long as he says nothing to the police. The audience, of course, knows as well as Hedda does what the price of his silence is going to be. The movement and the Judge's final position were designed to help the words communicate Hedda's situation and the power relationship that now exists between the two of them.

As with some of the visual elements discussed in the previous chapter, movement can create an emotional effect without any words being spoken. Long slow movements, for example, suggest relaxation, lack of tension; short quick movements suggest the reverse. One way of building the excitement of a scene is to increase the amount and speed of movement in it. Direction of movement also has significance. In real life we move toward things to which we take a positive attitude, away from things which we wish to evade or reject.

Movement is an element in picturization or composition. Indeed, a good deal of blocking consists of forming a picture, dissolving it and forming another. Some teachers of directing have said that if the action is stopped at any point in the play the audience ought to be looking at a perfectly composed picture. When the director composes stage pictures he has two considerations in mind — aesthetics and theatrical significance — the latter involving character relationships and motivation, the play's theme and emotional effect.

In forming a stage picture on the proscenium stage the aesthetic considerations are basically the same as those in a painting or photograph — unity, variety, balance, and emphasis. First of all the picture must hang

Figure 7–2. Note how the body positions of the actors compliment the scenery in *The Skin of Our Teeth*. (Westminster College, directed by Carolyn Coombs, designed by David Guthrie.)

together; every element must seem to belong there. At the same time that a picture is unified, however, it must have variety. A picture in which there is no variety, in which all the elements are perfectly regular, is likely to be dull to look at. That is why directors rarely use straight lines or semi-circles in arranging actors and why they typically try to be sure that too many actors are not standing in the same position and equal distances apart. Balance refers to the relatively equal distribution of weight on the stage. Too many people on one side of the stage, especially, if there is also heavy furniture there make the picture seem unbalanced. This is solved either by placing roughly equal masses an equal distance from the center point (symmetrical balance) or by placing the larger mass closer to the center point and the smaller farther away (assymmetrical balance). On the stage, there is another element that must be considered. Thus far, we have been talking about physical balance but we must also consider psychological balance. A very strong character on one side of the stage may out-balance six weaker characters on the other side, especially if he is placed in brighter light, is wearing a contrasting costume, or is elevated above the other characters. Emphasis involves two things. First of all, every picture has a focal point toward which the eye is automatically drawn. This can be seen by looking at almost any good representational painting or well-composed photograph. In the theatre, however, the director must be sure that the point of emphasis—the point toward which the audience's eye is led—in pictorial terms is also the point of emphasis in dramatic terms. Throughout the play there are things that the director particularly wants the audience to see and there are characters who should receive the most attention. Here his counterpart in the film has an advantage over him. Us-

123

Figure 7–3. Focus in a realistic grouping. *Hedda Gabler.* (Slippery Rock State College, Orley I. Holtan, director, Raymond Wallace, designer.)

ing the camera as an extension of the audience's eye, the film director can force them to look at what he wants them to see. The stage director must use other means. One such means is focus. People naturally tend to look where other people are looking, a point which is proved by the practical joke in which two people stand on a street corner and gaze up into the sky, eventually causing other passers-by to follow their gaze and look up. On the stage, if six characters are all looking at another character, the audience will also tend to look at him. This can be heightened by body position—by keeping the focal character open to the audience and causing other characters to stand with their backs partially to the audience, in closed positions. It can of course also be heightened by having the actors lean toward or point at the focal character. In the accompanying illustration from the Hillberry Theatre's production of *The Three Musketeers* notice how all of these pictorial elements have been achieved by the director's placement of characters. Of course here again, as in movement, the design of the set plays an important part. Pictorial composition on the arena or thrust stage is a different matter; what is perfectly balanced for one side of the audience will be out of balance for another side. The director on either of these stages cannot use the same elements of picture composition and must usually move his actors more often than the director for the proscenium. The principles here are much more complicated and the director must at least beware of bunching his actors so that each actor hides one or more players from parts of the audience and he must sometimes be careful of spreading them too far apart so that the audience cannot focus on the whole action.

124   The theatrical considerations of picturization must work hand-in-hand with the aesthetic. The way people arrange themselves in a room, for example, can tell us a great deal about them, about their reasons for being there and about their relationships. In an empty room such as a classroom or meeting hall, for example, a group of friends is likely to bunch together, while a group of strangers is likely to spread itself out over the room with each individual keeping a certain distance from every other. People who like each other will gather in a group and will maintain some distance between themselves and people that they dislike. Students of kinesics, or "body language," and proxemics, or the ways in which people use space, have noted that there are various zones of distance within any particular culture. There is, for example, an intimate distance that we share with family and close friends, an informal distance that we share with acquaintances, a formal distance that we maintain with strangers and so forth. In a group we are apt to open ourselves to—face toward—persons whom we wish to welcome to the group and close ourselves—turn partially away from—those who are unwelcome. In any group one person will usually be dominant and will take a position of emphasis, while the subordinate members of the group will yield to him. All of these things we probably learn very early and unconsciously so that as adults we are not always aware of them.[2] The director, however, can use

Figure 7–4. Notice how balance and focus are handled in this scene in *The Three Musketeers.* (Hilberry Theatre, Wayne State University, Richard Spear, director, Russell Smith, scenery, Saniel Field, costumes, Gary M. Witt, lights.)

Figure 7–5. Notice the elements of unity, balance, and variety in this composition in *Romeo and Juliet.* (Hilberry Theatre Repertory Company, Wayne State University. Directed by Robert T. Hazzard, setting by Joseph Falzetta, costumes by Helen Markovitch, and lighting by Gary M. Witt.)

them quite consciously to tell us in any given situation who is dominant, how the characters feel about each other, who fears or dislikes whom, who belongs and who is an outsider, etc. Harold Pinter's play, *The Homecoming* deals with a womanless family in London, ruled over by the father, Max. When the oldest son brings his wife home events transpire in such a way that at the end of the play she dominates all the men. When the son brings his wife in, he points to an armchair and says, "That's my father's chair." In one production of the play, when the wife was left alone for a moment she immediately sat in that chair and throughout the play she was the only character other than the father to sit in it. The aim of this was to psychologically prepare the audience through the use of placement of characters for the final scene of the play in which she again sat in that chair, this time with the men literally at her feet. In the terms we used in the previous chapter the chair is a metaphor for the father's position of dominance and the fact that the wife sits in it indicates that she has assumed that position and replaced him.

Rhythm and tempo are closely related. Tempo is sometimes also called pace and refers to the speed at which the action seems to proceed. That tempo or speed depends upon the type of play being done and the desired effect upon the audience. The tempo of comedy is usually brisk, for two reasons. First of all, the brisk pace heightens the fun; there seems to be a kind of psychological connection between humor and speed. Second, a good deal of comedy is dependent upon unreality, even absurdity.

If the audience were given time to think about what is being done or said they would have trouble in accepting the situation with which they are presented. Often crime or suspense melodramas are briskly paced for very similar reasons. The brisk pace heightens the tension and covers over the improbabilities and coincidences upon which such plays are frequently built. A serious or tragic play, however, should seem to move deliberately and slowly. In fact, a briskly paced play that seems to move very fast and a slowly paced one may frequently take exactly the same amount of time to play. Tempo is not so much a matter of actual time elapsed but of the audience's *feeling* of time. Many readers have probably had the experience of seeing a movie or perhaps a play which seemed to be over very quickly, only to find that you had spent two- and one-half hours in the theatre. In such a case the director had managed to pace the show so that you were not conscious of the passing time.

Whether a show is briskly or slowly paced, however, it cannot retain the same tempo all the way through, in every single scene. Rhythm may be defined as the variation of tempo—the alternate pulses of speeding up and slowing down which help to communicate the meaning or effect of the play and to keep the tempo from becoming monotonous. A play typically starts somewhat slowly and picks up in tempo as it approaches the final curtain. Within that overall pattern a fast scene may be followed by a slow one, allowing for a relaxation of audience tension, which is in turn followed by an even brisker one, etc.

Both tempo and rhythm are discovered within the play in each act, each scene, and each individual line. They are achieved in production by manipulating such things as speed and energy of movement, speed of line readings, and cue pick-ups. This last term is especially important. It means the actor's response to an audible or visual signal from another ac-

Figure 7–6. Harold Pinter's *The Homecoming.* (Slippery Rock State College, Orley I. Holtan, director, and Jeffrey Walker, designer.)

tor. Actor A says "Where are you going?" (cue) Actress B says, "I'm leaving you." (pick-up). The actor should always pick up his cues briskly but the faster the tempo of a play or scene the quicker that cue pick-up should be. By slowing or seeming to slow cue pick-ups—perhaps by allowing a physical reaction to intervene between the spoken cue and the spoken reply, the director can seem to slow a scene. He can retard the tempo by slowing the actual speaking of lines and by slowing down and decreasing the amount of movement. Of course the reverse effect is achieved by accelerating all of these things. The good director is sensitive to the tempos and rhythms contained within the script and uses them as consciously and deliberately as he does the elements of movement and picture to achieve his desired effects.

Key is closely related to rhythm and tempo and refers to the amount of emotional tension within a scene. Some scenes have a high key—i.e. a great amount of tension and others are very relaxed and have little tension. Actually, we recognize and use these terms in everyday life when we refer to someone for example as being "keyed up" or when we say that someone has a "low key" personality. Some plays—*Who's Afraid of Virginia Woolf?* is a good example—demand a high emotional key throughout. Others, such as *Our Town,* for instance, demand a relatively low key. Nevertheless, as with tempo, the key cannot remain constant. Even the relatively violent play needs its moments of quiet. If the key does not vary the audience is likely to become either bored or fatigued. The stimulus must be varied both within the play as a whole and within a particular scene. It is typical for a scene to begin on a low key, build to a high point of tension and then drop again. In many plays, also, each succeeding high key scene is a little higher than the one before. This heightening of tension or key is what an actor or director means when he says that a scene or a play "builds." Usually the director must be careful not to build the early scenes in the play too high so that his actors have no place to go later in the play where a heightening of tension is required. Obviously a scene can be built through the use of loud voices and violent action but it is important to remember that those things are not synonymous with high key. If key is defined as the amount of tension present, a scene in which a group of people wait quietly in a hospital corridor for the results of a serious operation being performed can be very high key.

A great deal of theatre as we know it depends upon the spoken word. Consequently sound is one of the important variables with which a director works. Primarily, he is concerned with the sound of the actor's voices, but there may be other sounds as well. A skilled director, working with the sound elements of loudness, pitch, quality, tempo and rhythm orchestrates a play much as the arranger or conductor orchestrates a piece of music. He can begin during the casting, by trying to achieve a balance of the actors' voices—some high, some low, some medium, some pleasant, some harsh, etc. In rehearsal he may wish the actor to produce a certain pitch level for the character and to vary that pitch with the situation and the meaning of the line. Volume and pitch both typically rise with excitement or anger and building a scene frequently involves a progressive increase in volume until a high point is reached and then a drop in volume. Quality refers to the pleasantness or unpleasantness of the voice and to the peculiar characteristics that identify it with one person. The director may make use of the actor's own voice quality or he may wish the actor to change it. Another important aspect of spoken sound is stress. In English sentences the words that carry the most important meaning usually receive a stronger stress than the other words and as the degree of emotion in the sentence rises the strength of the stress increases. Thus, stress may both change meaning or express shades of meaning and it may communicate emotion. A common exercise for actors involves asking them to vary the stress in a single simple sentence to express a variety of meanings. The following is an example:

I don't want to see you. (but he does)
I *don't* want to see you. (What made you think I did?)
I don't want to *see* you. (but I'll listen to you)
I don't want to see *you.* (I want to see someone else.)

Stress communicates other things as well. British English, for example, frequently has heavier and more varied stress than American English. The misplacing of stress on the wrong word or the wrong syllable is often one of the characteristics of a foreign accent. A greater variety of stress may occur in the speech of an affected or effeminate character. By manipulating stress or showing the actor how to manipulate it the director can communicate many subtle shades of meaning or feeling. The speed or tempo with which a line is spoken and the changes of tempo within a sequence of lines can communicate a great deal also about the character and the situation. Again, as with the overall play, tempo is the speed with which lines are spoken while rhythm is the variation in both tempo and stress. Lines read fast may communicate tension, excitement, or exuberance; lines read slowly may communicate relaxation, contemplation, laziness, or threat. As with movement and placement all of the above elements are used in everyday life, often without our being consciously aware of them. The director manipulates them quite deliberately for an artistic effect. If these elements are important in realistic drama, they are all the more so in poetic drama for the effect of spoken poetry is heavily dependent upon the manipulation of pitch, loudness, quality, stress, tempo and rhythm. There is perhaps no better example of the skillful use of these elements than the recordings of Dylan Thomas reading his own poetry.

Occasionally, the director needs not only to orchestrate the sounds of the actors' speeches but other sounds as well. Sometimes those sounds are produced mechanically — rainfall, explosions, sirens, etc. as discussed in the previous chapter. Sometimes they are produced on stage by the actors, even though they are not speech. Peter Weiss's play, *Marat/Sade* involves a group of mentally disturbed patients in an asylum acting out a play about the French Revolution. All of the actors in this play within the play are insane. In Peter Brook's production of *Marat/Sade* the dialogue carried on by the main characters was interspersed or interrupted by a relatively constant chorus of groans, cries, giggles, laughter, sobbing, and occasionally song. All of this had to be very carefully orchestrated so that the audience was aware of it and so that it built and subsided at the right places yet did not interfere with the spoken dialogue.

All of the director's "tools"—the elements of movement, picturization, tempo, rhythm, key, and sound—interact. From the preceding discussion it should be clear that key, for example, is built through using movement and sound, that fast tempo often involves high key, and so on. Just as it is difficult to separate scenery, lighting, acting, costume and the type of stage from the total theatrical experience, it is difficult if not impossible to detach one of these "tools" from the total effect of the direction.

The director in the theatre is the organizer of a very complex operation; he is the guiding artist who brings together actor, script, scenery, costumes, lighting, properties, and sound effects and creates out of them a theatrical experience for the audience. As such he has to possess a good many personal and professional qualities. Obviously he must love the theatre, for he has to spend many hours in preparation, in conference with his colleagues, in conducting auditions and rehearsals, not to mention those hours of thinking and worrying while he is away from the show and supposedly relaxing. He must be a person who gets along with others, for he has to work with a great many people and get the cooperation of all of them. He must be a person who is sensitive to and understands human nature, for not only does he have to understand the characters in the play but he must know how to approach many different actors and get from each his best performance. He must be familiar not only with the theatre and dramatic literature but with the other arts as well, for he may need to teach a dance or a song and he needs to use the elements of sculpture and pictorial composition in his everyday work. Finally, he must possess a large storehouse of miscellaneous information—how to fence or fight with knives, how to march, how to mix a martini, for example, as well as the manners and mores of other cultures and other periods of history.

The director has frequently been compared to the orchestra conductor in that he unites a great many separate elements to create an artistic effect which is the performance. It is true that he studies the script or score, that he interprets it, and that he rehearses his players to get them ready for the final performance. There is, however, an important difference. During the performance the orchestra conductor is in front of the orchestra with his baton controlling, at least to some degree, how the music is played. In this respect we could say that the director in the theatre is more like the football coach. He drills his players as thoroughly as he can but once the game begins he has little power to affect its outcome. The director, like the coach, must sit on the sidelines with his fingers crossed, his jaw clenched, and his stomach in knots. If, however, the director has done his work well the result is an exciting and enjoyable evening in the theatre and his greatest reward is knowing that he has provided such an experience for the audience.

Notes

[1]One of the best discussion of the evolution of the director and of Saxe-Meiningen's role in that development is found in Oscar G. Brockett and Robert R. Findlay, *Century of Innovation: A History of European and American Theatre and Drama Since 1870* (Englewood Cliffs: Prentice-Hall Inc., 1973), pp. 1–52. For a detailed discussion of the Meiningen Company see Max Grube, *The Story of the Meininger,* translated by Ann Marie Koller (Coral Gables, Fla.: University of Miami Press, 1963).

[2]The reader who is interested in this aspect of human behavior generally may find more information in Julius Fast, *Body Language* (New York: M. Evans, 1970) and Edward T. Hall, *The Hidden Dimension* (Garden City: Doubleday & Co., 1966).

Suggested Readings

COLE, TOBY AND HELEN KRICH CHINOY, EDS. *Directors on Directing.* Indianapolis, Indiana: Bobbs-Merrill Co., Inc., 1963.

GORCHAKOV, NICOLAI. *Stanislavsky Directs,* trans. Miriam Goldina. New York: Funk and Wagnalls Co., Inc., 1954.

GUTHRIE, TYRONE. "THE DIRECTOR" IN *A Life in the Theatre.* New York: McGraw-Hill, 1959.

HODGE, FRANCIS. *Play Directing: Analysis, Communication and Style.* Englewood Cliffs, New Jersey: Prentice-Hall, Inc., 1971.

PART THREE

THE
THEATRE
REFLECTS
LIFE

8

THE FORMS OF DRAMA

EVERY PLAY, MOVIE, OR TELEVISION DRAMATIC SHOW represents a way of looking at life. This is not to suggest that Shakespeare, Ibsen, Chekhov, Neil Simon, and the authors of *Gunsmoke,* and *All In The Family* are equal or that any or all of them have attempted deliberately to make philosophical statements about life, people, or the world around them. While some playwrights have clearly set out to make a significant comment about some aspect of life, others might argue that they are only interested in writing a good show or even in collecting a good pay check. Every artist, however, selects his material from life and human experience and arranges that material into a form according to a set of artistic conventions. His selection of a particular set of events out of all the possible events in life makes a comment about what he thinks is important and by choosing to arrange his material in a particular way he makes another comment about how he understands life. No matter how cynically the playwright approaches his material, no matter how strongly he argues that he is merely giving the public what it wants or pleasing the backers or sponsors, it is unlikely that he can keep himself and his way of looking at life completely out of his work. Furthermore, even if he could, he could still not prevent his audience from extracting their own meanings or comments upon life from the work. An example may be helpful here. Suppose a writer sets out deliberately to compose a commercial and sentimental comedy in which the poor but honest young man overcomes a series of obstacles and parental objections to marry the daughter of a very rich man. Regardless of his intentions, he has made a general statement about the possibilities for poor but honest young men. If, on the other hand, the rich girl in the story is selfish, bored, and spoiled, leads the young man on, induces him to fall in love with her, rejects him, and breaks his heart, the writer has made another and different kind of comment about the possibilities for such young men and the relationship of the social classes. Of course, not every member of the audience will accept either statement as true but in both stories a comment about life is implicitly there even if the writer did not set out deliberately to make it.

Most of the plays and playwrights we will be discussing in the following chapters have probably intended to make some kind of comment about life; even if they did not the plays still contain an implicit statement about human beings, human experience, the nature of reality, the world, the meaning of life. The kind of comment the playwright makes depends upon several factors. An obvious one is his own personality or temperament. If he is by nature optimistic and hopeful that fact will be reflected in his plays; if he is the opposite that too will affect his work. The playwright's experiences with life have a great deal to do both with his temperament and the kind of comment he is likely to make. Critics have said that the fact that Henrik Ibsen's father went bankrupt when he was a child is reflected again and again in the playwright's work. Certainly August Strindberg's loss of his mother, the poverty of his childhood home, and his three unhappy marriages are reflected in his plays. The American playwright, Eugene O'Neill, wrote himself and his family into several of his plays, most obviously in *Long Day's Journey Into Night* in which he changes few of the details of his own family experiences, only slightly disguising the names of the characters. Not all playwrights draw directly upon their own experience as did O'Neill and Strindberg, but their work cannot help but take on a certain coloration derived from their personalities and the way they look at life.

Another factor, closely related to the playwright's life experience, is the attitudes, beliefs, or value structures of his era. The Middle Ages, for example, were almost totally dominated by a religious point of view, by man's consciousness of himself as subservient to God, and by the expectation of the end of the world with the subsequent sorting out of the redeemed and the sinners into heaven and hell. Nearly all the anonymous plays of the Middle Ages were religious in theme and subject matter and it is not until near the end of the period that we find plays that are entirely secular. The Renaissance which followed marked an increase of interest in man, a greater feeling of individuality and freedom, and a spirit of adventure. The heroic characters of Christopher Marlowe, Shakespeare, and other Elizabethan playwrights are typical of the Renaissance, but would have been unimaginable in the Middle Ages. Closer to our own time, the scientific theories of Darwin in the middle nineteenth century and of Freud near the end of it, had a great impact upon the way people thought about themselves and their world and consequently on the work that artists produced. Similarly, two world wars, the Russian revolution, and the development of the atomic bomb have had a considerable influence upon the artists of our age.[1]

Occasionally, an artist surmises what may really be going on intellectually and spiritually in his time before the general public does and this may result in a drastic altering of the artistic conventions and an art that is "ahead of its time." As the previous statement suggests, a fourth consideration affecting the way in which an artist comments upon life is the theatrical conventions of his time and society. Shakespeare wrote for a theatre that had an open stage, was unroofed and depended upon the sun for light, that attracted people from all classes and walks of life, and that was, in addition to being an art form, a form of popular entertainment. The structure, the content, the language, and other elements of Shakespeare's drama are related not only to the society of his day, but to the kind of theatre for which he wrote. Ibsen wrote for an indoor theatre with increasingly sophisticated technical capabilities, and in which the tradition of the interior drawing room setting had already begun to be established. These factors as well as the life outside the theatre had their influence upon the kind of plays he wrote.

Obviously all of these factors influencing the playwright and the kind of comment he chooses to make upon life are interrelated. It is difficult, if not impossible, to separate one of them and identify it as the major influence upon the playwright's work. Temperament is formed partially out of personal experience, personal experience is in part governed by the prevailing attitudes of the age; the way an age sees itself and understands the world affect the conventions of its theatre and its other arts, and so on. The artist as a part of society both influences and is influenced by it. In the chapters that follow, we will consider some of the major developments in playwriting and the ways in which they have been related to the ages which produced them. As we do so, we shall see playwrights and theatre production techniques being influenced and affected by what was going on around them and in turn attempting to express these effects and to interpret the meaning and significance of events.

BASIC FORMS

It has been traditional practice among many theatre historians, critics, and literary scholars to classify drama into four basic categories. Those four categories are usually labeled, tragedy, comedy, melodrama, and farce. The first two forms can be said to have been invented by the Greeks and are labeled and discussed by Aristotle in his *Poetics*. His comments on comedy are very brief and sketchy but they do clearly identify it as a form distinct from tragedy. Farce, defined as a comic form involving a good deal of physical humor, "horseplay" and broad joking, is probably also ancient. Theatre historians are convinced that there were preliterary, improvised farces in Greece and the Italian peninsula probably before there was written comedy. The term "farce," as a label applied to a written form of comic play, however, is of much later origin. Similarly, the term "melodrama" and the specific kind of play to which it was regularly applied, dates to the late eighteenth century, but there were elements that could be called melodramatic in some of the earliest of the tragedies, especially those of Euripides. Both tragedy and melodrama can be called serious in the sense that the responses they seek from the audience are usually fear, pity, tension, tears. Comedy and farce, on the other hand, are light, in that they principally seek laughter as a response. Yet the purpose of tragedy *and* comedy may be to induce the audience to think seriously about life while that of melodrama and farce may be to provide escape. Thus, in another sense we might say that tragedy and comedy are serious while melodrama and farce are trivial. If the preceding seems confusing it may illustrate the point that the formal labels often are conveniences for critics and scholars more than they are accurate descriptions of particular plays. Nevertheless, there are general characteristics that define and identify each of the four types and there is a sense in which each of the four types represents a different interpretation of life or view of the world.

TRAGEDY

Tragedy, both the name and the dramatic form, comes to us from the ancient Greeks. No one knows exactly how tragedy originated for the evidence is too sketchy to allow any firm conclusions. One theory is that it originated from rituals celebrating the death and resurrection of the "year god" who, in Greece, was associated with the god of wine and vegetation, Dionysus. This year god, as mentioned in Chapter 1, was thought to govern the coming of the seasons and the fertility of plants, animals, and men. Since for a part of the year the earth lay dead and dormant and then experienced a renewed life in the spring, ancient men found it easy to conclude that the god who governed such matters had been killed by enemies, lay dead for a time, and then was resurrected. This year god myth, and ceremonies celebrating and reenacting it, was very common in the ancient Middle East. In ancient Greece the story of Dionysus was celebrated through the singing and dancing of a chorus of fifty, the song and dance being called the dithyrhamb. The theory holds that at some point a portion of the story was acted out rather than merely being narrated and that from this simple beginning evolved what we now call tragedy. The difficulty with this theory is that all but one of the Greek tragedies that we know about do not deal with Dionysus even indirectly, and the connecting link between the Dionysian ritual and the earliest tragedies is missing. One theory suggests that tragedies grew out of ceremonies honoring dead heroes, that they functioned as political devices designed to aid the transition in ancient Greece from a tribal to a political society. Other theories claim that tragedy simply developed as an effective way of telling a story. Each of these theories is fascinating to think about and each, when presented completely, makes a certain amount of sense. Unfortunately, there is no way that the accuracy of any of them can be proved and as a result we must remain in the dark as to how tragedy really originated. We do know that by 534 B.C. tragedy was a regular part of a festival held in Athens in the spring of the year, that a competition was held and prizes given, and that someone named Thespis won the prize that year. We also have a group of plays with certain common characteristics which were later summarized and discussed by Aristotle in the *Poetics*.

The term "tragedy" comes from a Greek root which means, roughly, "goat song." Many supporters of the ritual theory cite this as proof, pointing out that a part of Dionysian celebration involved men

Figure 8–1. Jean Paul Sartre's adaptation of Euripides' *The Trojan Women.* (Rocky Mountain College, D. E. Moffitt, director, Robert Morrison, designer.)

dressed as satyrs, i.e. creatures that were men from the waist up and goats from the waist down. Thus, the word meant a song *by* goats. Others have argued that in the early days of competition the prize for the winning tragedy was a goat and therefore conclude that its original meaning was song *for* a goat. As with the origin of tragedy there is no way to settle the argument. We are left with the fact that a certain type of play which originated in ancient Greece is called tragedy, whatever may have been the original significance of that word.[2]

Aristotle, in the *Poetics,* written roughly two thousand years ago, comprehensively described what tragedy among the Greeks *had been* and offered some suggestions for what an effective tragedy *might be.* Later critics, especially in the Renaissance, interpreted his suggestions and observations as rules or prescriptions for what a tragedy *had to be.* As a result, all subsequent tragedy is to some degree influenced by Aristotle's criteria and by the practice of the Greek playwrights. Aristotle says that a tragedy is an imitation of an action—by which he probably means something similar to the "basic pattern of events" which we discussed in Chapter 4. The action must be serious, it must be completed within the context of the tragedy and it must be of an appropriate length so that it can be taken in by an audience at one sitting. It should be written in verse with different kinds of verse being used in different parts of the play and it must imitate through enactment. The critical points here are that a tragedy must present a sequence of events that deals with the serious side of life and that it must be acted out—the events must be presented, not told about. His suggestions concerning verse, though they only described what Greek playwrights had done, had considerable influence, so that for hundreds of years playwrights and critics believed that the language of tragedy must be poetry. This belief prompted Maxwell Anderson, a twentieth-century American playwright, to compose *Winterset*, a dark tale of gangsters, murder, and revenge set in the slums of modern New York, in verse.

The proper function of tragedy is, according to Aristotle, to arouse the emotions of pity and fear and by so doing affect a *catharsis* or purgation of these emotions. A great many theories have been advanced to explain what Aristotle meant by this simple word. One of the most recent, and perhaps the most reasonable, suggests that the term comes from an ancient theory of medicine. Physically, the body was thought to contain certain fluids or humors, typically four, which, when in perfect balance, meant that the body was in a state of health. If one of these fluids became dominant, however, it caused illness and to restore health the excess fluid had to be drained off. This accounts for the practice of bleeding in medicine which was common until at least the eighteenth century.

Similarly the "soul" was thought to contain the "passions" and when one or more of them predominated it too had to be drained off in order to restore proper mental health and balance. Certain kinds of art and certain kinds of ritual were thought to bring about this draining off in a relatively harmless fashion. Though we no longer believe in the theory of humors or in the passions of the soul, we can still readily recognize the need for emotional release, and art, as well as other activities such as confessions, psychoanalysis, counseling, encounter groups, and perhaps even spectator sports, helps us to bring about that release. Though Aristotle wrote over two thousand years ago and based his ideas on a now obsolete medical theory he may not have been so far off the mark.[3]

Aristotle's discussion of the tragic hero is brief but full of interesting implications. The misfortune, he says must not fall upon a completely virtuous man, for that would merely be shocking and unexplainable. Nor can the tragic hero be a wicked man, for his descent from prosperity into misfortune would only be seen as richly deserved. What we have left, then, is a man who is basically good, maybe even a little bit better than most of us, who suffers a misfortune because of some "flaw" in his character. In fact, Aristotle says, the hero of tragedy must be an extraordinarily good man and that he should be a member, like Oedipus or Thyestes, of an illustrious family.

Aristotle's requirements for the tragic hero are based upon an aristocratic standard which involves a clear qualitative difference among people. Goodness or virtue is not the mere passive avoidance of evil, but the active development of all of one's potentialities. Furthermore, virtue is not a single quality; there are many virtues, a different one for each field of activity. For example, a student who is honest, truthful, chaste, etc., but who neglects his studies would not be considered virtuous by Aristotle. Part of the virtue of a student is to study conscientiously, as that of a soldier is to fight bravely, or that of a statesman to govern wisely. Families such as those of Thyeste or Oedipus did not become illustrious by birth, or by accident but because they conscientiously strove to fulfill their potential. This concept of goodness then is not quite the same as in the traditional Sunday School lesson. It may involve many of the common Christian virtues — honesty, truthfulness, loyalty, etc. — and it also involves a concept of duty, achievement and self-development. In fact, in his *Nichomachean Ethics* Aristotle argues that we become virtuous by practicing virtue, suggesting that a man *is* what he *does*. Of course, even the good person could make mistakes and this brings us to the concept of *hamartia* or tragic flaw, a word that has been argued over almost as much as has *catharsis*. It is not, as Aristotle makes clear, a vice such as greediness, cruelty, or lust. Rather it seems to be a kind of moral or intellectual error. Now, the practice of virtuous acts is not easy, especially since it does not, in Greek thought, involve merely following a set of rules or "Thou shalt nots." The good, Aristotle says, is a midpoint somewhere between two extremes; the virtue of bravery, thus, falls somewhere between cowardice and carelessness, thrift, somewhere between stinginess and extravagance. In different circumstances, however, that midpoint may be in a different place. Thrift, for example, may be different for a rich bachelor than it is for a family man of modest income, bravery, different for a soldier than for an ordinary citizen. Consequently, in any specific case the midpoint may not be easy to locate. *Hamartia,* then, may consist in missing the correct point in a particular set of circumstances. The tragic hero acts in a particular way because that is the kind of person he is, but that action, in this particular situation, may be the wrong one and may bring him misfortune.[4]

Perhaps a look at some actual tragedies will clarify some of the confusion. In both Greek and Elizabethan tragedies the leading character is frequently faced with a choice between two courses of action, either in the play or just before the play began. Oedipus can persist in his investigations or he can let the matter drop; Antigone can bury her brother against Creon's orders or she can forget it and be a dutiful citizen; Hamlet can avenge his father's supposed murder or he can ignore the Ghost and go back to Germany and the university. In each case, the choice is not one between a clearcut good and a clearcut evil, but one in which a reasonably good argument can be made for either side. Yet once the choice is made the other alternative is closed and the consequences must follow. Furthermore, the choice is often dictated by the kind of person one is. Oedipus' pride and stubbornness may have dictated not only the choice to investigate but also the other choices he makes; to run away from Corinth in order to escape the fate predicted for him by the oracle, to pursue the quarrel with the old man at the crossroads until it culminated in a fatal fight, to confront the Sphinx, etc. The case of Hamlet is a little more complex for, in a sense, he attempts to evade either choice. Had he acted straightforwardly and killed his uncle immediately his tragedy might not have occurred. However, the choice once made permits no turning back; if that choice leads to misfortune all one can do is accept. Tragedy, then, tends to be paradoxical. In one sense, man is free; he makes choices between alternatives. In another sense he is a captive, not of fate, but of his own character which influences the choices he makes.

It is clear too that in tragedy actions have consequences. This is another idea that is not altogether popular in our day and age. Many feel that we should be excused for our actions, that we should receive amnesty or forgiveness or that we can "pass the buck" to someone or something else — our human nature, our parents, society, the system, fate, God. What seems to emerge from tragedy, both classic and later forms, is that man must suffer the consequence of his actions and face his destiny. The Greeks seemed to be aware that no matter how clever, powerful, or inventive man was he was also a creature who could, through his own careless or dishonorable actions, bring misfortune upon himself. Yet even when he does he can still be admirable provided that he has the courage to face up to that misfortune in the proper way. In his *Ethics* Aristotle argues that happiness is the end or goal of all men, but happiness, he insists, cannot be defined in terms of material prosperity or good fortune. Life is too uncertain for that; the man that depends upon such things may tomorrow lose all that he has. Yet, says Aristotle:

> . . . true nobility shines out even here, if a multitude of great misfortunes be borne with calmness — not, to be sure, with the calmness of insensibility, but of nobility and greatness of soul

and again,

> For we hold that the truly good and wise man will bear with dignity whatever fortune sends and will always make the best of his circumstances.[5]

The quality of bearing misfortune with dignity is common to most tragic heroes.

What, then, is the view of man and of the universe presented in tragedy? Put simply, it seems to be that the universe is a moral order and that within this order man has a moral and ethical responsibility. He must act and choose between courses of action without always knowing the end results of his choices. Furthermore, these actions and choices have inevitable consequences. Wrong choice, the refusal to choose, even perhaps right choice, can destroy. Eric Bentley argues that tragedy is concerned with the question of justice and with man's attempt to justify himself in the face of the cosmos.[6] In tragedy man places himself on trial; he conducts an argument with the universe. Why should the innocent suffer as does Desdemona in *Othello* or Cordelia in *King Lear*? Why, even if one is guilty of error, should the punishment seem to exceed the crime? The fact is, however, even in life the innocent suffer as the result of others' actions and the consequences of actions for the doer may be far more severe than the action warranted. This is what brings tragedy closer to reality than perhaps any other form of drama. It is for this reason that the tragic flaw is not a vice but a quality that in another person, in other circumstances, or possessed in greater moderation might even be good. While the fate of Richard III for example, might be a just punishment for the murders he has committed, the fate of Oedipus, Antigone, Hamlet, or Lear strikes us differently. Each could justifiably ask, "What have I done to deserve this?" But if they ever raise such a question they transcend it and accept what befalls them as part of the inevitable mystery of existence. The issue of ethical responsibility and the necessity of facing misfortune with dignity makes the tragic hero's status as king, queen, prince, member of an illustrious family more than just a historical quirk. By virtue of their status and position the responsibilities of such persons are greater and the effects of their choices more significant. Not only are kingdoms frequently involved in their fates but they are also examples to those who do not occupy such high positions.

In short, the function of tragedy seems to be to remind man that he lives in an uneasy world, one in which his choices reverberate or spread

Figure 8–2. The most famous of Elizabethan Tragedies, *Hamlet.* (The Hilberry Repertory Company, Wayne State University, directed by Richard Spear, scenery designed by James Knight, costumes designed by Daniel Thomas Field, and lighting by Gary M. Witt.)

out like ripples when a stone is thrown into a pool of water. Yet, however uncertain and risky the world of tragedy may be, it is not indifferent to man. In Greek tragedy the gods are fairly regularly involved in men's actions and in Shakespearean tragedy human actions may actually disturb the universe. In *Macbeth* the following exchange takes place between Ross and an Old Man on the morning following the king's murder:

OLD MAN:
> Threescore and ten I can remember well:
> Within the volume of which time I have seen
> Hours dreadful and things strange; but this sore night
> Hath trifled former knowings.

ROSS:
> Ah, good father,
> Thou seest the heavens, as troubled with man's act,
> Threaten his bloody stage. By the clock 'tis day,
> And yet dark night strangles the traveling lamp.
> Is't night's predominance, or the day's shame,
> That darkness does the face of earth entomb,
> When living light should kiss it?

Many critics have argued that it is difficult, if not impossible to write tragedy in our modern age. This difficulty arises out of two or three circumstances alluded to earlier. First of all, we tend not to value one person over another. In seeking legal and political equality, which are very important, we have gone on to imply that there is no ethical or qualitative difference between people. The Romantics, reformers, and liberals of the eighteenth and nineteenth centuries, reacting against a society in which privilege was arbitrarily assigned on the basis of birth or wealth, tended to argue that an individual is significant and valuable simply because he exists and then occasionally to extend the argument to suggest that the *less* status one has the *more* significant one is. A good deal of modern literature and drama has tended to deal with the outcasts, the dregs, or the lower depths of society. Such a literature may have been necessary as a corrective in a society where little or no attention was paid to the common people, but the attitude that produced it is not the one that produced classic tragedy. For paradoxically in valuing everyone equally we may conclude by valuing no one very much. Yet the qualities of the tragic hero are precisely those that set him apart from and above other people. His very superiority is what makes his tragic fate more fearful and pitiable.[7] In relatively recent times an argument arose over whether or not Arthur Miller's *Death of a Salesman* was a tragedy. Miller contended that a salesman could be a tragic figure because he was a human being and because he was representative of most men in our society. On the other hand, if we define tragedy as we have in the preceding pages the crucial question becomes whether Willy Loman, salesman or not, has those special qualities of goodness and dignity that qualify him as a tragic hero or whether he is merely a victim of outside forces that he never comes to grips with or understands.

Second, we live in an ethically relativistic world. We are exceedingly unwilling to make clearcut distinctions between good and evil and we even question the existence of such categories. It is more convenient, perhaps, to blame evil deeds on sickness, bad upbringing, social or economic deprivation, etc., or to rationalize them on the basis of good intentions or of necessity. Thus, Adolf Hitler was convinced that he was saving the world from Communism and Adolf Eichmann and Lieutenant Calley were merely following orders. Yet, as we have seen, the tragic hero may lament but he does not try to shift the blame or to make excuses for himself. It is rare to find a modern play in which the hero so resolutely faces reality and accepts the blame for and the consequences of his actions as did the heroes of classic tragedy. To produce a satisfactory tragedy in our day it seems that we must rediscover greatness and responsibility in man, and several critics have contended that it cannot be done.[8]

MELODRAMA

The other traditional form that purports to treat life seriously, at least in the sense that it deals with grim events and does not seek laughter as a response, is melodrama. Melodrama as a distinct form originated around the time of the French Revolution and dominated the European and American stages for many years thereafter. Melodramatic elements, however, can be found in drama as far back as tragedies of Euripides, in Shakespearean and other Elizabethan plays, and in a form that was called domestic or bourgeois tragedy. Euripides' *The Bacchae,* for example, contains a final scene in which a mother, having killed her own son in a mad frenzy, comes on stage carrying his severed head; in the same playwright's *Iphigenia in Taurus* there is a last minute escape from a threatening enemy that is quite typical of melodrama. Shakespeare's Richard III and Iago can both be seen as melodramatic villains and one can see melodrama even in *Hamlet* in the machinery of poisoned cups and swords and the accidents which conclude the play. The first true melodrama, however, is usually credited to a Frenchman named Guilbert de Pixrecourt and was written in 1798. The name "melodrama" was coined because it was common to accompany each performance with music for the purpose of heightening the mood, a practice which was continued in films.

Melodrama as a distinct form has a number of identifying characteristics. One of the most obvious of these is a set of stock characters which may be almost interchangeable from play to play. At least three such stock characters must usually be present – a heroine who is threatened by a villain, and a hero who rescues her and defeats the villain. In the melodrama of the nineteenth century that heroine was pure and innocent. She might be a dutiful and virginal daughter or orphan girl, or she might be a virtuous wife. In some cases she is in love with the hero while in others she may have scorned or ignored him until he performs his act of rescue. The villain is a character of unalloyed evil. He may be handsome and charming but if so those qualities are used to advance his villainy. There is little or no suggestion in melodrama that the villain might be misunderstood, that he might be the victim of circumstances, or that some good might be hidden deep within his wicked nature. He may seek to gain money, power, the heroine's sexual favors, or a combination of the three and he may use blackmail, threats of force, or deception to gain those ends. The hero is usually a male version of the heroine. He need not be quite so innocent of the ways of the world, but he is usually untainted by vice. That he is always courageous and manly goes without saying and he bests the villain either by greater cleverness, greater courage and fortitude, or greater physical strength. Beside these three obligatory characters there may be certain others. The heroine, for example, may have a brother or a father who is in trouble and it is often this very trouble that the villain uses in order to gain his way with her. There may be another female, a woman less pure than the heroine who allies herself with the villain because the hero has spurned her. The hero may occasionally have a trusty "sidekick" who may also function as comic relief. Of all the characters the villain is the indispensable one, for it is his scheming that keeps the plot going.

Central to the plot of melodrama is the threat of evil. The good characters must be placed in danger by the villain and that danger must seem almost undefeatable. Its final escape or defeat must, furthermore, be held off until the last few minutes of the play and often things must appear absolutely hopeless before the villain is finally defeated. This danger, however, need not always be physical. A variant on the pattern just described is one in which the danger is moral; the virtuous wife is led astray by a smooth talking seducer who then either abandons her or turns into a brute who tyrannizes over her. She may be rescued and reclaimed or she may manage to get back home only to die, having repented of her folly and having been forgiven by her loving husband. This is the pattern of one of the most famous melodramas of all time, a nineteenth century English play called *East Lynne*.

The basic pattern we have been considering is capable of a great many variations but central to all must be the villain and some form of threat. When nineteenth century melodramas such as *East Lynne, The Ticket of Leave Man, Uncle Tom's Cabin,* etc. are done today they are often burlesqued; even if they are not they may strike modern audiences as funny. What is funny, however, is usually only the nineteenth century social and dramatic conventions. If we strip away some of the moralizing speeches, some of the sentimentality and some of the moral and social attitudes of a previous age, we find the melodramatic form still present in the theatre and especially in the films and television of today. It is easy to recognize the three obligatory characters in the James Bond film, for example. The heroine, of course, need not be virginal, nor is Bond ostentatiously virtuous, but both are still within the boundaries of what we generally consider to be good. The villain, Dr. No or Auric Goldfinger, is fully as vicious as his counterpart of the nineteenth century, even though he no longer slinks about wearing a cape and twirling his mustache. The modern form that is perhaps closest in spirit to the melodrama of the nineteenth century is the traditional western movie in which the hero was absolutely pure and loved no one but his horse, while the villain was the personification of evil. That form, too, however, has tended to be replaced by the so-called "adult western" which is probably no less melodramatic but in which the "good" characters are allowed some human vices. Probably the master of melodrama on the screen in this century is Alfred Hitchcock; he handles the form with sufficient skill that even the most sophisticated film goer is caught up in the work and does not see the creaky melodramatic machinery behind it. Melodrama is probably much more common today on the movie house and television screens than it is in the live theatre, but it is still present there. One of the most popular plays of not too many years ago which was subsequently made into a movie and which has also enjoyed great popularity in college and community theatres, was Frederick Knott's *Wait Until Dark*. In it, a blind girl is menaced by a set of thoroughly evil gangsters who are trying to obtain a doll that has accidentally come into her husband's possession. The doll is, of course, hollow and filled with heroin. She manages to hold them off until the very last minutes of the play when she is saved by her husband who bursts through the door accompanied by the police.

The world-view presented by melodrama is somewhat different from that presented by tragedy. As in tragedy the world is certainly a dangerous place. The danger, however, is always external; if the hero or heroine is destroyed or threatened with destruction it is not due to any fault of his or her own. The destruction comes from an outside force — criminals, foreign spies, or monsters. However as frightening as the world might be, melodrama is ultimately optimistic. Villainy is always defeated even if it seems victorious until three minutes before the final curtain. Furthermore, conventional values and morals tend to be supported and endorsed by melodrama. The good, in our understanding of the term, always wins out. Even in cases such as that of *East Lynne* in which the hero or the heroine has "sinned" the act is always followed by recognition of its evil nature and by repentance. The melodramas of past ages may seem ridiculous to us largely because our concepts of morality and virtue have changed. In an age in which women have become much more independent and in which sex need not be completely hidden the heroine need not be totally innocent. Yet in the modern melodrama even if the heroine has committed acts that would have been unthinkable in the nineteenth century she has often done so for a "good" reason. She may, for example, have formed a liaison with the villain to protect someone in her family or to take revenge for an injury he has done to her family. In some cases, too, her apparent lapses from conventional morality may be deceptive; she has not done what everyone, including the hero, thinks she has done. In other cases, no matter what kind of life she leads she is basically "good at heart." Similarly, even if the hero, as in the James Bond films, commits acts that are morally questionable, he is good in the sense that he is on "our side." Generally speaking melodrama can be said to endorse the conventional values such as home, family, patriotism, honesty, and bravery. Melodrama does not deny the evil in the world. Indeed, it may present an evil more horrifying than that which we encounter in tragedy. But it is nonetheless comforting for two reasons. First it makes a clearcut distinction between the "bad guys" and the "good guys," and the latter are always ourselves. In American melodrama of the nineteenth century, for example, the villain was frequently a foreigner or an American who had adopted foreign ways and thus ceased to be a "true American." The villains, furthermore, are clearly villainous and we, as audience, do not have to worry about subtleties or psychological complexities. Even if the villain may temporarily appear to be honest and virtuous, we know better. Second, evil is always defeated. No matter how bad things may look, how powerful the villain, or how helpless the heroine, we know that something will happen to save the day. Of course, such a picture of the world is not true. The police do not always arrive at the last minute and there are undoubtedly a good many villains walking around unpunished and maybe even occupying positions of power and influence. Perhaps we do not even believe that it is true — at least not outside the context of the show itself. For a couple of hours, however, we can allow ourselves to be frightened, comforted with the knowledge that things will turn out all right. The villain will be caught and justice will triumph. The fear in melodrama, then, is not the same as that in tragedy for it is not inherent in the nature of the universe or of man himself. It is temporary, it is external, and it can always be overcome.

Melodrama, however, must have some roots in reality. Our newspapers and radio and television newscasts over the past many years have contained a large number of persons who could qualify as melodramatic villains — Charles Starkweather, Richard Speck, Charles Manson and his "family", and the Houston mass murderer to name just a few. And where in the pages of melodrama could one find greater villains than Adolf Hitler and some of the other Nazi leaders? Nevertheless, melodrama tends to simplify villainy and heroism and to reassure us in our desire to believe that justice does exist in the universe. We could perhaps argue that the melodrama is the adult's version of the child's fairy tale, with gangsters, international spies or mad scientists substituting for wicked witches, cruel stepmothers, giants, and ogres. It may be that the melodramatic formula satisfies some deep human need and provides a means, however false and overly optimistic, of coming to grips with the evil that obviously does exist in real life.

COMEDY AND FARCE

It is much more difficult to make the same kind of arbitrary and sharp separation between comedy and farce that we made between tragedy and melodrama. Some of the same general differences exist; comedy, for example, tends to place more emphasis on character, farce on situation or plot; comedy is perhaps more believable while farce depends more heavily on coincidence. Nevertheless, it is not so easy to see the two as distinctly different versions of existence or pictures of the world. The differences that exist are more of degree than of kind. It is more reasonable therefore, to talk in terms of a kind of ladder of comedy types with comedy at the top and farce at the bottom. The discussion of the nature and purpose of the comic, with which we shall begin, applies to both of them.

Comedy, above all, is designed to make men laugh. We do not need to have lived very long to have discovered that there are a good many frustrations in life. Some of the most annoying of those frustrations come from the circumstance of having constantly to live with other people — parents, teachers, wives, husbands, mothers-in-law, bosses, etc. In countless little ways and in a few big ones we find our wills thwarted and our desires frustrated. We could take all these frustrations seriously; we could cry, curse, rage, foam at the mouth, and eventually develop ulcers or high blood pressure or go mad. The less destructive way is to treat all or most of them as funny. We stated earlier that human beings are the only animals who use language. They are also the only animals that laugh. The central character in Robert Heinlein's novel, *Stranger in a Strange Land* is a human who was raised from infancy among Martians and brought to Earth as a young man. As a result, though he is physically an earth man, he is psychologically a Martian. In many respects he is superior to his fellow humans and adapts quite easily to their customs and way of life. Human laughter, however, puzzles and frightens him. Then one day, after being on earth for some time, he visits a zoo and while watching a cage of monkeys he laughs — so hard that he frightens his girl friend, Jill. Later he explains to her why he could suddenly laugh and what he has learned from the experience:

> I grok people. I *am* people . . . so now I can say it in people talk. I've found out why people laugh. They laugh because it hurts. . . . because it's the only thing that'll make it stop hurting.
>
> I had thought — I had been told — that a "funny" thing is a thing of goodness. It isn't. Not ever is it funny to the person it happens to. . . . The goodness is in the laughing. I grok it is a bravery. . . . and a sharing against pain and sorrow and defeat.[9]

150

What Michael Valentine Smith is saying here is what other learned critics have said, that laughter is a way not only of overcoming or dealing with the many minor frustrations of life but even with the major one—our mortality.

Comedy is, first of all, then, a celebration of life. A great many comedies revolve around marriage, sex, and procreation and, indeed, the form is thought to have originated in fertility rituals in ancient Greece. Marriage and sex are probably the most vigorous and vital affirmations of life and thus the firmest denials of death. Tragedy focuses on death and the misfortunes and destruction that can fall on the unwary, while comedy shows us man affirming life, somehow muddling through, and even managing to be a little happy in spite of the misfortunes.

One mode of accepting life is to reconcile ourselves with society and the social strictures that frustrate us; to do this it is often necessary to see that a prime source of our frustration is frequently in ourselves. Norman DeWitt, formerly a professor of Classics at the University of Minnesota, used to remark to his classes that both the tragic hero and the comic character are in a sense misfits. To illustrate this point he would ask his students to try to visualize tragic heroes at a weekend houseparty; Macbeth would be seeing ghosts and visions, Hamlet constantly contemplating suicide, Oedipus trying to discover the truth, Othello suspiciously watching his wife, and so on. This illustrates, too, that it requires only a slight shift of perspective to make the tragic seem comic and vice versa. In tragedy we sympathize with the hero and take his obsession seriously. In comedy we see that same obsession as ridiculous and sympathize with society. Moliere's *The Miser,* for example, deals with a rich old man who is so in love with money that he denies himself and his family even the most ordinary of luxuries. He strives to marry his children off to older partners both of whom are expected to bring an additional fortune into the family. Prior to the dinner party that he must give for these prospective marriage partners he instructs his servants not to respond too quickly when the guests want more food or wine. When one of them complains that he needs a new pair of breeches because he has a hole in the seat of those he is wearing, Harpagon tells him to stand with his back to the wall so that the hole will not show. Clearly Harpagon has turned the ordinary virtue of thrift into an obsession that makes him a sort of monster, a misfit in society. At last his children best him, marry the partners they wish, and leave him alone to lament over the money which his servant has stolen. In the same playwright's *The Misanthrope,* the central character, Alceste, is disgusted with all the lying and pretense that goes on in polite society. Alceste, however, is so devoted to telling the truth that he loses all but the most loyal of friends. He will not make the slightest concession to the necessity to bend the truth slightly, out of courtesy. At last he is forced to conclude that he cannot live in such a false society and must go off by himself to the desert. Both plays are comic, *The Miser* more obviously so, but both could be tragic if we shifted our sympathies to the miser or the compulsive truth-teller. Some comedy of this type might be regarded as cruel in that the obsessed character is dealt with rather harshly, but in other cases the comic character recognizes that his own error is the source of his problems and is reconciled to society.

There is, however, another kind of comedy that is not so much aimed at reinforcing social norms as at gently satirizing or violently overturning them. Comedy can be one of the ways in which we can safely attack people and forces which oppress and frustrate us. Oppressed peoples and minority groups have frequently produced a rich vein of humor. Much of the humor in the Western world, for example, is Jewish in origin, and blacks also have a rich humor of which whites are often unaware because they are the target of it. Consider also how many jokes there are in which the butt of the humor is a professor, a dean, a boss, a top-sergeant or a mother-in-law. Another good example is the standup comic's line, "Take my wife—please!" and, in deference to the women's movement, Phyllis Diller's routine about her husband, Fang. The comic writer's aim may often be to take all that we are supposed to think of as normal and desirable and turn it upside down, sometimes in the interest of what he sees as a higher sanity, sometimes in the interest of the repressed individual.

Critics and scholars who write about comedy often break it up into different types and often disagree in their categories and labeling. It might be useful to think of comedy as a kind of continuum ranging from "high" to "low." There are some difficulties with this approach, however. The first is that the terms high and low are not intended as value judgments— i.e. high comedy is good, low comedy bad—but instead refer to the kind of characters involved, the kind of humor, and the kind of laughter sought. High comedy typically involves upper or upper middle-class people, people who at least have pretensions to social status and appear to be wealthy. Low comedy deals with characters farther down the social scale. High comedy employs a more intellectual humor, aimed at the mind and often requiring a certain knowledge or sophistication on the part of the audience; low comedy, on the other hand, is strongly physical and at the extreme end depends upon the "sight gag"—the slapstick, the pie in the face, the slip on the banana peel. High comedy may seek a smile or a chuckle, at most a kind of gentle laughter, while low comedy goes for the "belly laugh." These distinctions are a bit arbitrary for in practice we are likely to find that the types overlap. Within a play that can be labeled high comedy we may well find low comedy elements; even in low comedy we may find humor that is not always broad and physical. In the traditional division into comedy and farce we are likely to find comedy being roughly synonymous with high comedy and farce with low comedy.

One type of high comedy is commonly called *comedy of manners*. As the name suggests its humor is derived from poking fun at the manners and social conventions of a particular social group by exaggerating them

Figure 8–3. *The Country Wife,* a Restoration comedy of manners. (Hilberry Theatre, Wayne State University, directed by Richard Spear, scenery designed by Russell Paquette, costumes designed by Vic Leverett and Helen Markovitch, and lighting by Gary M. Witt.)

just sufficiently to make them ridiculous. Though the social conventions of any group can probably appear ridiculous if we look at them closely enough and from the right perspective, comedy of manners usually deals with the upper classes. It is naturally best suited to a society in which social distinctions and classes are quite sharply defined and that is one of the reasons that the best comedy of manners in our language has come from England. Historically, a high point in the comedy of manners was during the Restoration, that period after 1660 when Charles II had been brought back to the throne of England after roughly twenty years of Puritan rule. The Restoration comedy dealt almost exclusively with the doings of the aristocrats and court dandies of London—the same people, in fact, who went to see them. The plots often revolved around sex, with a young gallant trying to woo a reluctant lady or trying to find a way of getting together with another man's wife who, incidentally, was usually not unwilling provided that the opportunity could be arranged. One of the best of such comedies was William Congreve's *The Country Wife,* though its moral tone grossly offended the Puritans of its time and could still upset more conservative American communities today. Another fine comedy of that period is William Wycherly's *The Way of the World.* It is cleverer than *The Country Wife* and not as suggestive.

Restoration comedies tend not to be extremely popular today, especially in this country, because to appreciate them fully one needs to know **153** something of the manners and mores of the period depicted. Closer to our own time and therefore more readily appreciated is Oscar Wilde's *The Importance of Being Earnest*. Written in the late nineteenth century, it portrays upper class society of the Edwardian day in which life was treated as a game, form was everything, and social position played a very important role. The story involves a young man named Jack Worthing who has invented a fictitious elder brother named Earnest so that he can have an excuse to get away from his ward and his home in the country and enjoy a life of pleasure in London. In the city he falls in love with and proposes to Gwendolyn Fairfax, who confesses to him that she has fallen in love with him because his name is Earnest and that she could not love a man with any other name. The fact that his real name is Jack, then, causes the first complication; the second is the fact that he does not know his parents. He was found in a handbag that had been checked at a London railway station, and was adopted by the elderly gentleman who found him. To complicate matters further, his friend, Algernon Moncrieff, goes to Jack's home in the country, passes himself off as brother Earnest, and falls in love with Jack's ward, Cecily Cardew. Cecily, however, has also always held the ideal of marrying a man named Earnest. Without going into further detail, suffice it to say that the plot is eventually worked out through the discovery of Jack's real identity and both young men are permitted to marry the women of their choice. The crucial factor in the plot is the importance of family position for marriage and the silly idealism of the young girls that leads them to conclude that the only really safe name for a husband is Earnest. A bit of the flavor of the comedy can be seen in the lines that follow. At the end of second act, after the young men's real names have been discovered and they have had a fight with their respective fiancees, Jack and Algy are sitting at the tea table in the garden:

JACK:
> How you can sit there, calmly eating muffins, when we are in this terrible trouble, I can't imagine.

ALGY:
> One can't eat muffins in an agitated manner. The butter would probably get on one's cuffs. One must always eat muffins quite calmly. It is the only way to eat them.

The young men are furious at each other, they seem to have lost their fiancees, and yet their quarrel revolves around the eating of muffins.

Another Englishman, Noel Coward, is certainly one of the best writers of high comedy in this century, though his plays often contain elements that could be identified with farce. His plays, too, deal with the British upper class or at least with the wealthy and sophisticated class. A frequent feature of his plays is that of the natural man or woman breaking through the surface of sophistication and good manners. In Coward's *Private Lives* Amanda and Elyot, who have been divorced from each other and have remarried other people, meet by accident on the adjoining balconies of their honeymoon suites in a French hotel. They decide that they are still desperately in love with one another and run off to Amanda's flat in Paris, leaving his wife, Sibyl, and her husband, Victor, behind. It was the quick tempers of both, however, and their tendency to get into violent quarrels that led to the divorce in the first place and after a few days of illicit bliss the old problem returns. The end of the second act finds them rolling on the floor, kicking and punching at each other, as Victor and Sibyl enter. One of the funniest scenes in the play occurs the next morning when all four are at breakfast together trying very hard to maintain a "civilized" polite conversation while passions are seething underneath. Eventually, Amanda can contain herself no longer and shoves her buttered roll into Elyot's face. At the end of the play, however, Elyot and Amanda have made up and slip away quietly, while Victor and Sibyl, the "normal" couple are on the verge of a knock-down, drag-out brawl.

In *Blithe Spirit,* another of Coward's plays, a writer employs a medium to perform a seance because he wishes to use such a seance in his next book. Unfortunately the medium succeeds in materializing the ghost of his ex-wife, whom only he can see. This, of course, creates many hilarious complications with his second wife, especially when she learns that it is not nearly so easy to get rid of a ghost as it is to materialize one. Again, the strain of the situation strips away the veneer of politeness and sophistication and the couple begin to shout at each other. Eventually the second wife is killed also and the writer is now afflicted with *two* ghosts. At last, however, he and the medium succeed in dematerializing them and the writer now reveals that he is glad to be rid of both wives so that he can enjoy life without being dominated by a female. Some critics have accused Coward of being trivial and it is true that he never concerns himself with the political and social issues of his time. Yet over and over his plays illustrate the point that the shallow, playful, noncaring attitude his characters try to portray is not so easy to maintain in the face of crises. Under the surfaces of the sophisticated ladies and gentlemen are people who be-

Figure 8–4. A modern comedy of manners, Noel Coward's *Blithe Spirit.* (Westminster College, directed by Carolyn Coombs, and designed by James Arnaman.)

have no more reasonably or politely than anyone else when the pressure is applied, and that, perhaps, is a thing worth realizing.

Another form that is usually considered high comedy is *satire.* Satire aims at the correction, or at least the identification, of human foolishness and stupidity by treating them comically; often it aims at particular institutions or beliefs and exaggerates them so that they appear in a ridiculous light. In this sense it is, of course, aimed at the mind. The satirist hopes that we will see how stupid are many of the things we do and change our ways or he may feel that we will never really change but still wish to show us that we are stupid. This can be done very obviously or very subtly. Perhaps the greatest satirist in the history of theatrical comedy was the ancient Greek, Aristophanes. Maybe his best known play is *Lysistrata* in which the women of both sides decide to go on a sex strike until their husbands agree to end the Peloponnesian War. The possibilities for very broad and earthy comedy in this are obvious and Aristophanes exploited them to the full. At the same time, his plays contained comments and attacks on contemporary political and literary figures by name, including Socrates, as well as some very excellent parodies of other writers that can be fully appreciated only by a person who knows both the ancient Greek literature and the language. In our own time broad satire has been present in films such as Stanley Kubrick's *Dr. Strangelove: or How I Learned to Stop Worrying and Love the Bomb,* or *M.A.S.H.* and is present also in T.V. shows such as *All in the Family.*

Figure 8–5. Aristophanic comedy, *The Birds.* (A student thesis production at Ohio University, directed by Larry Sutton, scenery by James Lauricella, costumes by Cletus Anderson, photo courtesy Larry Sutton.)

As with other forms of high comedy the British are excellent at satire. Some very good examples are to be found in the review from the 1960s called *Beyond the Fringe* and its sequel which opened in New York in the fall of 1973 under the title, *Good Evening.* Perhaps the best of British satirists was George Bernard Shaw, who is also considered a writer of comedy of manners. His most commonly known play is *Pygmalion,* though most know it in Lerner and Loewe's musical version, *My Fair Lady.* The element of satire is present in this story of a cockney flower seller who is taught standard speech and passed off among the aristocracy as a duchess, but it is not as obvious as in some of Shaw's other comedies. In *Arms and the Man* he satirizes the romantic attitude toward war by depicting a soldier who is not afraid to admit that he runs away when the situation seems to require it and who carries chocolates in his cartridge box because he realizes that a soldier is more often likely to get hungry than to run out of ammunition. In *Major Barbara* he satirizes both the Salvation Army and the munitions industry. In *The Devil's Disciple* he suggests that the British lost the American Revolution because an officer in the British war office was in such a hurry to get away for his weekend in the country that he forgot to dispatch an important set of orders. Shaw's plays are at the same time comedy of manners and attacks on society and the institutions it holds dear.

Another type of comedy, as we move along the continuum, may be labeled *character comedy*. Here the humor derives largely from the eccentricities of a particular character or set of characters. Shakespeare's contemporary, Ben Jonson, may perhaps be included here, though he must also be considered a satirist and at times a very savage one. Jonson's comedy was based upon the theory of humors in which the dominance of one of the four fluids or humors was supposed to produce a certain kind of personality. Each of Jonson's characters was a walking illustration of the dominance of one of the humors; they were all eccentric to the point of being grotesque. A modern example of this character comedy is the very popular *You Can't Take it With You* which is frequently done in high schools. The head of the family, Grandpa Vanderhoff has as his chief occupation in life going to graduation ceremonies — it does not matter where, or who is graduating. One of his sons makes fireworks in the basement of their house, one daughter devotes herself to modern dance, though she is much too old to have any future, and each other member of the family, with the exception of one granddaughter, has a similar eccentricity. Somewhat like Moliere's characters, they possess normal human characteristics, exaggerated or twisted out of normal. There is a good deal of farce in the play as well, but the major comic effect comes from this collection of weird but lovable characters. A theme that frequently runs through comedy of this type (though not in Jonson's) is that if these characters are insane they are not much more so than the so-called normal people and perhaps they are better in that they admit their eccentricities.

When we deal with *situation comedy* we are getting quite close to farce. The humor here does not arise primarily from a set of strange characters but from relatively normal people finding themselves in an absurd situation. The characters may, in fact, be relatively stock types—a typical couple, family, etc. Much of the dramatic comedy on television is of this type, employing a group of basic characters week after week and straining the imagination of writers to create ever new comic situations. An example of a situation comedy is the quite successful play of the late 1950s called *The Marriage-Go-Round.* The two principal characters are a husband and wife both college professors, both very stable, ordinary, and devoted to each other. They are anticipating the arrival of a Swedish professor friend and his daughter. When she arrives she is not the girl in pigtails they remember, but a very mature young lady. She tells them that her father is not coming and later reveals to the husband that she has decided that the two of them together should conceive the perfect child. The reader can imagine the complications that arise from her little scheme and it is not necessary to relate the rest of the plot. The point is that the characters are not inherently comic in themselves; the play is funny because some quite ordinary people are placed in a ridiculous situation.

Farce *is* situation comedy and the more outrageous and improbable the situation the better the farce is likely to be. It depends heavily upon coincidence, misunderstanding, and mistaken identity—either deliberate or accidental. Essential to farce is a group of characters with whom, however exaggerated they may be, we can identify, in whom we can see ourselves or people we know. Typically these characters are faced with a problem to which they must provide a solution and that solution is often an extremely far-fetched one. In many cases, indeed, there may be a quite logical and sensible alternative to the far-fetched solution, but for some reason the characters of farce do not think of it. *Charley's Aunt,* written in the nineteenth century by an Oxford undergraduate, is one of the classic farces of all time. The plot involves two students who have invited two young ladies to tea in their rooms. At the time such a meeting was improper unless a chaperone were present. In this case the chaperone is to be Charley's wealthy aunt from Brazil. Unfortunately, the old lady is detained and the young men are faced with the alternative of giving up their date. As a solution to their dilemma they persuade a fellow student (male, of course) to impersonate the aunt. A further complication arises when the middle-aged guardian of one of the young ladies falls for the bogus aunt and spends a good deal of time chasing him around the stage. Needless to say at the end of the play everything is sorted out, but in the meantime all sorts of hilarious complications occur. The attempt to deal with a problem by imaginative but illogical and ridiculous means is characteristic of farce. Occasionally, however, the complications of farce are not caused entirely by the characters. One of the oldest of farces is Plautus' *The Meneachmi,* from ancient Rome. Here the complications arise partly from the fact that twin brothers were separated in infancy and do not know of each others' existence. One of them has a wife and a mistress, both of whom are making life difficult for him. When his identical twin arrives in town he is attacked by both women and it takes the rest of the play to get the misunderstandings and mistaken identities sorted out. Shakespeare based his *Comedy of Errors* on the same idea, doubling the complication by giving each brother a servant who is also a twin. As this suggests, farce like melodrama, often employs stock characters and certain basic formulas or plots upon which variations can be created. The misunderstood husband, the deceived wife, the interfering father or mother, the tricky servant have all been stock characters of farce since Roman times.

The humor of farce, in addition to being based on coincidence and misunderstanding, is often physical. Beatings, chases, pratfalls, men dressing as women, men or women being caught in a state of semiundress or other embarrassing circumstances are all staples of farce. In fact, a device used to administer comic beatings in early farces has given its name to this physical humor. The "slapstick" consisted of two thin and flexible strips of wood attached to a handle so that when swung they made a loud crack without inflicting much pain or damage. Slapstick comedy, while not identical with farce, often plays an important part in it.

There are implications involved in the content of farce. In at least two important senses farce can be called comedy of misrule. It was earlier suggested that some comedy aims at upsetting or overturning social norms, sometimes violently; that aim is characteristic of farce. The most staid and sober-minded individual has probably occasionally felt the urge to thumb his nose at the authority figures in society, to do something outrageous. The characters of farce do so. Bosses, wives, mothers-in-law, parents, policemen, politicians, and first sergeants all get their "comeuppance" in farce. Thus Eric Bentley has described it as an attack on our most cherished institutions.[10] Farce, however, is not merely aggressive. George Kernodle has said that farce reassures that we really do not need

Figure 8-6. An ancient farce—Plautus' *The Meneachmi.* (St. Olaf College, Ralph Haugen, director and designer.)

to fear the authority figures because we see that they are often stupid, clumsy and inept.[11] If they do not defeat themselves they can frequently be outwitted by one who is brash and clever enough. Second, farce is comedy of misrule in the sense that it is based so heavily on accident and coincidence. It presents us with a world of disorder in which things do not work out as planned and in which all sorts of improbable events can and do occur. Farce, however, is not pessimistic for the improbable occurrences may as likely be in our favor as in that of the people who oppose us. In direct opposition to tragedy, the characters of farce are often of very low status; in Roman comedy the most sympathetic characters were frequently slaves. The world of farce, then, is one in which the most ordinary people can usually muddle through—no matter how horrible the mess into which they get themselves.

Some critics have argued that comic drama is designed to correct social evils by making them appear ridiculous and have further asserted that the comic attitude implies a superiority over and a contempt for the characters of comedy. While this is certainly true of some comedy it is not true of all of it. A good deal of comedy, including farce, seems to suggest that perhaps social evils and human imperfections cannot be corrected and that we ought to learn to live with them. A lot of comedy, too, seems to involve affection rather than contempt for its characters, as it recognizes that we are all at different times and to varying degrees foolish and

Figure 8–7. A modern farce, *A Flea in Her Ear* by Georges Feydeau. (Hilberry Theatre, Wayne State University. Directed by Richard Spear, scenery designed by William Rowe, costumes designed by Stephanie Schoelzel, and lighting by Gary M. Witt.)

imperfect. In a sense comic and tragic drama can be seen as opposite sides of the same coin. If tragedy cautions us that we live in an insecure world in which a misstep can lead to disaster, comedy reassures us that such disasters do not occur to most of us, and even when they do they are perhaps not so great as we had imagined.

TRAGICOMEDY

In addition to the four basic forms we have discussed there is another which began perhaps with Euripides, perhaps with the Italian Renaissance, and has come more and more to dominate modern drama. It involves a mingling of tragedy and comedy in the same play. Shakespeare included scenes of comic relief in his tragedies, such as the porter scene in *Macbeth* or the gravedigger scene in *Hamlet*. Tragicomedy, however, goes beyond this in intermingling tragic and comic material in the same play to the extent that the difference is not clearly perceivable. We may find ourselves laughing at something and simultaneously shuddering or realizing later that the thing we laughed at is really horrifying. Or we may be jolted violently from laughter to horror. Earlier we quoted Michael Valentine Smith as saying that the "funny" thing is never funny to the person to whom it happens. We also said that often only a slight shift of perspective is necessary to make the tragic seem comic and vice-versa. Thus, in Israel Horovitz's long one-act play, *The Indian Wants the Bronx,* two street corner toughs come upon an old East Indian who has become lost in New York, wishes to contact his son, and does not speak English. The two boys argue with each other, play games with and torment the Indian and yet at times seem on the point of helping him. Much of what they say is funny; the Indian's insecurity and fear is even funny to us, but not to him. Finally, at the end of the play the more violent of the two draws a switchblade and slashes the Indian's hand. They then run off leaving him pathetically holding out his blood stained hand and repeating the few English phrases they have taught him, "Thank you. You're welcome. How are you?" Tragicomedy sees the tragic and the comic as so intermingled in real life that it is often impossible to see the difference. As a form it may present a situation that appears to be comic and then give it a sudden tragic twist. It may, as in the film, *Dr. Strangelove,* take a grim subject such as atomic annihilation and overlay it with a comic treatment. It may alternate very rapidly between the comic and the tragic in the same play. Perhaps one of the finest examples of tragicomedy in the modern theatre is Edward Albee's *Who's Afraid of Virginia Woolf?* There are many laughs in the play, but many people are also deeply upset by it and by the end of the third act its mood has become distinctly serious. Vicious marital battling may be funny to detached observers as it is, for example, in Coward's *Private Lives*. But Albee does not allow his audience to remain detached observers. The battling becomes too real and too lacerating to allow them to continue comfortably to laugh. More and more serious playwrights today employ this mingling of comic and tragic, among them Friedrich Duerrenmatt and Max Frisch in Switzerland, Harold Pinter in England, and Albee in the United States. The reason for the growth of tragicomedy may be found in our earlier discussion of the difficulties involved in writing tragedy for our time. Duerrenmatt, indeed, has suggested that we have in the twentieth century become so numbed by real horrors that the tragic can have little effect on us and can only be rediscovered by approaching it through comedy.[12]

In this chapter we have discussed four basic forms of drama and have also considered a fifth which has come more and more to dominate modern theatre. These types represent different ways of looking at life and each presents a world picture that is perhaps still relevant to our own time. Though we have stressed the difficulties of writing tragedy in our own day tragedies from past ages have proved still to be effective in the theatre, suggesting that there may still be some sympathy with the tragic view of life. Comedy is always popular and, though styles and subject matter may change through the ages, the comic view of life makes it possible for man to live with his own imperfections and those of the universe he inhabits. Melodrama reassures us that evil can be overcome and that justice does occasionally triumph. In absolute terms that may be a fairy tale, but fairy tales too have their uses if they enable us, even temporarily, to escape from or overcome the very real evils of the world. Tragicomedy reflects the very complex nature of modern reality, the difficulties of seeing events consistently in tragic or comic terms. Most of these basic forms, however, can be presented in different styles and in some cases the modern theatre has evolved new styles that may not correspond to any of them. The chapters that follow consider some of these styles that have arisen out of new conditions and reflect new ways of looking at the world.

Notes

[1]The following chapters discuss in more detail these developments and their influence upon the drama and theatre.

[2]The ritual theory is based largely on James G. Fraser's *The Golden Bough* and the subsequent research by a group of scholars at Cambridge University—Gilbert Murray, F. M. Cornford and others. A particularly full account is found in Theodore Gaster, *Thespis: Ritual, Myth and Drama in the Ancient Near East* (New York: Doubleday, 1961). Gerald F. Else, however, presents a very persuasive attack on the ritual theory in *The Origin and Early Form of Greek Tragedy* (Cambridge, Mass.: Harvard University Press, 1965).

[3]G. M. A. Grube, "Editor's Introduction" Aristotle, *On Poetry and Style* (New York: Bobbs-Merrill, 1958), pp. xiv–xvii.

[4]Some contemporary scholars have argued, however, that *hamartia* meant simply "mistaken identity,"—i.e. the tragic hero fails to recognize someone. This theory has been advanced by Else in his study of the *Poetics* and is mentioned also by Richmond A. Lattimore in *Story Patterns in Greek Tragedy* (Ann Arbor, Mich.: University of Michigan Press, 1965), p. 10.

[5]Aristotle, "The Nichomachean Ethics" in Philip Wheelwright, ed. and trans. *Aristotle* (New York: The Odyssey Press, 1951), p. 176.

[6]Eric Bentley, *The Life of the Drama* (New York: Athenaeum, 1967), p. 260.

[7]Lattimore argues in the work mentioned above that the idea that even the greatest of men is vulnerable to destruction not by an outside force but by himself, is the truth and moral lesson of tragedy. (pp. 54–55).

[8]Joseph Wood Krutch has advanced this argument in an essay entitled "The Tragic Fallacy" in Corrigan, Robert W. (ed.) *Tragedy: Vision and Form* (San Francisco: Chandler, 1965). And Friedrich Duerrenmatt has done so even more strongly in a piece entitled "Problems of the Theatre." Both selections are widely anthologized. The Duerrenmatt article appears in Corrigan, Robert W. (ed.) *The Context and Craft of Drama* (San Francisco: Chandler, 1965).

[9]Robert A. Heinlein, *Stranger in a Strange Land* (New York: Berkeley, 1968), pp. 299–300.

[10]See his chapter entitled "Farce" in the work cited above. Bentley places great stress on the aggressive tendency of farce and sees its motive force as hostility, an argument which he may push too far.

[11]In a paper entitled "What Do You Know: Comic Perception" Presented at the annual convention of the American Theatre Association in Minneapolis, August, 1974.

[12]Duerrenmatt advances this argument in his essay "Problems of the Theatre" in *note #8*. As a German speaking Swiss who came of age during World War II he is, of course, particularly sensitive to the horrors of the Nazi era.

Suggested Readings

The theoretical and critical literature on tragedy is vast and a bibliography of works on comedy, while not as long, would still include many dozen sources. The student who is seriously interested in tragedy should, of course, read Aristotle's *Poetics*. Two good collections of essays on tragedy and comedy are:

CORRIGAN, ROBERT W. *Tragedy: Vision and Form*. San Francisco: Chandler Publishing Co., 1965.

CORRIGAN, ROBERT W. *Comedy: Meaning and Form*. San Francisco: Chandler Publishing Co., 1965.

Two excellent books on melodrama are:

RAHILL, FRANK. *The World of Melodrama*. University Park, Pa.: The Pennsylvania State University Press, 1967.

GRIMSTED, DAVID. *Melodrama Unveiled: American Theatre and Culture*. Chicago: The University of Chicago Press, 1968.

Bentley's *The Life of the Drama,* cited several times in the notes, contains chapters on all of the four major forms and one on tragicomedy.

The following list of plays are representative samples only. The instructor may wish to suggest others.

Tragedy:
    SOPHOCLES, *Oedipus the King*
    SHAKESPEARE, *Hamlet*

Melodrama:
    Burton, *East Lynne*

Comedy and Farce:
    MOLIERE, *The Miser*
    WILDE, *The Importance of Being Earnest*
    SHAW, *Arms and the Man*
    COWARD, *Private Lives*
    PLAUTUS, *The Meneachmi*
    THOMAS, *Charley's Aunt*

Tragicomedy:
    ALBEE, *Who's Afraid of Virginia Woolf?*
    HOROVITZ, *The Indian Wants the Bronx*

9

REALISM AND NATURALISM

THE BASIC FORMS DISCUSSED in the previous chapter underlie all drama. The distinctions between tragedy and melodrama, comedy and farce, even serious and comic may not always be as clearly drawn as we have arbitrarily done, but every play probably builds from one or more of these basic forms. Even while employing the basic forms, however, different playwrights and different periods of playwriting may present their material in different styles. The word "style" is much abused in theatre and often suggests externals such as the fluttering of lace handkerchiefs, affected speech and gesture, and the posing and posturing which are so prevalent in period plays. Style does, of course, involve certain externals, in the theatre as elsewhere. It is closely connected with what we have previously called theatrical convention. It goes beyond that, however, as it reflects a different way of perceiving the world and consequently a different method of communicating that perception. We know very little about the performing style of the Greek theatre, but we know that the plays were presented before huge audiences many of whom were a long distance from the actors, we know that they involved song and dance and that the actors wore masks. Shakespeare's plays were presented on a stage that was quite close to the audience, that could represent anyplace the playwright wished, and that probably made little use of scenery. The acting was probably energetic and vigorous. The comedy of the Restoration was presented on an indoor stage in front of painted two-dimensional scenery and the actors were very conscious of their diction, their movement, and their physical appearance. There is historical evidence to indicate that they probably postured and posed much as did the court dandies and ladies of fashion that they portrayed. There had been many styles in the theatre and drama prior to the middle of the nineteenth century, but they all had two things in common. First, they assumed a distinction between art and life, so that dramatic dialogue, stage speech, movement, body position, and the grouping of actors were all somewhat artificial and "theatrical." Closely related to this attitude was the fact that theatrical conventions did not call for the audience to assume that they were watching real and ordinary people going about their everyday business and doing real things in real surroundings. The audience was always aware that it was watching performers in a theatre. In the years following 1850, however, a new style based upon a different set of assumptions about the theatre and about life began to appear in the theatres of Europe. That

style, realism, came so to dominate European and American thinking
about the theatre in the past hundred years that it served, at least for the
public mind, as a standard against which all other kinds of theatre were to
be judged. Even today the dominant style of commercial productions in
New York and London and of the vast majority of community theatre
productions in the United States is realism.

REALISM: A BEGINNING DEFINITION

Realism, like other styles of the theatre, is a mode of perceiving and presenting the world around us. We must bear in mind that realism can mean
three things. First, when we speak of realism we can mean a *scenic style*.
To employ our earlier terminology, we expect to see a set that documents
or provides information fully and completely about time, place, social
status and so on. We expect to see a room in a St. Louis tenement, a Pari-
sian hotel or a Midwestern farm house that looks as much as possible like
the thing it is supposed to be. Second, we mean a *style of playwriting*
which depicts representative or "typical" people from everyday life, who
talk and act pretty as much as those people would in real life. Third, we
frequently mean *a combination of the above* which depicts events and
people that we believe, that seem to reflect the world outside the theatre
as we know and understand it. When we say that a play is "realistic,"
then, we usually have in mind at least one and probably all three of these
conditions.

Figure 9–1. Realism of setting and content—*Ceremonies in Dark Old Men* by Lonne
Elder III. (Bonstelle Theatre, Wayne State University. Directed by Martin Molson, scenery designed by Jim Seemann, technical direction by Charles Vornberger, costumes
designed by Sharon Larkey, and lighting by Bill Drake.)

In each of them, however, there are potential problems. First of all, we must recognize that a stage set is never completely realistic. No matter to what lengths the director and the designer may go, there always remains the basic *un*reality of the missing fourth wall through which we are witnessing the events.[1] Second, dramatic characters are rarely or never ordinary people in ordinary circumstances. Albee's George and Martha, Williams's Blanche DuBois and Stanley Kowalski, Miller's Willie Loman may *resemble* people that we might know but they are likely to be somewhat heightened, somewhat exaggerated, somewhat more extreme simply because they are dramatic characters. Nor is stage action an exact representation of real events. In discussing the script we said that a play involves a basic pattern of events which strikes the audience as significant; in order to do so that pattern must usually be more tightly organized than real life, frequently around some sort of crisis or a significant point in the lives of the characters. Dramatic dialogue, too, is usually more direct and more tightly organized than is real life speech. A tape recording of a conversation, a social gathering, even an argument is not likely to serve as dramatic dialogue, at least not without a good deal of editing and rewriting; it is likely to ramble, to be repetitious, to stray from the topic and to leave things only partially expressed. Dramatic dialogue, on the other hand, even if it seems to ramble, is much more tightly structured. The third problem is a more serious one. It is quite easy for us to reject as unrealistic those characters and events which do not conform to our own personal experience. If we are widely traveled, extremely perceptive or have come into contact with many different kinds of people this may not be a problem, but the narrower the range of our experience the more likely we are to be wrong. While the characters and events of certain plays may seem to us to be strange and unbelievable, we must not be too quick to dismiss them as unrealistic. Policemen, psychiatrists, priests, and doctors can frequently tell tales that are as bizarre as any depicted on stage or screen. In spite of the difficulties, however, these three criteria, scenic style, style of playwriting and performance, and believability in terms of our own experience, do constitute a good working definition of realism.

We are principally concerned here with the way in which realism functions as a mode of perception and with the image of the world that it presents. In order to understand it from this perspective it would be wise to look briefly at its historical development and some of the influences that brought it about.

SOCIAL BACKGROUNDS OF REALISM

The characters of classic and Elizabethan serious drama were almost always kings, princes, generals, heroes, and their female counterparts. The ordinary citizen, the man in the street, the kind of person most of us know, was thought fit only to be a subject for comedy. With the Renaissance, however, a new class of people began to gain power in society; this development was accelerated with the rise of trade and especially with the Industrial Revolution. To put it simply, power and influence in European society began to shift from those titled aristocrats who owned land to men who owned ships, factories, and shops and even to some of those who worked in those ships, factories and shops. The middle class or *bourgeoisie* began to attain power politically, socially and economically. The rate at which this occurred varied from country to country, coming earliest, perhaps, in England. In some places it was accomplished relatively painlessly; in others, such as France, it required a bloody revolution. Nonetheless, by the end of the eighteenth century a new class was emerging and demanding to be taken seriously, in the theatre as elsewhere. Having money to spend on theatre tickets, many of these people wanted to see themselves, their attitudes, and their values depicted on stage. This gave rise to a form called *bourgeois* tragedy or domestic drama. There had even been a few examples of this in the late Elizabethan period, but one of the most significant plays in the development of the form was written in the eighteenth century by George Lillo. It was entitled *The London Merchant, or the Tragical History of George Barnwell* and told the story of a young apprentice who is seduced by a wicked woman and led by her to steal from his employer and ultimately to murder his uncle. It is sentimental, full of high flown moralizing, written alternately in prose and verse, and for today's audience is extremely easy to burlesque, but it still marks an advance in the direction of realism. Instead of kings, palaces, courts, and military encampments, it brings upon the stage the world of counting houses and shops, of merchants and apprentices — the same world to which the London merchants who went to the theatre would return the next day. More importantly, perhaps, it presented upon the stage the values of that world — hard work, thrift, honesty, the shunning of idle pleasures — and presented business as both a worthy and an ennobling activity. The *bourgeois* tragedy, then, set a trend for the introduction of the ordinary man and his values in serious plays which continued into the next century.

The rise of the middle class was, however, only one such influence. Another was the development of science, especially developments in biology, medicine, and psychology. Of particular impact were the theories of Darwin who argued that the evolution of the creature called man proceeded through a process of natural selection through accidental variations. Of crucial importance in this theory was the ability of an animal to adapt to its environment. For example, if food were scarce on the lower branches of trees only the longer necked giraffes would survive. They would then mate and pass on the long neck to their offspring who in turn would pass it on to theirs. Man, too, was a product of such a process.[2] If this necessarily weakened his religious faith it did not weaken his faith that man could be understood by the application of the scientific method of objective observation and description of his behavior. It implied that environment played a key role in the development and behavior of animal species, including man. Psychology, too, in these pre-Freudian days, tended to conclude that man could be understood from outside by studying traits, behavior patterns and the influences of environment. Thus, we find in the 1870s a group of innovative theatre and literary people calling for a "slice of life" to be put on the stage. It was, furthermore, to be presented with total objectivity and the audience was to study it as though it were a laboratory specimen. The fallacy of calling for a play to be presented with total objectivity should be obvious. Nevertheless, the notion that man could be understood on the basis of external signs persisted until it was seriously questioned by Freud and predecessors and destroyed on the stage by August Strindberg.

Yet another influence was the continuing social and political struggle. The French Revolution of 1798 had not brought equality and wiped out injustice, nor had the revolutions of 1848. Throughout much of Europe and also in America there were continuing struggles between the ruler and the ruled, the rich and the poor, the employer and the employee, man and woman, and faith and science. Social problems abounded; crime, vice, drink, poverty, child labor, antiquated laws relating to property and marriage, etc. Many members of the intellectual and literary community were deeply concerned with these problems, some of them taking direct political action. During the latter half of the nineteenth century Georg Brandes, an influential Danish critic and intellectual historian, said in a lecture that it was the function of modern literature to put problems into debate. Very shortly thereafter plays began to appear which dealt forthrightly and honestly with such social problems as prostitution, drunkenness, slum landlordism, labor abuses, and many others. The greatest of such plays, those which have survived to the present, were obviously not exclusively concerned with the social problems they depicted; indeed they may not have been primarily concerned with those problems at all. There were, however, many dramatists who were willing to take up the gauntlet flung down by Brandes and to attack the social evils of their day.

The rise of realism was, of course, not an overnight phenomenon, nor is it likely that a playwright sat down one day and said, "I'm going to write a realistic play." Rather it was a slow development, resulting, not so much from conscious decisions as from a shifting of perception. Nineteenth-century man began to see his world and his place in it differently. The new middle class and the revolutions throughout Europe had brought the aristocrats down and the common man up. Science and technology had a paradoxical effect. On the one hand they had undermined to a considerable degree the old religious faith and the old social order. In some ways this reduced man's stature. He found it much more difficult, in the light of scientific developments, to regard himself as a special sort of being, created in the image of God and destined for personal salvation. At the same time, and herein lies the paradox, technology had given him greater control over his physical universe than he had ever before experienced and thus, enhanced his confidence. Revolutionary movements and science together had challenged prevailing moral codes and social values, so that it is perhaps quite accurate to describe nineteenth-century man in Matthew Arnold's phrase as "wandering between two worlds; one dead, the other powerless to be born."[3]

REALISM IN PLAYWRITING

It is beyond the scope of this book to discuss in detail the evolution of realistic drama. The student who is interested in this evolution is referred to the supplementary readings listed at the end of the chapter. Here, only a few of the highlights in this evolution are presented. We have already mentioned Lillo's *The London Merchant*. Among his contemporaries and followers were, in France, Denis Diderot and in Germany, Gotthold Ephraim Lessing. Both of these men pioneered in the *bourgeois* drama of middle class life, the former with two plays entitled *The Father of the Family* and *The Illegitimate Son,* the latter with *Miss Sara Sampson.* Romantic drama and melodrama, however, tended to overshadow these early attempts at realism. In 1844 a German playwright named Friedrich Hebbel wrote at least a proto-realistic play called *Maria Magdalena.* It deals with a series of troubles that befall the family of an old carpenter, a stiff and proper German dedicated to the traditional religious and social morality. When his daughter is seduced and made pregnant he threatens to kill her rather than submit to the ridicule and disapproval of his neighbors. He reacts in a similarly rigid fashion when his son is accused of theft. The daughter's true lover challenges the seducer to a duel and kills him, but is fatally wounded himself. The girl commits suicide. When her body is brought in at the end of the play, the old man, still a prisoner of his traditional morality, looks at the wreck of his family and says, "I don't understand the world anymore."

Also during the 1840s early attempts at realism appeared in Russia. Ivan Turgenev, better known perhaps as a novelist and writer of short stories, wrote a play called *A Month in the Country* which, however, was not produced until many years later. As the title suggests it is set on a Russian country estate, one of the type to which the aristocracy went in the summer. It deals primarily with a complicated triangular love affair between a mother, her daughter, and the daughter's tutor, but in the process it quite accurately depicts the daily life of the Russian country estate. At about the same time, another Russian, Alexander Ostrovsky, was experimenting with a realistic form, most notably in a play called *The Thunderstorm.*

In mid-nineteenth-century France, the dominant playwrights were Eugene Scribe, Alexandre Dumas *fils* and Emile Augier. Scribe was the inventor of a form known as the "well-made" play, a very carefully and skillfully constructed drama which followed closely the triangular structure described in Chapter 4. He cannot be called a realist, but the form he developed had a great influence upon certain of the realistic playwrights, especially Ibsen. Of the three, Dumas *fils* is the most famous, chiefly because he wrote *The Lady of the Camellias,* better known as *Camille,* which became a starring vehicle for actresses from Sarah Bernhardt to Greta Garbo. It is a story of a tubercular courtesan—today we would think of her as a high-class call girl—who falls in love with a young man of good family, but gives him up in order to avoid damaging his and his family's reputation. He thinks she has deserted him for another man and berates her savagely; at last, however, he learns the truth and arrives at her death bed just in time for her to cough away her life in his arms. The sentimental tone is obvious, but, however syrupy the play may be, it must not be forgotten that it broke new ground in the direction of realism by presenting on stage not only prostitution but the whole society of prostitutes, procurers, show girls, playboys, and men about town that the French call the *demi-monde.* It presented this "half-world," furthermore, not comically but seriously. Dumas *fils* wrote other plays, as did Augier, dealing with this *demi-monde,* as well as with other taboo subjects such as illegitimacy, corruption in politics and journalism, and social climbing. In all of these plays, however, there is too much intrigue, too much dependence on coincidence, and too much solemn moralizing. Truly realistic drama was yet to come.

When at last it did come it came from an unlikely source. Instead of appearing, as one would expect, from near the center of European culture—France, England or perhaps Germany—it came from a Norwegian playwright named Henrik Ibsen. Ibsen had earlier written romantic dramas, historical dramas, and poetic dramas. What turned him to realism is unclear but after a couple of experiments with the form he electrified the literary, theatrical, and social worlds with a play called *A Doll's House* (1879). It tells the story of Nora Helmer who, years before, had borrowed money illegally, forging her father's name to the note, in order to provide a holiday in Italy for her husband, Torvald, who needed the stay in the Mediterranean sunshine to recover from a respiratory illness. Torvald knows nothing about this and would not approve if he did. Nora, however, is threatened by a blackmailer with exposure; throughout the play she tries to forestall the revelation but when it comes she expects her husband to be magnanimous, to forgive her, perhaps to take the blame for the forgery upon himself. Instead he turns on her, accusing her of disgracing him and his good name, even though she is the one in danger of going to jail. And finally, when he learns that the villain has relented and is not going to the police after all, he cries out, "*I* am saved, Nora!" At this point Nora sees her marriage in its true light and in the climactic scene she tells Torvald that she has been living like a plaything in a doll's house and that in order to find her true self she must leave her husband and children. To us, this may not seem so scandalous; in many respects it is very contemporary. However, it was a scandal in the nineteenth century. The play was greeted with cheers by the feminist movement and with cries of outrage by the traditionalists. Ibsen was castigated by critics and damned from pulpits from one end of the Western world to the other, but in spite of the rage of some segments of society he became the idol of all the rebels, iconoclasts, and *avant-garde* playwrights, actors, and directors throughout Europe. The outcry was even louder at his next play, *Ghosts,* in which he alluded to, though he never mentioned the word, syphilis. The play, however, was not *about* syphilis. It was about a woman's attempt to free herself not, this time, from marriage, but from dead and worn-out-beliefs, attitudes, and superstitions. This play was followed by *An Enemy of the People,* discussed in Chapter 4, and eight more plays, among which are such masterpieces as *The Wild Duck, Hedda Gabler,* and *The Master Builder.* Some of these later plays began to edge away from realism, though they never left it completely.

If we must look for a "father" of realism in playwriting Ibsen is without doubt that father, and his influence is still felt in the modern theatre. He was not, however, alone. Another Scandinavian, this time a Swede, August Strindberg, can also be classified as one of the great practitioners of realism. Though he wrote a great many plays his reputation as a realist rests chiefly on two of them, *The Father* (1887) and *Miss Julie* (1888). The former depicts, as Strindberg often did, a power struggle between husband and wife which culminates with the wife driving her husband insane. *Miss Julie* depicts the seduction of a young countess by her father's valet and its consequences—a suicide. Again we have a power struggle, this time a double one between the sexes and the social classes. The basis for the play had been found in a newspaper story, but Strindberg managed to imbue it with his own kind of emotional intensity. Both plays are serious, even tragic, but they also contain a sardonic kind of humor. Indeed, the plays of both Ibsen and Strindberg show a tendency toward that blending of comic and serious material that is found in tragicomedy.[4]

An important figure in that species of realism known as naturalism was the French man of letters, Emil Zola. Zola was primarily a novelist and essayist, though he did write a few plays in which he attempted to work out his new ideas of theatre. His most important ideas, however, were expressed in two critical works entitled *Naturalism in the Theatre* (1881) and *The Experimental Novel* (1881). In addition to literature, Zola was strongly interested in the science of his day, especially as it applied to human behavior. Thus, he was particularly concerned with the laws of heredity and the influences of environment. These shaping forces had to be studied in order that their operation could be controlled or directed for the betterment of humanity. It was the task of literature and art as well as of science to seek that betterment. Consequently, Zola called for a naturalistic drama that would study man objectively according to the scientific method. Each play was, in a sense, an experiment through which the

Figure 9–2. A scene from Strindberg's *Miss Julie.* (Slippery Rock State College, directed by Orley I. Holtan, designed by Raymond Wallace, photo by Raymond Wallace.)

causes and results of human actions could be observed. Zola's own plays were not very successful and it is doubtful that he had any influence on Ibsen's work. He did, however, influence Strindberg to some degree and also a number of other French playwrights. His most important influence, though, was probably upon André Antoine and the production practices he employed.

The early realists were serious minded men who, like the Greek tragedians, wanted to say something significant about existence and about contemporary social conditions. There are two important playwrights, however, who do not quite fit this pattern; the Russian, Anton Chekhov, and the Irishman/Englishman, George Bernard Shaw. In one respect Chekhov's plays are more profoundly realistic than those of Ibsen. We observed earlier that dramatic dialogue is tighter and more organized than everyday conversation. Chekhov's dialogue seems more like that of life. It wanders, it changes direction abruptly, and often seems to be addressed to no one in particular. Characters speak but they do not seem to be speaking or listening to each other. The action rambles and seems to go nowhere. A common criticism of Chekhov's plays is that "nothing happens." Actually, a great deal happens but much of the action is interior and below the surface of the text. All the plays—there are only four full length finished ones—deal with a decaying and rather helpless Russian aristocracy. These plays have usually been seen as sad, yet Chekhov insisted that they were comedies. Perhaps it is more correct to call them tragicomedies. Probably his most famous play is *The Cherry Orchard.* It deals with an aristocratic and once rich family which is faced with the prospect of losing the country home that they have owned for generations. This threat exists because they have never been practical about money and have always depended upon loans and fortunate marriages to see them through. Throughout the play they futilely discuss ways in which they might save the estate but take no decisive action. Furthermore, they reject the most practical solution—dividing part of the property into lots and selling them to people who want to build summer villas. At last one of their own former peasants buys the estate from their creditors and does just that, forcing them to leave, though he had no wish to do so. He had waited and hoped that they would take some action to save their home, but when it became clear that they were not going to, he bought it rather than let it fall into the hands of someone who had never lived on it. The plight of the family is certainly sad, perhaps tragic, yet the characters are also comic in that they are so completely and ludicrously out of touch with the reality of their situation. When the play is well done, as it was at Minneapolis's Guthrie Theatre, both the comic and the tragic elements clearly emerge.

Shaw was a true comic, but a comic with a social purpose. As a young man he was much taken with Ibsen, though contemporary scholars feel that he may have grossly misunderstood him. When Shaw began to write plays he was directly concerned with social problems, but he wished to deal with them comically, hoping, perhaps to laugh people into correct behavior if they could not be shamed into it. Among his plays are *Widower's Houses,* which dealt with slum landlords, *Mrs. Warren's Profession,* which dealt with prostitution, *Major Barbara,* concerned with the munitions industry, and *Arms and the Man*, which dealt with the "glory" of war. Almost all of Shaw's plays are realistic, though the realistic context is presented comically. Shaw lived to be well over ninety and continued to write plays, though his best work was done, according to most critics, in his early period, around the years of World War I.

REALISM IN PRODUCTION

Realism as a production style can be said really to have started with the Duke of Saxe-Meiningen. There were a few isolated earlier attempts at realism, but it was the Duke's concern with being as meticulously correct as possible in every detail of production that broke the crucial ground. This involved extensive research into architecture, decor, furnishings, costumes, weaponry, and a host of other subjects. It also involved thorough rehearsal and stress on ensemble acting—i.e., every part, even the smallest, was to be as carefully prepared and meticulously acted as every other part. The Duke's repertoire, however, was not confined to, or even heavily committed to, realistic drama. It remained for a young amateur director, actor, and employee of the Paris Gas Company, André Antoine, to take the first decisive step in bringing the realistic play and the realistic production style together. He and a group of his friends founded the *Thèâtre Libre*, or Free Theatre, for the purpose of producing plays that were not being done in the commercial Paris theatres. To escape the government censorship they organized as a private club and sold memberships rather than tickets. It was this theatre that brought Ibsen to the attention of the French public, but, more importantly, Antoine stressed a new approach to staging and acting. The aim of the scenery and the set properties was to create as fully as possible the illusion of reality. To do this he used the box set — though he was not the first to do so — and made it completely three dimensional; he did not merely paint on the walls such units as cabinets or fireplaces, but used the solid three dimensional pieces. In a play called *The Butchers* he is said to have used actual sides of beef as part of his setting. On occasion he would arrange furniture along the edge of the stage, its backs to the audience as though it were set against the imaginary fourth wall. In his style of acting, too, he discouraged declamation, demanded realistic actions and speech, and even encouraged his actors to turn their backs on the audience, something that was rarely done in the theatre prior to his time. The *Thèâtre Libre* lasted only eight years (1887–1895), but it created a precedent for such groups all over Europe. Within two years of the founding of Antoine's theatre a similar group had been founded in Berlin by Otto Brahm. Called the *Freie Bühne*, it opened in 1889 with Ibsen's *Ghosts* and in the following years produced plays by Strindberg, Tolstoy, Zola and Gerhart Hauptmann, whose work it introduced to the theatrical world. In 1891, J. T. Grein opened the Independent Theatre in London, again with Ibsen's *Ghosts*. This too was a short-lived operation and its most significant achievement was to introduce George Bernard Shaw to the English public with *Widower's Houses*. Ironically, when Shaw produced *Mrs. Warren's Profession* a few years later, J. T. Grein, then a critic, was one of the chief objectors to it on the grounds that it was obscene and immoral.[5] The United States did not really catch up with this movement until 1912. There had been a good deal of realism in stage scenery and lighting earlier, chiefly through the efforts of producer-director, David Belasco, but Belasco employed his extreme realism of setting in the service of some very poor plays. In the years between 1912 and 1917, however, a number of independent theatres were founded in various parts of the country, the most important of which were the Neighborhood Playhouse and the Washington Square Players in New York and the Provincetown Players in Provincetown, Massachusetts. The Washington Square Players eventually became the Theatre Guild, one of America's most respected theatres, and the Provincetown Players gave birth to perhaps America's greatest playwright, Eugene O'Neill.

In terms of its longterm influence on the theatre of the Western world, however, the most important of these new groups was probably the Moscow Art Theatre. It was born out of a conversation between a young would-be actor named Konstantin Stanislavski and a young critic, Vladimir Nemirovich-Danchenko. Their theater was opened in 1898, a completely professional operation dedicated to truth and realism in production. As a director, Stanislavski was meticulous, paying attention to the smallest detail and working on a play sometimes for months before he opened it.[6] Photos of the sets used in the Moscow Art Theatre show extreme realism of detail. The two most important contributions of this theatre, however, were (1) the introduction of Anton Chekhov with a highly successful production of *The Sea Gull* and (2) Stanislavski's "system" of acting. It is difficult briefly to summarize the Stanislavski system. Fundamentally, it came out of his extreme concern for artistic truth. Stanislavski hated anything in the theatre that seemed false or smacked of trickery. Artistic truth was to be attained by the actor's trying as much as possible to immerse himself in the "given circumstances" of the role and the play. Much of the approach to the study of a role described in Chapter Three is based upon the Stanislavski system. Perhaps the two key words in the system were *justification* and *belief*. The actor had to be able to justify everything he said and did on the stage. In other words, he did not simply say lines and perform business; he always spoke and acted with, in the back of his mind, the phrase, "I am doing this because . . . " To clarify further, if he uses Stanislavski's approach an actor does not say to himself, "I am pacing the floor in this scene because the director told me to look nervous." Instead he says, "I am nervous. I am afraid my wife will discover that I lost the rent money at the race track." and that thought leads him to pace the floor. Closely related to the above is the fact that the actor must believe everything he does on the stage, for only by believing it himself can he make other people believe it. This is not to say that the actor, like a mental patient, literally believes that he *is* Julius Caesar. It only means that everything he does *as* Caesar must be something that he believes Caesar could and might do. The performances by the actors of the Moscow Art Theatre were widely and highly praised for their realism and inner truth. While not all actors and directors have followed the system literally and exactly, it is probably safe to say that there are few actors in Europe and the United States under the age of approximately seventy, who have not been influenced by it to some extent.

Since their origins in the mid-nineteenth century and especially in the years following approximately 1870, realism in playwriting, realism in acting, and realism in scenic style have become standard in Western theatre. While realism has not gone unchallenged it has tended to form the standard against which other forms of theatre have been judged and evaluated. Furthermore, stage realism tended to be adopted in this century as the basic style of that new art form, the film, and eventually by television.

Consequently, when the average person goes to the theatre he finds the realistic style most understandable and acceptable and is often puzzled, put off, or offended by variations from it.

REALISM: IMPLICATIONS AND PROBLEMS

A presentation of the world-view of realism is a little more difficult than it was with the traditional forms. This is so not only because of the potential confusion of the three common meanings of the term with which we began this chapter, but also because, as a style of playwriting and production, it embodies many of the contradictions and conflicts of the age in which it developed. At least it does so if it is in the hands of a serious dramatist. The task is complicated also by the fact that, though we tend to think of all three together, a realistic script, realistic acting, and realistic stagecraft can be separated. In other words, a realistic play by Ibsen, Chekhov, O'Neill, or Miller probably *demands* realistic acting but does not necessarily require realistic scenery. In fact, excellent productions of Ibsen's *The Master Builder* and Chekhov's *The Cherry Orchard* were done on the thrust stage of the Guthrie Theatre where scenery is necessarily limited to furniture and set props and at most a few minimal pieces. Furthermore, realism as a production and acting style is not necessarily restricted to the realistic play, at least if we define realism as having some basic element of truth, some resemblance to what happens in real life. David Belasco, as we have mentioned, employed extreme realism of scenery in the service of some extremely artificial formula melodramas. If we think of the realism of films and television—frequently consisting of the actual locations—this becomes even more obvious. However real the locale and however believable the acting, we must recognize that many of the events depicted bear small resemblance to anything that actually happens.[7] Indeed, realism of acting and of setting may be applied to poetic plays such as those of Shakespeare. On stage, of course, producing Shakespeare in realistic settings is very cumbersome, but it has been done very successfully on at least two occasions on film, the Laurence Olivier film of *Hamlet* in the late 1940s and the more recent Franco Zefferelli production of *Romeo and Juliet*.

Perhaps the best way to attack the problem is to reconsider some of the influences that led into realism. The first of these was the increasing influence of the middle class. This entry of the middle class brought about a shift of focus within the drama, a change which is not immediately obvious to us because we have always lived with it but which, in its time, was a radical departure. Fundamentally, that change involved the nature and situation of the hero. The tragic hero, as we have indicated, struggled with fate or with a powerful human adversary and his struggle involved such large questions as "Is there justice in the universe?" The central character of the middle-class drama was more likely to struggle with social institutions, codes of behavior, or traditions, and the questions were more likely to involve the nature of marriage, the ethics of business, or the responsibility of government. These are not unimportant questions, but they are clearly smaller ones than those posed by tragedy. The tragic hero, furthermore, was likely to be an autonomous individual; if he did not control his fate completely he was at least independent of human institutions and decided questions of right and wrong for himself. The protagonist of the bourgeois drama, on the other hand, tended to be at the mercy of social institutions and forces and uncertain about the course he should take. The art historian, Arnold Hauser, puts it this way:

> Classical tragedy sees man isolated and describes him as an independent, autonomous intellectual entity, in merely external contact with the material world and never influenced by it in his innermost self. The bourgeois drama, on the other hand, thinks of him as a part and function of his environment and depicts him as a being who, instead of controlling concrete reality, as in classical tragedy, is himself controlled and absorbed by it. The milieu ceases to be simply the background and external framework and now takes an active part in the shaping of human destiny.[8]

This attitude toward man and his place in the scheme of things was reinforced by the scientific developments referred to earlier. If, after all, man was a product of evolution, of natural selection from accidental variations, his independence and control over his own fate was questionable. Other intellectual developments of the nineteenth century—the phi-

Figure 9–3. A realistic play done on a nonrealistic set. Arthur Miller's *The Crucible*. (Slippery Rock State College, Milton Carless, director, Raymond Wallace, designer.)

losophy of history most clearly expressed by Hegel, and early developments in sociology and psychology — tended to have a similar effect. Man's sense of personal worth is diminished. He could very well see himself as an object or a pawn in a game played by nature, history, or institutions. The movement called naturalism, really a species of extreme realism, arose out of such influences and stressed the vital role played by environment in the fate of the individual. As we have indicated, Zola and his followers were not pessimistic about the possibilities of improving mankind. Nonetheless, if forces such as heredity and environment are as strong as the naturalists argued they were, the ability of the individual human being to control his own destiny becomes distinctly lessened.

One aspect of realism, then, becomes the reduction in stature and influence of the central character. The emphasis tends to shift from the individual to the social or the collective. Rather than hero, the protagonist of realistic drama often becomes the victim of social institutions, of nature, or of history.[9] The tragic hero was very much alone and society played little or no part in his downfall. There were, of course, other characters in the plays but they too were present as individuals, not as representatives of the social order within which the hero moved. We know next to nothing about the society of Thebes in *Oedipus* nor of Elsinore in *Hamlet* and we really do not need to. In the realistic play, however, the environment is always present and often plays an important part in the action. A set of laws made it necessary in the first place for Nora Helmer to forge her father's name in order to borrow money. The attitudes of society make the threat of revelation such a dreadful thing both for her and her husband. The same kind of observation can be made about *Ghosts, An Enemy of the People, The Wild Duck, Hedda Gabler,* and probably about the vast majority of other realistic plays. In many of the serious plays the protagonist loses the struggle but, unlike tragedy in which the hero's fate occurs because of his own nature and is inevitable, here we feel that the defeat need not have occurred had social conditions only been different.

Clearly, then, another significant aspect of realism involves a revolutionary attack on existing social institutions and modes of thought. Some of the early playwrights of realism were primarily concerned with social, political, and economic revolution. As a result, of course, realism tended to be strongly opposed by those critics and other public figures who represented the conservative establishment. This concern for change tended to create plays of two types: one focused on the lower classes, on the downtrodden and oppressed, as the group in society most in need of change, while the other focused on the middle and upper classes exposing the supposed hypocrisy and selfishness of their attitudes and behavior. In the first group we find such playwrights as Hauptmann and the Russian, Maxim Gorky, while in the second we find Ibsen, Henri Becque, and Shaw.

Still a third characteristic of realism is the emphasis on the ordinary and everyday. Tragedy, or, for that matter, even melodrama to some extent, had dealt with heroic figures and unusual situations. Serious art was thought, until the mid-nineteenth century, to require idealization and elevation; it was expected to be larger than life. Zola and his followers disputed that claim, arguing that there was as much drama in a tenement room as in a palace and that a shopkeeper or a factory worker was as worthy of being a subject for serious drama as a king or a prince. This idea has become so common to us that we no longer find it very surprising. When we go to a serious play or film today we expect to see people pretty much like ourselves and behavior pretty much like that on the streets from which we came. Thus, in recent years we have had plays about a salesman, set in a shabby New York suburb *(Death of a Salesman);* a machinist, his wife and sister-in-law, set in a New Orleans slum *(A Streetcar Named Desire);* a mid-western widow and her two daughters *(Picnic),* and so on.

For realism, the goal of the theatre is to create the illusion of reality. The scenery creates for us a highly recognizable milieu, the room with the visible walls covered with wallpaper and hung with paintings, the floor covered with carpet, the room filled with furniture. In some extreme cases we have the refrigerator that actually works, the pipes that contain running water, the stove with the real fire. The object of the designer and the director is to make us see, feel, smell, to experience as completely as possible the atmosphere and texture of the place in which the action occurs. Costumes carry the same purpose. They are, or at least seem to be, the kind of clothes worn by the people the actors represent. Acting is designed to create the illusion of real people doing real things. It is often deliberately *un*theatrical. The audience at such a play is cast in the role of eavesdroppers, peering through a keyhole or a curtain at people who do not know they are there. The lighting technician, too, takes great pains to create the color, quantity, and quality of light that would be found in the real situation and even to create supposedly real sources within the scene for that light. In a sense, then, realism presents us with a comfortable world, one we recognize, one to which we have little trouble adjusting and which we do not have to figure out or interpret. Even the characters are understandable for, with the stress on psychology and the influences of the environment, the motivating forces, whether internal or external, are there for us to see. Many realistic plays contain a "self-revelation" scene or speech in which the character explains what has caused him to behave as he does. If such a world is not always pleasant, it is at least one in which we are not presented with unanswerable mysteries. Even though it may depict human beings in miserable situations, it is not completely pessimistic or hopeless, for what people can understand society can correct.[10]

We might be tempted to argue that such a theatre is the ideal. Art, after all, is supposed to reflect life. Did not Shakespeare say that the function of the theatre was to "hold the mirror up to nature?" Undeniably, realism is easier to relate to than other forms or styles of drama. One does not have to puzzle over it; one does not have to try to interpret the language; one can recognize the situation and follow the plot immediately. For this reason we might say that the artist can convey his message more quickly and effectively to more people. We might also argue that a form which depicts life as it is is a more valuable and useful art than one which idealizes. Much of the original impetus behind realism was the argument that the age of tragedy and romantic drama was out-of-date and had no relevance to the nineteenth-century world in which the theatre then existed. An important contribution of realism was the fact that it brought new people and new subject matter to the stage; it made audiences and critics aware that the theatre did not have to deal with the aristocracy on the one hand or to present fairy tales, full of improbable events and set in a romantic never-never land, on the other. The best realistic plays — those of Ibsen, Strindberg, and Chekhov, for example — made comments on life that are as significant as those made by any other plays and certainly more so than those made by the formula melodramas that they replaced.

At the same time there are some difficulties with realism which eventually caused a number of movements away from it in search of new forms. One of these difficulties, as many people have seen it, is the very restriction of its focus. As we have already suggested realism may be said to have reduced the stature of man, made him less heroic, less individually responsible, less free. In doing so, of course, realism was reflecting the attitudes of its age, attitudes which are largely shared in our time. Yet in depicting man as victim, in presenting him as a pawn of larger forces, whether social, historical, or natural, it can be accused of robbing him of nobility and dignity.[11]

Indeed, the characters presented by many realistic plays are notably lacking in such qualities, and that has given rise to another objection to realism. Some critics might ask whether it is possible for us to identify with a mentally disturbed, faded Southern belle or with a broken-down salesman who, all his life, has deluded himself. More bluntly, they might ask if these people are worth our sympathy and concern. Such criticism can, of course, reflect negatively upon the critics. It may reveal a kind of snobbishness, a desire to separate one's self from ordinary humanity. To those who ask why we should care about Willie Loman, in *Death of a Salesman,* Miller, through Willie's wife, offers one answer, "He's a human being. Some attention must be paid." In another sense, this kind of criticism may be seen as an evasion. Many people would rather not be reminded of the sordid, the ugly, the unjust, or the cruel. Realistic drama may force them to look at an aspect of life that they would rather ignore. At the same time, however, there may be some value in this kind of criticism. While the finest of realistic plays do transcend the ordinary and deal with significant themes and questions, there is always the problem of making something out of nothing. Without denying that the misunderstood housewife, the divorcee, the alienated teenager, the homosexual, or the neurotic deserve our sympathy, we might be justified in asking whether there may not be more important problems in life than whether, for example, Jane Doe has a satisfactory sex life or Johnny Jones gets along with his mother. It is easy for the realistic playwright to cross the line from significance into banality and triviality. The novelist, Saul Bellow, once made an interesting comment on precisely this problem of art. "There is grandeur," he said, "in cursing the heavens, but when we curse our socks we must not expect to be taken seriously."[12]

Closely related to this problem is the tendency for realistic drama to be too much bound by time and place. The play that addresses itself to specific social problems may perform a valuable service in its own day but it also runs the risk of being quickly outdated. If a play sets out, for example, to depict the suffering of children working in factories and mills it no longer has anything to say once child labor laws are passed. It may still be of some interest to the historian but to the general public it is as dead as last week's newspaper. Ibsen has survived because he was not primarily interested in such problems as marriage, pollution, liberal politics, or financial skulduggery, but with larger ones such as freedom, responsibility, and the individual's right to fulfill himself. Many of his contemporaries, like Björnstjerne Björnson, who were primarily concerned with immediate issues have disappeared almost completely. Their names are known to no one except theatre and literary historians and there is no reason that they should be. Many of the plays and films inspired by World War II, to cite another example, seem at best merely curious and at worst funny to us now, unless they had some other value than their direct concern with the war.

Another significant criticism of realism is based not so much on its subject matter as upon its effect in the theatre. If one of the purposes of art is to take man away from the ordinary and to expand his horizons so that he may live a richer and fuller life, it may be argued that realism, which presents him with the ordinary and everyday, fails in that purpose. There is something in all of us that craves stimulation, both emotional and intellectual. This is not merely a longing for escape, but a desire to be thrilled, aroused, excited, and perhaps, in the process, enlightened. There are those who would argue that the deliberately *un*theatrical quality of many realistic performances robs us of that opportunity.

Along with the disappearance of theatricality, if we allow for the sake of the discussion that such a loss really occurs in realism, goes the separation of the actor and the audience. When we go to a realistic play we sit in the dark and watch a lighted stage. The actors pretend that we are not there and we pretend that we are spying upon events from real life.

In an earlier chapter of this book the theatre was distinguished from film by the presence of the living actor. This makes possible interaction between actor and spectator which is not possible in a film. When, however, we enter into a mutual agreement with the actor to pretend that we are not there, we lose that contact. Thus, many of the objections to the proscenium stage discussed in Chapter 5 apply as well to the realistic performance.

Perhaps the most important objection to realism, however, centers on the nature and importance of reality or truth. It is this objection that has largely given rise to many of the movements we shall discuss in the following chapters. All serious artists, after all, in some way seek truth. Truth, though, is an extremely slippery concept that may be defined in a variety of ways. A legitimate philosophical question can be raised as to whether that which we observe objectively is necessarily more true than that which we experience subjectively. Indeed, students of perception, of language, and of psychology have been telling us for some time that we see as real or true that which we want to see, that which we have been trained to see, or that which our language makes it possible for us to see. Realism does cast us in the role of outside observers and assumes a fairly simple and straightforward relationship between what we perceive and "reality." Scientific and philosophical developments of the twentieth century, as well as everyday experience, have increasingly suggested that the relationship may be a good deal more complicated and that "reality" may not be so firm and tangible as we have supposed.

Realistic drama, then, is a way of looking at and interpreting experience. As such it reflects the assumptions of the society and the age in which it developed, assumptions which are still held in the twentieth century. The great achievement of realism was to expand the possibilities of theatre, to bring into it aspects of experience that had not previously been considered worthy of art. The great realistic plays, those by Ibsen, Strindberg, Chekhov, Shaw, O'Neill, perhaps Tennessee Williams and Arthur Miller, perhaps others, have made significant comments upon experience and have provided richly rewarding theatre. Perhaps many of them will endure and be read and produced in future ages as Shakespeare and the Greeks are today. At the same time, realism has also been accused of limiting the theatre and of presenting too restricted a view of experience. Thus, in the years since around 1900 a number of new movements have developed which reflect reality and experience in very different ways.

Notes

[1]This unreality persists also in the film. The camera intrudes into the most intimate situations where it is highly unrealistic for an observer to be.

[2]A particularly good discussion of the influence of Darwin on nineteenth-century and modern thought is to be found in Jacques Barzun, *Darwin, Marx, and Wagner: Critique of a Heritage* (Garden City, N.Y.: Doubleday & Company Inc., 1958), pp. 25–126.

[3]In "Stanzas from the Grande Chartreuse," written between September, 1851 and March, 1855.

[4]One scholar discusses Ibsen's *The Wild Duck* as a classic of contemporary tragicomedy. Karl S. Guthke, *Modern Tragicomedy: An Investigation into the Nature of the Genre* (New York: Random House, 1966), pp. 144ff.

[5]The "Independent Theatre Movement" is discussed at considerable length in the Brockett and Findlay book *Century of Innovation* (Englewood Cliffs, N.J.: Prentice-Hall, Inc., 1973) mentioned in connection with Chapter Seven and even more completely in Anna Irene Miller, *The Independent Theatre of Europe: 1887 to the Present* (New York: Ray Long and Richard Smith Inc., 1931).

[6]Stanislavsky's acting theory is quite completely presented in his three books, *An Actor Prepares, Building a Character* and *Creating a Role* all published by Theatre Arts Books. His work as a director is described in Nicolai Gorchakov, *Stanislavsky Directs* (New York: Funk & Wagnalls Company, 1954).

[7]If one contrasts the film versions of the James Bond stories with that of John LeCarre's novel, *The Spy Who Came in from the Cold* one can readily see this point. Despite realism of setting the former are romantic fantasies, while the latter is much closer to the real experience of the spy.

[8]Arnold Hauser, *The Social History of Art* vol. III (New York: Vintage Books, 1951), p. 89.

[9]Wylie Sypher has seen the decline of the individualistic self as a major characteristic of modern society and modern developments in the arts. See *Loss of the Self in Modern Literature and Art* (New York: Vintage Books, 1964). Another detailed discussion of the antiindividualistic tendencies of nineteenth- and twentieth-century science and technology is to be found in Floyd W. Matson, *The Broken Image: Man, Science and Society* (New York: Anchor Books, 1964).

[10]That particular form of realism which was the approved theatrical form in the Soviet Union — "socialist realism" — demanded an optimistic theme. The playwright ran grave risks if he implied that social conditions in Communist societies were not improving.

[11]One contemporary psychologist has, in fact, suggested that such concepts as freedom and dignity are outmoded and must be dispensed with in order to create a safe and a happy society. See B. F. Skinner, *Beyond Freedom and Dignity* (New York: Knopf, 1971).

[12]In an article entitled "The Writer as Moralist" *The Atlantic* (March, 1963).

Suggested Readings

Books:

BENTLEY, ERIC. *The Playwright as Thinker.* New York: Harcourt Brace Jovanovich, Inc., 1948.

BROCKETT, OSCAR G. AND ROBERT R. FINDLAY. *Century of Innovation: A History of European and American Theater and Drama Since 1870.* Englewood Cliffs, N.J.: Prentice-Hall, Inc., 1973.

COLE, TOBY, ed. *Playwrights on Playwriting: The Meaning and Making of Modern Drama from Ibsen to Ionesco.* New York: Hill and Wang, 1961.

GASSNER, JOHN. *Directions in Modern Theatre and Drama.* New York: Holt, Rinehart and Winston, Inc., 1965.

Plays:*

CHEKHOV, ANTON. *The Cherry Orchard*
IBSEN, HENRIK. *A Doll's House*
MILLER, ARTHUR. *Death of a Salesman*
STRINDBERG, AUGUST. *Miss Julie*
WILLIAMS, TENNESSEE. *A Streetcar Named Desire.*

*The above plays represent a sampling of those which can be considered realistic. Your instructor may wish to suggest others. The translation by Leonard Kipnis of *The Cherry Orchard* is particularly good as is that by Rolf Fjelde of *A Doll's House.*

10

ALTERNATIVES TO REALISM

There was a faith healer of Deal
Who said, "Although pain isn't real,
When I sit on a pin
And it punctures my skin,
I dislike what I fancy I feel."

THIS ANONYMOUS LIMERICK points out one of the major objections to realism and naturalism, an objection that was raised quite early by theatre artists as well as others. Fundamentally it is rooted in the question, just what is real anyway and how do we know it to be real? Realism, it was argued by many, is too narrow a way of viewing the world; it leaves too much out of account. It insists that only that which we can touch, hear, taste or smell is real. It has room in its world-view only for that which makes logical sense, for perceivable cause-effect relationships. It views man from outside as an object manipulated by largely external forces. Consequently, it has no room for the *subjective* —for emotional states, feelings, dreams, the illogical and the irrational, the mysterious, or the supernatural. It ignores a large portion of human experience. Of even greater importance, however, is the question of whether we can know reality objectively at all. Even the devices through which we perceive the supposedly real can play tricks on us. Thus, like the faith healer of Deal, our senses may contradict our concept of what is real or not real.

SOCIAL AND PHILOSOPHICAL BACKGROUND

Many theatre historians treat this objection as a product of the late nineteenth century when it had its greatest influence, but in fact it can be traced back much earlier to the movement called Romanticism and beyond that to the philosophy of Immanuel Kant. In the late eighteenth century Kant set out in a very systematic way to determine exactly what we know and how we come to know it. This search forms the substance of his two influential books, *The Critique of Pure Reason* and *The Critique of Practical Reason*. All knowledge of the outside world, he concluded, comes to us through our senses. Whatever we know, even about our own beings, is received through sight, hearing, touch, taste, and smell. Even that which is reported to us in conversation, a lecture, or a book was perceived through someone else's senses and is interpreted through our own.

Here we encounter an enormous problem, though at first it may not seem like one. Every individual is different from every other individual; his senses are different and his experience is different. Consequently, when A and B look at the same scene or object they do not see exactly the same thing. One may see beauty, the other ugliness; one may see a useful object, the other an unidentifiable chunk of metal. Furthermore, there is no way that we can adequately verify what our senses perceive. A cannot enter into B's mind and see what he sees. He can only depend upon what B *reports* that he sees. Most of us, then, bow to majority consensus and accept as real that which the people around us take to be real. The color blind person learns to accept that what he sees as green is actually blue and perhaps to distrust his senses in the matter of colors. Indeed, we tend to perceive those things which we have been taught to perceive and not to see those which we have not. A standard example in this context is the Eskimo who has learned to perceive, and has names in his language for, many different kinds of snow. If this is true of tangible objects, how much more true is it of *sensations,* such as pain, of *abstract qualities,* such as beauty, or of *values,* such as good? In short, Kant argued that knowledge is subjective; it is a personal possession. Indeed, the very existence of Immanuel Kant is reported to us by someone else, through a chain of someone elses back to someone who presumably knew him. We accept on trust the fact that he did exist, but we cannot *know* it with absolute certainty.

We can now take this a step further. Our senses, through which we perceive reality, may play tricks upon us. Most readers of this book will have seen those optical illusions in which one line appears to be longer than another, though both are exactly the same. Most of us, also, have had the experience of seeing someone that we thought we knew, only to realize that we were mistaken. Many of us of have probably had the experience known as *deja-vu* — the strong sensation that we have been in a place before, even though we know we have not — and many of us have had dreams so vivid that upon waking we had to tell ourselves that it was after all only a dream. We could add to the list many other things such as mirages, hallucinations, hunches, ESP, and precognition.

Thus, the objectors to realism argued from Kant's position that what we take to be real is a highly personal thing. This is not to say that nothing *is* real; it is merely to question the confidence with which we assume that we *know* what is real. They argued further that those who want to be realists simply screen out, ignore, or dismiss all those things which do not fit their vision of the world or which they cannot explain.

The movement called Romanticism, which had its beginnings in the late eighteenth century, had always stressed that feelings, personal subjective experiences, were more real and significant than the logical and rational. Some literary and intellectual historians date Romanticism from approximately the late 1780s to around 1850. Jacques Barzun argues that it has not yet ended.[1] Certainly, there has been a tendency among artists, writers, and philosophers up to the present day to emphasize the subjective side of man and to display great interest in the strange, the mysterious, and the bizarre. Tom Driver, in a recent book, has distinguished between two strains of Romanticism which he refers to as Romanticism of the Dream and Romanticism of the Here and Now. The former stresses the subjective, the occult, the supernatural, the historically and geographically remote, while the latter includes what we think of as realism.[2] The Romanticists of the first variety were not content to view things from the outside and to approach life rationally. They wanted to plunge beneath surfaces and to escape ordinary reality in search of a deeper and more profound one. These tendencies are certainly apparent in the poetry of Wordsworth and Shelley, in the music and the critical writings of Richard Wagner, and in the philosophical works of Nietszche. If Driver's theory is correct, the history of Western thought, at least of nonscientific thought, in the nineteenth and twentieth centuries has been the history of an alteration back and forth between these two kinds of Romanticism.

Other influences were at work at this same time, even in some of the sciences, to create this shift in perspective. Psychology, which up to this time had been primarily interested in the observation of man's behavior and the discovery of human instincts, began, in the late nineteenth century to take off in previously unexplored directions. One which greatly interested psychologists and laymen alike was the power of mind over matter and will, especially as it manifested itself in hypnotic suggestion. Another of their interests was the power of the mind to create or distort reality in a hallucinatory state. Even supposed realists such as Ibsen displayed a strong fascination with such things. While vacationing in Denmark during the summer before he wrote *The Lady From the Sea* Ibsen attended several hypnotic demonstrations and collected a number of strange stories about events that had supposedly occurred in the district. One such story, which formed the basis for his play, was of a minister's wife who had supposedly allowed herself to be hypnotized by a former lover into leaving her husband and children. Ellida Wangel, the central character in *The Lady From the Sea,* believes that her former seaman lover—who may even be a ghost—has a mysterious power in his eyes which she cannot resist. Similar themes and ideas occur in his later plays, especially *The Master Builder* and *Little Eyolf.* Strindberg, too, became intrigued with the idea of thought-power and in one of his plays, *Crimes and Crimes,* toys with the idea that a child may have been wished to death by her father.

More important, perhaps, than these earlier developments in psychology were the theories of Sigmund Freud. For Freud, the mind consisted of three levels; one, the conscious, rational, controlling aspect of the personality, he called the super-ego; the second, the source of perceptions and decisions, he labeled the ego, and the third, the animalistic drives and desires, he called the id. As we grow up and become socialized these animalistic desires are repressed by the more conscious states, but they are not destroyed. They continue to exist and often motivate our behavior without our knowing it. This may also be true of certain elements of the ego which have been repressed. Thus, what we think we do for rational reasons may in fact be motivated by unconscious impulses. In some instances, also, we act in ways that we know to be irrational but which we can explain only by saying, "I don't know what made me do that." One of Freud's followers, Carl G. Jung, went even farther and suggested that not only do we have a personal unconscious into which we have repressed aspects of our individual experience, but a collective unconscious which contains the repressed memories, fears, and drives of the human race. These things then come out in symbolic form in myths, dreams, hallucinations, and certain kinds of art.

If human beings are this complex, then, how can we say that we can evaluate their reality by observing their actions from outside? What problems does this create for the dramatist who wishes to portray "real" people? A quiet, modest, respectable person, perhaps a good husband, father, and church-goer, suddenly commits a horrible crime. One reality clashes with another and people ask, "How could he do such a thing?" Such events frequently occur in life. Obviously, then, on stage, as in life, what we see the character do and what we hear him say may be only one reality, a portion of reality, or even unreality.

During these same years there was another strong movement affecting European artists and intellectuals. In Paris especially, but also in other capitals, there was a strong and growing interest in the occult. Mysticism, astrology, alchemy, witchcraft, dream interpretation—all were becoming increasingly fashionable. People dabbled in fortune-telling, especially through the use of the Tarot cards, and in spiritualism. In Paris, an American woman of Polish descent, one Madame Blavatsky, was preaching her own particular version of Oriental mysticism, called theosophy, which laid heavy stress on reincarnation. The Irish poet and playwright, W. B. Yeats, wrote a book entitled *A Vision* which he claimed was dictated to him by the spirits. Some of these artists and writers embraced Catholicism, especially of the mystic sort, while others, among them August Strindberg, were influenced by the writings of an eighteenth-century Swedish mystic named Emmanuel Swedenborg who had described visions of heaven and of an invisible world lying behind the visible and tangible one. The works of William Blake and Edgar Allan Poe were extremely popular. Still other artists, writers, and intellectuals sought mystical visions through the use of drugs or heavy indulgence in alcohol.

Political and social events also had a hand in prompting a revolt against realism. It is customary for laymen to think of the years prior to World War I, roughly 1890–1914 as a kind of Golden Age of peace and order. Contemporary historians know, however, that whatever may have been the surface appearance, there was a great deal of underground disorder lurking and boiling and occasionally breaking forth. Strikes and demonstrations were bloody and frequent, including a couple of notable ones in the United States. The years between 1881–1914 saw the assassinations of Czar Alexander II of Russia, President Carnot of France, Premier Canovas of Spain, the Empress Elizabeth of Austria, King Humbert of Italy, President McKinley of the United States, King Alexander of Serbia and finally, in an obscure little town called Serajevo, of Franz-Ferdinand of Austria-Hungary. Those were the years also of the famous Dreyfus Affair in which a young Jewish officer of the French army was falsely accused of treason and espionage. The legal, political, and sometimes physical battles over his guilt or innocence raged over a period of five years and divided France into two armed camps. One of the prominent figures who came to his defense, incidentally, was Emile Zola. In short, the period when the revolts against realism occurred was one of turmoil and strife, a period in which the concept of an orderly and understandable world and of the progress of man toward a better future seemed more and more to be a fiction.[3]

All of the arts were affected by these various influences. During these years there appeared in painting the Impressionists, such as Cezanne, Matisse, Degas and Gauguin, the Expressionists, such as Van Gogh and Edvard Munch and, a little later, the Cubists, led by Picasso and Georges Braque. In music it was first the era of Debussy, Ravel, and Mahler and later of Stravinsky and Bartok. Stravinsky's *Rites of Spring* caused a riot when it was first performed in Paris in 1913. In dance it was the era of Isadora Duncan who broke drastically with traditional ballet and adopted her own free, interpretive style which became the basis for what is now called modern dance.[4]

SYMBOLISM

In the theatre the first of the departures from realism came with a group known as the symbolists. Actually Ibsen had already moved from realism in the direction of symbolism in his later plays. From *The Wild Duck* onward, his plays, though still rooted in realism, become more and more strange and puzzling. His later plays, especially *The Master Builder* and *When We Dead Awaken* were greatly admired by Maurice Maeterlinck, the foremost of the symbolists, and by James Joyce, who was himself to break important new ground with the novel.

The symbolist movement as such, however, had a kind of program and was centered in Paris. Foremost among its spokesmen was the poet, Stephane Mallarmé. Mallarmé was not a major playwright, but he was deeply interested in the theatre and presented his ideas about it in a series of essays written in 1885 and 1886. Theatre, he claimed, could be the highest form of literature, portraying at its best, as in tragedy, the struggle between man's spirituality and the realities of the world. The theatre of realism, he argued, had ignored metaphysics and thus presented a one-sided view of man. The theatre should save man but in order to do so it had to adopt some of the characteristics of music and of the mass. The theatre, then, should be a kind of communion and its effect should be akin to that of religion.

For the symbolists, the reality of outward appearances was an unimportant thing. The truer reality lay in the internal, the subjective, and the mysterious. Such reality, however, could not be directly presented through dialogue, action, and scenery, but must be hinted at and evoked through the use of symbols, metaphors, and myths. They aimed primarily at creating a mood or an aura of feeling through which the true reality would be indirectly perceived. The most important of the pure symbolist playwrights was Maurice Maeterlinck. His best plays, *The Intruder, The Blind* and *Pelleas and Melisande* are not so much concerned with telling a story or depicting a set of social conditions as they are with creating such a mood. To do this they are set in places that are not geographically identifiable and frequently in some indeterminate long ago; they employ poetic and evocative language and recurrent symbols. The effect of reading Maeterlinck, and probably of seeing his plays, is one of seeing the events through a kind of mist or haze. Every scene, every action, every word, seems weighted with a mysterious and inexpressable meaning. Indeed, the less definable in specific terms is the symbol, the more effective it would be thought to be. Consequently, symbolism may be the most difficult of these forms to discuss because, if the symbolic play or film could be clearly defined and discussed, it would probably no longer be symbolic. The plays of Maeterlinck and the other symbolists are rarely done today, at least in the United States, though the technique is occasionally used in supposedly realistic plays. Thus, the paper lantern that Blanche places over the light bulb in Williams' *Streetcar Named Desire* is a touch of symbolism, as is the old woman who appears selling "flowers for the dead" when Blanche is on the verge of a breakdown in the same play. Indeed, the very title of the play, and the name of the slum neighborhood in which the play is set — the Elysian Fields — are also bits of symbolism. Occasionally, in contemporary film, one can see a good example of pure symbolism. Federico Fellini's *Juliet of the Spirits, 8-1/2,* and *La Dolce Vita* have that quality, as does Antonioni's *Blow-up.* Symbolism, however, is difficult to make work and in its pure form is not likely to be very popular except among those who like to be puzzled and tantalized.

EXPRESSIONISM

Another and, in the long run, probably more significant form can largely be credited to the Swede, August Strindberg, who is certainly one of the most important and influential playwrights of the last hundred years. In order fully to understand his contribution it is necessary briefly to consider his life and career just before he struck off in new directions. The life is a fascinating one in itself, but Strindberg's experiences are probably more closely tied to his art than is the case with any other playwright. After his early attempts at realism and naturalism he experienced a series of troubles, marital, financial, legal, and critical. His first marriage broke up, his works were severely criticized in Sweden and made him little money, and he was even hailed into court on a blasphemy charge arising out of a relatively innocent reference to communion wafers in a collection of short stories called *Getting Married*. Some months after the onset of all these troubles Strindberg found himself in Berlin, divorced, broke, and in a high state of nervous tension. There he associated himself with a group of artists and intellectuals, mostly Scandinavian, who frequented a tavern that he nicknamed the Black Pig. This tavern boasted that it stocked over nine hundred brands of liquor imported from all over the world, and it may have seemed that Strindberg and his friends intended to drink it all. Among the other patrons at that tavern was the Norwegian expressionist painter, Edvard Munch. This group drank and talked away night after night and drifted in and out of affairs with various liberated females, one of whom is the subject of several of Munch's paintings. All of this frenzied activity did Strindberg's nervous state no good and after a hasty marriage with an Austrian journalist named Frieda Uhl and very short stay with her, he drifted to Paris. There he devoted himself to alchemy, became convinced that he had discovered the secret of transforming base metals into gold, and also became deeply involved with the various occult and spiritualist movements. Apparently during this period he went through a number of emotional crises which may have verged upon insanity, during which he saw signs and omens in the most ordinary events, suffered persecution mania and at last became convinced that he was being punished for his agnosticism by "powers" sent from God.[5] After this experience, which he called his Inferno and described in a novel by that name, he wrote an entirely new kind of play, dealing not with everyday experience and the concerns of daily life, but with subjective and spiritual matters. In essence, he tried to recreate on the stage two things: the suffering of the soul in its search for God or for some spiritual anchor, and the feverish, semimad experience of the dream. The most famous of these plays, in fact, is called *A Dream Play*. In it events occur in the seemingly unconnected and irrational way that they do in dreams, held together, as Strindberg says in his preface, only by the consciousness of the dreamer. Characters change identity—one of the central characters is by turns the Officer, the Lawyer, and the Poet and at one point is even returned to his schoolroom and suffers over the same examinations he took as a boy. Time is collapsed or extended almost at random, the scene shifts from one place to another with no apparent logic, and symbols pop up, disappear, and resurface. One such symbol is the growing castle, which is supposed to be rising out of mud and manure and which has on top a large chrysanthemum bud. Another is the clover-leaf door, which appears in scene after scene and is supposed to conceal behind it the meaning of life. A constant theme that runs through the play is "Man is to be pitied." While other plays that Strindberg wrote during these later years may not have been as extreme, all of them seem to have behind them, as Strindberg once commented to a friend, a "terrifying half-reality." Strindberg's major contribution to the theatre, then, was his attempt not to portray external and objective, but internal and subjective reality. The symbolists attempted to do this by creating a mysterious and intangible mood; Strindberg does it by almost forcibly trying to yank the audience inside his central character and forcing them to see the world through his eyes. It is rare in the United States to see a production of one of Strindberg's post-Inferno plays, though they are frequently done in Sweden and his influence on Swedish literature and drama is very strong. The Strindbergian style appears over and over again in the films of Ingmar Bergman, especially in *Wild Strawberries, The Seventh Seal, The Magician,* and *Hour of the Wolf.* [6]

Strindberg's influence on twentieth-century drama and theatre is especially strong. He, with some help from a German named Frank Wedekind, was principally responsible for beginning a movement in theatre that came to be known as Expressionism. German Expressionism began in the years immediately preceding World War I and lasted as a pure form until about 1924. Like Strindberg, the German Expressionists were interested in portraying the tortured, unhappy, often near psychotic inner states of their central characters and forcing the audience to experience their mental states with them. The German movement, however, split in two directions, one following Strindberg in emphasizing the religious and spiritual

Figure 10–1. In Arthur Kopit's *Indians,* Buffalo Bill Cody confronts his memories of past glories. The play becomes an expressionistic, dreamlike tapestry of the whole history of the West. (Hilberry Theatre, Wayne State University, directed by Don Blakely, scenery by Russell Paquette, costumes by Vic Leveritt, lighting by Gary M. Witt.)

and the other more strongly stressing themes of social, political, and economic protest. Needless to say a number of the Expressionists, especially of this second group were imprisoned, killed, or driven out of Germany when Hitler came to power in the 1930s.

DADA AND SURREALISM

Dada and Surrealism are two movements in playwriting styles that can be treated together since they both developed within a few years of each other, involved some of the same people, and tended to overlap considerably. World War I, in which the carnage and destruction reached greater heights than it ever had before, was a profound shock to the European psyche. Many of the young, especially in Germany, reacted strongly, completely rejecting all the prewar values such as morality, materialism, patriotism, and nationalism — that they thought had brought about the war. A number of young refugees from Germany settled in Zurich, Switzerland, and there, in a tavern called the Cabaret Voltaire, Dada was born. Under the leadership of a poet, Tristan Tzara, this group of disillusioned and embittered young men decided that since the world was meaningless the only proper response to it was an art that was also meaningless. The movement was completely nihilistic and was, in a sense, a defiant thumbing of the nose at polite society and accepted values, including artistic values. If the bourgeoisie wanted beauty in art, they would give them ugliness. If they wanted logic and sense, the Dadaists would provide chaos and disorder. If the bourgeoisie sought beautiful objects and wished to hear pleasant music the Dadaists would provide junk and the raucous noises of the street. In short, they attempted to destroy all traditional artistic standards in order to convey to the bourgeoisie how ugly and insane their world was. If the Dadaists affirmed any positive values at all, they were only those of pure spontaneity and the innocence of childhood. Even the name Dada is said to have been picked at random from the dictionary and is the French child's name for hobbyhorse. This fact implies also that Dada was not an entirely grim affair. In spite of its nihilism there was a kind of humor or playfulness associated with the movement, though not a kind that was likely to be appreciated by the middle-class traditionalists at whom it was aimed. The very nature of their beliefs prevented the Dadaists from writing plays in the traditional sense. Instead they staged "manifestations" in which they performed various spontaneous and senseless acts. A group of them might gather, for example, in a public place where one would read poetry aloud, another might tear up a piece of paper into tiny strips and a third walk backward in circles repeating the same four letter word over and over. A good example of Dada in the visual arts is the famous "sculpture" by Marcel Duchamp, consisting of a urinal taken from a public restroom and mounted on a board.

Many of the people who became a part of the Surrealist movement graduated from Dada, but the motives of the later movement were slightly different. Like Expressionism and Symbolism, Surrealism started from the premise that the external reality we see is only the surface; indeed, it may be a false reality that we project onto the universe by making arbitrary connections between random events. The Surrealists wished to get at a deeper or greater realism. In fact, the prefix, "sur" in French means "super." One of the strongest influences upon André Bréton, who was a leader of the group, was Freudian psychology, which led him to argue that the deeper and more profound truths were contained in the unconscious and that a way must be found in which to set them free. One approach to this was through "automatic writing." The aim was to turn off the conscious mind and let the contents of the unconscious pour out spontaneously, much as a patient would do when he free-associates orally on the psychiatrist's couch. Again, Surrealism did not become a major movement in the theatre, but it did produce at least two playwrights of some significance, Jean Cocteau and Guillaume Apollinaire. Perhaps the best way of making clear the nature of Surrealistic theatre is to quote directly from the stage directions and opening dialogue of Cocteau's *The Eiffel Tower Wedding Party:*

> The first platform of the Eiffel Tower, The backdrop represents a bird's-eye view of Paris. Upstage right, a camera at eye level: the black funnel forms a corridor extending to the wings, and the camera front opens like a door to permit the entrances and exits of the characters. Downstage, right and left, half hidden by the proscenium arch, two actors costumed as Phonographs: their bodies are the cabinets, their mouths the horns. It is these Phonographs which comment on the action and recite the lines of the characters. They should speak very loudly and quickly, pronouncing each syllable distinctly. The action is simultaneous with the comments of the Phonographs.
>
> The curtain rises with the drum-roll which ends the overture. Empty set.
>
> PHONO I.
> You are on the first platform of the Eiffel Tower.
> PHONO II.
> Look! An ostrich. She crosses the stage. She goes off. And here's the hunter. He's tracking the ostrich. He looks up. He sees something. He raises his gun. He fires.
> PHONO I.
> Heavens! A radiogram.
>
> *A large blue radiogram falls from above.*
>
> PHONO II.
> The shot wakes up the Manager of the Eiffel Tower. He appears.
> PHONO I.
> Hey, Mac, where do you think you are—hunting?
> PHONO II.
> I was trailing an ostrich. I thought I saw it on the cables of the Eiffel Tower.

PHONO I.
    And you killed me a radiogram!
PHONO II.
    I didn't mean to do it.
PHONO I.
    End of the dialogue.[7]

The play goes on in this same vein, with a General describing how he tried to eat a pie which was covered with wasps but when he attempted to brush them away they turned into tigers, a cyclist appearing, asking for directions and riding off again, a dance performed by a Bathing Beauty, and other bizarre events. Apollinaire wrote a short play called *The Breasts of Teiresias,* supposedly loosely based on the legend of the ancient Greek seer who was both a woman and a man. At a crucial point in the play Teiresias releases two inflated balloons from under his-her dress, allowing them to float off up to the ceiling. Few pure Surrealist plays are done anymore, though elements of Surrealism have crept into more traditional forms. One of the best available examples of Surrealism is a film by Salvador Dali and Luis Buñuel, entitled *The Andalusian Dog* — no dog ever appears in it — which is frequently shown in film courses and by college film societies. A newer film which contains a good deal of Surrealism is Stanley Kubrick's *A Clockwork Orange.*

STAGING

The staging of these various movements naturally puts considerable strain on the director, the designer, and the actors. It is much easier to create a realistic interior and for the actors to behave as much as possible like people in everyday life. The Symbolist, the Expressionist, or the Surrealist cannot depend upon such simplicity. Thus, the scenery is frequently strange, evocative, symbolic, or bizarre. Lighting plays an important part in Symbolism, especially that subtle combination of light and shadow that is called *Chiaroscuro.* The theories of Appia, calling for a theatre lighting that operated to create and control mood in the same way as did music or poetry, are important here. So are Gordon Craig's designs for scenery resembling huge obelisks or granite blocks. In connection with this kind of theatre Gorelik's concept of scenery as metaphor (see Chapter 6) is perhaps most important. These innovators were not interested in documenting time and place; they were interested in creating mood or emotional effect and the scenery and lighting would thus necessarily be to some extent metaphoric. Scenery in Expressionistic plays was often violently distorted in order to depict a violently distorted mind (see fig. 6–5b, p. 91). Acting cannot be extremely realistic either. The actor's aim in this kind of theatre is to make a point or create an impression, not to appear to be a real person. Thus, for example, Cocteau's description of the Phonographs speaking loudly, quickly, and distinctly. Acting in such plays may be dreamlike, frenzied, or mechanical, but it is rarely realistic.

PROBLEMS AND IMPLICATIONS

All of the movements we have discussed have their roots in the idea that reality is subjective and personal as well as objective and public. Any movement in the arts, then, which attempts to restrict itself to the objective actually distorts rather than depicts reality. Personal turmoil, psychological and other scientific developments, and social and political conflict caused many artists, around the turn of the century and in the new one, to turn inward and to try to depict the world as *experienced* rather than the world as *observed*. If the aim of classic drama was to present an ordered universe in which justice prevails, one aim of this movement was to present a mad, disordered, and chaotic world. If the aim of realism was to present a world that was logical, sensible and governed by scientific laws, the aim of the departures from realism was to present a subjective world of the spirit in which logic, sense, and scientific law were irrelevant.

Distinguishing among these forms is often difficult, especially since each of them tends to spring from a very similar impulse. How does one tell, for instance, whether a particular play is to be categorized as Symbolism, Expressionism, or Surrealism? Such classification may, in fact, be quite arbitrary. and it may be that only critics and scholars need be seriously concerned with fitting plays into appropriate pigeonholes. Nevertheless, there are some rules of thumb that may be helpful. Symbolism is usually rooted in reality. The characters, events and places are not distinctly *un*real; they may even be quite recognizable, but within that realistic context, objects, characters, and events seem to take on strange meanings or emotional colorations. Typically in watching such a play we feel that something is being said that we cannot quite grasp. Another way of saying it is to go back to the analogy with language with which this book began. All art, like all language, employs symbols. Language is, indeed, nothing but symbols. In Symbolist art, however, the symbols are less clear, the referents or meanings less precisely identifiable. In Symbolism, we are not sure whether a rose is just a rose, or whether it is beauty, purity, innocence, love, fragility, or all of them at the same time. In Ibsen's *The Wild Duck,* we know that the duck is a real bird. The crucial question is, what else is it? In Expressionism we move a little farther from tangible reality and a little deeper into the subjective. Now reality becomes distorted and logical or sensible connections between events become vague or disappear altogether. We tend to feel, however, that we are viewing reality through a pair of eyes, usually those of somebody in the cast. In *The Dream Play,* for example, we feel that we are seeing reality through the eyes of Strindberg, who is also the Officer, the Lawyer, and the Poet.

199 Surrealism may be equally distorted and illogical or even more so. The crucial difference is that the "point-of-view" character seems to be missing. In a sense, we are in the same role as the audience at a realistic play. We are watchers, but the events we watch are strange, bizarre, distorted, and illogical. We are expected to make the connections and discover the deeper or truer reality behind the strangeness.

Each of these departures from realism is an attempt to get at a deeper order of reality or to express a different kind of truth. At the same time they may contain within them certain disadvantages. While it is true that truth and reality are to some extent subjective and individual, there is at the same time some common element to all those separate images; if there were not we could not communicate at all. It is precisely in this stress on the subjectivity of experience that the problem arises, for theatre is a communal activity and if the artist insists too strongly upon his own personal vision he runs the risk of alienating and losing his audience. He may, of course, eventually lead them to see the world in his way and this is certainly a legitimate function of art. Strindberg's work, for example, was not widely accepted until some time after his death, when the general experiences of Europeans made his personal view more acceptable and understandable. There is typically a lag between the most experimental forms of art and their general acceptance. It is quite possible, however, and this is the risk that the Symbolist, Expressionist, or Surrealist runs, that his personal fantasies and subjective reactions will never communicate to a larger public.

This personalization of the art form leads to another potential problem. That is the creation of a coterie art, a form that appeals only to a small sympathetic clique. Though we cannot be completely sure about Shakespeare's audiences and even less sure about those of the Greek dramatists it seems likely that Shakespeare, especially, provided something for everybody; a story, excitement, spectacle, and humor for the crowd and something more for those who had the wit, intelligence, sophistication, or education to get it. Today's theatre has apparently split into two theatres—one made up of the Broadway farce and melodrama and musical comedy for the masses and another, perhaps more serious, at least in intent, for artists and intellectuals. The one, in spite of its financial difficulties, does provide a good living for the few and entertainment for the many, while the other often operates on a shoestring and is confined to the poorer neighborhoods of large cities or to college and university campuses. The former, too, though it may provide a degree of fame and fortune for some of its participants, often creates artistic frustration, for actors and directors recognize that it is frequently trivial and lightweight and does not provide them with real challenges. The solution may lie in at least two different directions. The first involves educating the general public to what the serious *avant-garde* artist is trying to do while the second may require the artist himself to try to seek greater contact or community with a larger audience.

Figure 10–2. In Arthur Miller's *After the Fall* the play becomes a blend of realism and expressionism with the action taking place in the protagonist's memory. (Wayne State University Theatre, directed by Robert T. Hazzard.)

In this chapter we have considered several new forms of theatre that arose out of new experiences and new ways of looking at the world. None of these movements maintained itself long as an independent form. Elements of all of them, with the possible exception of Dada, tended to get absorbed into the more traditional forms and to influence contemporary playwriting and production techniques. We have mentioned the use of symbolism as a technique in *A Streetcar Named Desire.* Expressionist techniques have been similarly incorporated into realism. In Miller's *Death of a Salesman,* for example, we are taken inside Willie Loman's mind as he goes back into his memories or as he imagines dialogues with his long vanished brother, Ben. The use of dance music and a revolver shot as sound effects in *Streetcar* serve a similar purpose. The whole of Miller's *After the Fall* takes place in Quentin's head as he journeys back into his own memories. It is easier technically for the film to do this sort of thing and we have become so accustomed to the flashback and hallucination scenes in that medium that we rarely stop to think that they are not "realistic." Even some of the more bizarre elements of Dada and Surrealism have reappeared under other names in recent artistic movements to play a part in some of the more modern movements. Thus far these new movements have not replaced realism; on the contrary they have in many ways enriched it and they have also provided an alternate way of dealing with experience which can exist alongside realism.

201

Notes

[1]Jacques Barzun, *Classic, Romantic and Modern* (New York: Doubleday & Company, Inc., 1961), *passim*.

[2]Tom Driver, *The History of Modern Theatre: Romantic Quest and Modern Query* (New York: Delta, 1971), *passim*.

[3]The chaotic history of this period is well told in Barbara W. Tuchman, *The Proud Tower* (New York: The MacMillan Company, 1966).

[4]The early history of the artistic developments, especially leading to Surrealism and Dada, of this period is well discussed in Roger Shattuck, *The Banquet Years: The Origins of the Avant-Gard in France, 1885 to World War I*. (New York: Vintage Books, 1968).

[5]Strindberg wrote a number of semiautobiographical novels recounting many of his experiences. The one dealing with this period is entitled *The Inferno* and the new translation by Evert Sprinchorn (New York: Doubleday Anchor Books, 1968), contains a long introduction that is packed with fascinating details about his stay in Berlin and Paris. Additional detail is provided in a novel called *The Cloister* newly edited in Swedish by C. G. Bjurström, translated by Mary Sandbach (London: Secker & Warburg, 1969).

[6]While many of these films are now quite old and were shown in small "art" theatres, many of them are available in screenplay form in paperback and they are also frequently shown by college and university film societies.

[7]Jean Cocteau, "The Eiffel Tower Wedding Party" (trans., Dudley Fitts) in *The Infernal Machine and Other Plays* (New York: New Directions, 1963), pp. 161–63. © 1963 by New Directions Publishing Corp. Reprinted by permission of New Directions Publishing Corp.

Suggested Readings

Books:

BENTLEY, ERIC. *The Playwright as Thinker* (New York: Harcourt Brace Jovanovich Inc., 1948.

BROCKETT AND FINDLAY. *Century of Innovation:* Englewood Cliffs, N.J.: Prentice-Hall, 1973.

GASSNER, JOHN. *Directions in Modern Theatre and Drama* New York: Holt, Rinehart & Winston, Inc., 1965.

SHATTUCK, ROGER. *The Banquet Years* New York: Vintage Books, 1968.

Plays:

MAETERLINCK, MAURICE. *Pelleas and Melisande*

STRINDBERG, AUGUST. *The Dream Play*

O'NEILL, EUGENE. *The Hairy Ape"*

RICE, ELMER. *The Adding Machine"*

"These last two are American versions of Expressionism and as such are probably a little easier to identify with than the works of the German Expressionists.

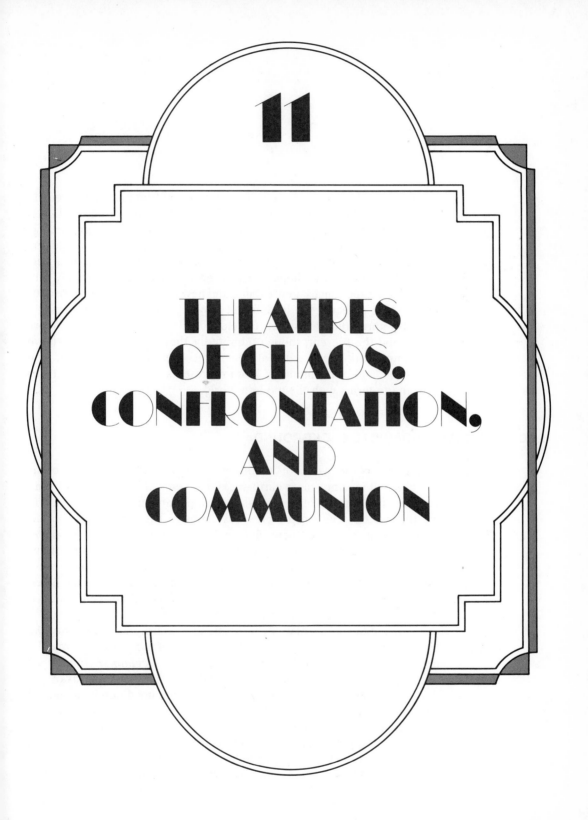

11

THEATRES OF CHAOS, CONFRONTATION, AND COMMUNION

WORLD WAR I had an enormous impact upon the European mind, society, and the arts and, to an extent, that influence was felt also in the United States. The events that followed the war had an even greater impact. The world that had preceded 1914 seemed permanently to have vanished and, though many people had hoped that a new and better one had been brought into being, that hope suffered repeated shocks in the years after 1917. New experiences, new events, and new developments gave rise to a theatre that reflected life in different ways. In a broad sense, there are probably three theatres which developed in the period between World War I and the present, though admittedly they overlap. At the risk of oversimplification, we can call them the theatres of chaos, of confrontation, and of communion. Each represents a different way of trying to come to terms with the modern world.

SOCIAL AND PHILOSOPHICAL BACKGROUND

The history of the twentieth century has been marked by a number of disturbing, and in some cases earth-shaking, events. There has also been a continuation of many of the trends toward the diminishing of the individual that we observed in the previous century. These events and trends have in turn stimulated new philosophical movements and new developments in the arts. The crowding into roughly sixty-five years of two world wars, major revolutions in various parts of the globe, and a set of astonishing scientific developments including one that provides the potential for the complete destruction of the planet, could not help but have drastic effects upon values and ways of thought.

One of these effects was a widespread insecurity or uncertainty. Social scientists have recently made frequent use of the word, "anomie," to describe our society. *Webster's Seventh New Collegiate Dictionary* defines that term as "a state of society in which normative standards of conduct and belief are weak or lacking" or "a similar condition in an individual commonly characterized by disorientation, anxiety, and isolation." Normative standards of belief and conduct had already suffered a severe shock in the orgy of killing that had been World War I. Even before the Armistice and the Peace of Versailles, revolution had broken out in Russia. The old Czarist regime was overthrown and replaced briefly by a democratic government. This was in turn overthrown by the Bolsheviks or, as we know them today, Communists. Many people in Europe and America expected the Communist regime to collapse quickly; when it did not there was increasing fear, especially among the privileged classes, of the "Red Menace," a fear which has not entirely disappeared in our own time.

Shortly after the end of the war, Europe began to suffer extreme economic hardships. Defeated Germany was the first and one of the worst sufferers, but following the stock market crash of 1929 the United States and the rest of the "victorious" nations were plunged into economic depression. The economic disaster and the Red threat made it possible for Benito Mussolini and Adolf Hitler to assume dictatorial power in Italy and Germany. For a time the rest of the world thought of them as funny little men who posed no serious danger. In spite of Mussolini's invasion of defenceless Ethiopia and Hitler's systematic terror campaign against Communists, Jews, and other "undesirables," many people persisted, as late as the Spanish Civil War in 1936, in ignoring the danger. The Second World War which at last broke out in 1938, raged for seven years and eventually involved most of the nations in the world. This war caused more havoc, death, and destruction than ever before in man's history. Furthermore, it was only after the war that its full horror was revealed. Over six million Jews and others had been systematically slaughtered in places like Dachau, Auschwitz, Belsen, and Treblinka. Medical experiments of the cruelest sort had been carried out on living victims. All of this had been done by a nation that many had considered to be the most civilized in Europe while other non-Germans and non-Nazis had either cooperated or passively watched.[1]

Those who had suffered and those who had merely seen the suffering had to ask themselves, how could human beings do these things to one another? How could supposedly civilized and Christian Europeans systematically and cold bloodedly murder millions of their fellows and how could a supposedly loving God let it happen? They could find few satisfactory answers. These questions naturally became of enormous importance to artists and intellectuals who had witnessed the horrors.

As in 1918, the end of the war did not bring peace and tranquility. The secret of the atomic bomb which had ended the war was quickly discovered by the Russians. At the height of the Cold War the peoples of the world were overshadowed by two huge nuclear powers, standing each other off with what has aptly been termed a balance of terror. The years since 1945 also saw a series of shocks, disruptions, wars, and revolutions in places like Berlin, the Middle East, Korea, Vietnam, Cuba, Greece, and Algeria. War, revolution, and the threat of nuclear annihilation caused a mood of deep pessimism to infect Europe in the 1950s and the United States was not untouched by it.[2]

Related to anomie is a second trend, increasingly characteristic of the post-World War I world, commonly called alienation. It is at once a sociological, philosophical, and psychological term and is consequently difficult to define. Put as simply as possible, however, it means that the individual feels separated or cut off from his existence, from society, from his work, even from himself. We have already mentioned the Darwinian revolution and the increasing scientific movement and its effect on man's sense of his own importance. This movement did not diminish in our century and, though religion is by no means a thing of the past, accumulating scientific evidence and the emotional shocks of World War II and its aftermath made it increasingly difficult for man to maintain his old religious faith and to think of himself as a child of God. But if man is not a child of God, what is he? If he is merely a cosmic accident or a naked ape, what happens to the whole structure of values and traditions that had sustained him since the Middle Ages? This was the question that many sensitive thinkers and artists found themselves asking as the century progressed. Yet it was not so much even the philosophical questioning that was significant as it was the sense of rootlessness that many men felt, even men who could not articulate the problem.

The experience of social alienation is one that is more familiar to most of us. With the growth of technology, industrialization, and urbanization the Western world experienced a shift from what one German sociologist called the *Gemeinschaft* to the *Gesellschaft* — i.e., from the small, self-contained and tightly knit community to the large, anonymous organization. Modern citizens often live in large cities and work for large corporations. One obvious result of such conditions is loneliness, for city dwellers often do not know their next door neighbors, workers in a large corporation are often not well acquainted with their fellow workers, and both are far removed from the sources of power that affect their lives. The anthropologist, Margaret Mead, has commented that modern communities tend to be too homogeneous; the residents of many suburban communities vary only slightly in age, the children are isolated in schools, the old people in homes or retirement communities, and the processes of both birth and death are hidden away.[3] This growth of large organizations affects us even in our work. Workers and craftsmen of previous ages could point with pride to something they had made, having followed the whole process from start to finish. Today's worker often works on an assembly line, performing a small part in a large operation, or deals entirely with abstractions rather than with either products or people. Thus, many contemporary philosophers and social critics have argued that modern man does not feel a part of his community nor of his work and often feels that he has little or no control over his own existence. It was feelings of this sort that led protesting students in the 1960s to carry placards which read, "I am a human being. Do not fold, staple, or mutilate."[4]

In summary, twentieth century man seems more and more to have come to the point of regarding himself as a thing, an object manipulated by forces over which he has no control, for reasons that he does not understand. He does not make things happen; things happen to him. This is a quite different thing from the concept of fate held by the ancient Greeks. Man, for the Greeks, could not *ultimately* control his destiny, but he did have an appointed place in the scheme of things and within it he could take decisive action. Indeed, it was usually the taking of a wrong action that brought on the tragedy. Analogically, we could say that the Greek attitude pictured man as walking through a swamp and having to exercise care that he did not step off into water too deep for him. By contrast modern man might be seen as being whirled and tossed around in the strong currects of a river, having little control over his direction or speed. This feeling of thingness, coupled with the uncertainty and insecurity described earlier in this chapter tends to make life seem unreal, strange, senseless, absurd. Recall that anomie as related to the individual was defined as "characterized by disorientation, anxiety, and isolation." Out of this confusion, anxiety, rootlessness and alienation, especially after World War II, come the theatres that form the subject of this chapter.

ANTONIN ARTAUD

Before we can begin our discussion of the theatres of chaos, confrontation, and communion we must consider one man who, though never successful as a playwright, has perhaps had more influence on the contemporary theatre than any other person, save one.[5] His thinking and his writings on the theatre have touched, in one way or another, all three of the movements that constitute our concern in this chapter. Artaud was a Frenchman, born to a middle-class family in Marseilles in 1896. He was educated in his home town, was a good student, and was deeply interested in modern art and literature. From his arrival in Paris in 1920 until his death in 1948 he was a poet, an actor, a director, an artist, and a critic. At none of these but the last was he outstandingly successful. He suffered constantly from ill health, and even spent nine years in a mental institution, but his writings on the theatre, principally collected under the title, *The Theater and its Double,* constitute one of the most important bodies of theatre theory and criticism to be published in this century.

Artaud objected strongly to the theatre he knew, which he saw as having three principal faults: it was too devoted to masterpieces of the past, it failed to move us deeply because of its shallowness and triviality, and it was too devoted to the word, that is, too literary. In contrast he proposed a "theatre of cruelty," an idea which is easy to misunderstand unless one reads Artaud carefully and reflects long over what he says. This theatre of cruelty does not necessarily imply, as we might immediately conclude, acts of extreme and grotesque violence; its subject matter need not be murder, torture, and mayhem. It is "cruel" in the sense that it makes us uncomfortable, that it grips and moves us deeply, that it does not allow us to dismiss it as merely "pleasant" or "entertaining." In the opening essay of *The Theater and its Double,* Artaud compares the theatre to the Black Plague which ravaged Europe in the Middle Ages. The Plague was extremely contagious, severe in its symptoms, and almost always fatal. It completely decimated whole districts in many parts of Europe. Its psychological effect, however, is what concerns Artaud. Under the pressure of so many deaths, the survivors often abandoned all traditional rules and mores. Since it frequently seemed that no one would survive, they launched themselves upon orgies of lust and greed. In short, the plague liberated or released all the dark forces of the soul that normally civilized people keep in check. It revealed to people those acts of which they are capable, that they might otherwise have denied. Artaud sees in this a curative function, perhaps similar to, though more drastic than, that of psychoanalysis, for as we are forced to see that we can be cruel, murderous, and lustful, as we recognize the existence of these potentialities within us, we may better be able to control them. "It appears," says Artaud, "that by means of the plague, a gigantic abcess, as much moral as social has been collectively drained; and that like the plague, the theatre has been created to drain abcesses collectively."[6] A theatre that is vital and useful should accomplish this by forcefully showing us what we are and of what we are capable. In a later essay entitled "No More Masterpieces," Artaud advances the argument that most of the masterpieces of the past may have been good for their own time, but have nothing to say to us. This is so primarily because they are too literary, they have become art for art's sake and appeal to the mind rather than to the senses. In this context he defines theatre of cruelty more completely and adds to it another element:

> But *"theater of cruelty"* means a theater difficult and cruel for myself first of all. And on the level of performance, it is not the cruelty we can exercise upon each other by hacking at each other's bodies, carving up our personal anatomies, or, like Assyrian emperors, sending parcels of human ears, noses, or neatly detached nostrils through the mail, but the much more terrible and necessary cruelty which things can exercise against us. We are not free. And the sky can still fall on our heads. And the theater has been created to teach us that first of all.[7]

Theatre of cruelty, then, seems to involve not merely the draining of collective abcesses—an idea which seems not very far removed from Aristotle's *catharsis*—but also teaching us that we live in an insecure world in which calamities are always possible. In theory Artaud's theatre does not seem very different from Greek tragedy. In form, however, it may be quite different.

The theatre of the past, Artaud argues, has become fixed and so encrusted over by traditional forms and by academic criticism that we can no longer see it. In the essay just quoted he makes a statement that would horrify many professors and perhaps delight many students. If *Oedipus the King* has nothing to say to a modern generation, he says, we should put the blame upon the play, not upon the audience. The modern theatre, on the other hand, at least the commercial theatre with which Artaud was familiar, is too trivial and shallow:

> Given the theater as we see it here, one would say there is nothing more to life than knowing whether we can make love skilfully, whether we will go to war or are cowardly enough to make peace, how we cope with our little pangs of conscience, and whether we will become conscious of our "complexes" . . . or if indeed our "complexes" will do us in. Rarely, moreover, does the debate rise to a social level, rarely do we question our social and moral system. Our theater never goes so far as to ask whether this social and moral system might not by chance be iniquitous.[8]

Artaud was strongly influenced by a visiting group of Balinese performers that he saw in Paris in 1931, and by semi-primitive Indian ceremonials that he saw during a visit to Mexico. The former especially, suggested to him a theatre that was not dependent upon the poetry of words that appeal primarily to the mind, but on a theatre poetry, employing all of the elements of scenery, lighting, architecture, and above all the moving body in space. Such a theatre would at least relegate language to second place if it did not eliminate it altogether, and would have a direct impact upon the senses. To employ popular slang it would evoke a "gut level" rather than an intellectual response. If the emphasis of the traditional theatre was on poetry, the emphasis of Artaud's theatre would be on spectacle.

The most important and suggestive of Artaud's attempts to realize his theatre of cruelty in concrete terms is the scenario for a spectacle to be entitled "The Conquest of Mexico," also contained in *The Theater and its Double.* It was never produced and does not even seem to be finished, but in its theme of colonization and the clash of Christianity with paganism, it may have influenced Peter Shaffer's play, *The Royal Hunt of the Sun,* which deals with the Spanish conquest of Peru. In fact, though Artaud cannot be considered successful as a playwright, he influenced not only Shaffer but many other playwrights and directors, among them Jean Genet, Eugene Ionesco, Harold Pinter, Peter Weiss, Peter Brook, Julian Beck and Judith Malina, and Tom O'Horgan. Perhaps no one has fully realized Artaud's concept of theatre of cruelty as he envisioned it, but it is safe to say that the modern theatre would not be the same without him.[9]

THE THEATRE OF CHAOS

The theatre of chaos reflects a disintegrating, insane, and senseless society and world. In some respects it can be said to have been influenced by Dada, though as a theatre movement Dada did not come to much.

A major root of the theatre of chaos, which gave birth to a small group of plays, is a philosophical movement called existentialism. Thousands of words have been written attempting to define this very complex philosophy and it would be beyond our purposes to discuss it in detail here. Its most influential branch, at least as far as the theatre is concerned,

209

follows the thinking of Jean Paul Sartre. Sartre begins with the premise that there is no God; consequently there are no external restraints on man and no meaning in the universe. Man, therefore, is free; he can do anything he likes, but because he exists he must do something. He can only escape the obligation to act by ceasing to exist. By our choices, by the actions we typically take, we define or create ourselves and also impose upon our world the only kind of meaning it can ever have. Thus, the man who habitually acts in a cowardly fashion is a coward, no matter what he may *think* or *say* he is, a point which Sartre makes in his most famous play, *No Exit.* Upon this structure, however, Sartre is able to build an ethical and social philosophy by pointing out that we do not live in this world alone. However free we may be from metaphysical restraints, our actions cannot be completely irresponsible because they have consequences for other people. Man is therefore both free and forced to act but he is also obligated to take the responsibility for his actions. Sartre is both a serious philosopher and a playwright. Indeed, the nature of his philosophy may have required him, for the sake of clarity, to express it in dramatic form. In addition to *No Exit* he has written a number of other plays, among them *The Flies, Dirty Hands,* and *The Condemned of Altona.* Each of them, in various ways, involves questions of choice, action, and ethical responsibility. Closely related to Sartre is another Frenchman, Albert Camus. There is some disagreement about whether Camus should properly be called an existentialist, but he is usually so classified and he certainly shared some of Sartre's ideas and preoccupations. His most famous play is *Caligula.* It deals with the Roman emperor of that name who, following the sudden death of his sister, set out by gratuitous acts of crime and cruelty to discover whether there is any meaning in the world. The simple idea which sets him off upon this course is summed up in the sentence, "Men die and they are not happy." Both Sartre and Camus, however, stayed basically within the realistic tradition in playwriting. Philosophically, though both posited a meaningless world, they also tried to find a rationale for a human action. Though they argued that there was neither a natural or a divine order in the universe, they still felt that man could create a human order.[10]

The other major root of the theatre of chaos goes all the way back to a very strange play produced in Paris in 1896, written by Alfred Jarry and entitled *Ubu Roi. Ubu* was a grotesque, broad, obscene, and childish parody on the heroic, romantic drama, some of which was still around. Its central character is a Polish noble, who like Macbeth, kills the king in order to take the throne himself. He is, for all practical purposes, a big, stupid, spoiled child who carries a toilet plunger for a sceptre and begins the play by shouting the French equivalent of the English four letter word for excrement. Aside from its deliberate obscenity and parody, the play has the tone one might expect if a fairly bright ten-year-old sat down to write a Shakespearean play. So far as we know *Ubu* had no direct descendants, though it did have some influence on the Dada movement and was later rediscovered by and strongly influenced the playwrights we have come to call Absurdists. Mingled with the influence of Jarry and Dada were elements of the circus, the burlesque comedians, and the music hall to form a theatre that had similar philosophical premises to the existentialist drama, but was very different in form.

The Absurdists, in essence, accepted the pessimistic premises of existentialism and ignored its positive side. If there is no God, no purpose, no order, natural or divine, then life is meaningless. It is an unwanted gift forced upon man for no reason that he can understand, which will one day be terminated by an equally meaningless death. In a famous essay Camus likened the condition of man to that of the Greek demi-god, Sisyphus, who, because he had offended Zeus, was condemned to roll a huge rock to the top of a hill. Just as he was about to reach the top, however, his strength failed and the rock came rolling back down to the bottom, so that he had to begin all over again. Camus saw a kind of strange triumph in the fact that Sisyphus knew he had almost made it, that at least he had struggled. The Absurdists saw only the meaninglessness of the task. All of our philosophy, rituals, religions, languages, and sciences, they felt, are nothing but our attempts to hide the absurdity of existence.

The so called Theatre of the Absurd never developed as a unified school. Rather, it consists of a group of playwrights who appeared at about the same time and expressed pretty much the same view of life. What made them significant was not that they expressed a pessimistic view of existence; that had been done before, all the way back to Euripides. What was significant was the fact that they attempted to match the form of the drama with its theme or content. That is, they seemed to believe that if life is meaningless and absurd, its absurdity can only be expressed through a form that is equally meaningless and absurd. In this sense, they were the artistic heirs of the Dadaists.

Perhaps the two most famous of these playwrights are Samuel Beckett and Eugene Ionesco. Though they write differently, they tend to express a similar view of existence through equally absurd form. Beckett is an Irishman who first came to Paris between the wars as secretary and companion to the novelist, James Joyce. There he stayed and he has written almost all of his major works, novels, plays, and poetry, in French. His most famous play is *Waiting for Godot,* which we discussed briefly in Chapter 4. Two tramps wait by the side of the road for Mr. Godot. They do not know who he is, they do not know why he is coming, they do not know why they are waiting. One character says that Godot is coming "to save us," but when the other asks, "to save us from what?" the first replies, "I don't know." They occupy their waiting time with inane chatter, with petty quarrels, and occasionally with questions that seem to have some philosophical significance. One of them, for example, is bothered by the fact that of the two thieves who were crucified with Christ, one is damned and the other saved. Like all their other topics of conversation, however, this one goes nowhere. The only other major characters in the

Figure 11-1. Pozzo's slave, Lucky, in Becket's *Waiting for Godot.* (St. Olaf College, Ralph Haugen, director and designer.)

play are Pozzo and his slave, Lucky. When they first meet in Act One, Pozzo is a confident man of the world, occupying himself with his pipe, his food, his wine, and other material comforts, and dragging his abused slave around on a long rope. In Act Two things have changed; Pozzo is blind and helpless and Lucky must now lead him around by the same rope. At the end of each of the two acts a messenger arrives to say that Godot is not coming today but that he may come tomorrow. There has been a great deal of discussion and criticism of the play, attempting to discover what it means, and there is no generally agreed upon answer. One aspect of the human condition that it focuses upon is the act of waiting itself. All of us, perhaps, spend a great deal of time waiting for things to get better—for the degree, for the right boy or girl, for the right job, for the children to grow up, etc. It may be that Beckett is suggesting that life consists of such meaningless waiting. There is also an interesting religious interpretation of the play. If, after all, we strike off the last two letters of Godot, it is obvious what we have left. When we couple that with the idea of salvation mentioned earlier and all of the other Biblical references in the play, we have a strong argument that Beckett was concerned with the problem of faith. The fact that Godot never comes, however, is not very optimistic. Pessimism and pointless activity play a major part in Beckett's other plays as well. In *End Game* four people are living in a house in the middle of a desolate landscape. They may be the only human beings left alive. Hamm is blind and confined to a wheel chair; Clov, his son, can walk and see but he is crippled; Nag and Nell, Hamm's mother and father, are kept in trash cans. In *Happy Days* a woman is buried up to her waist in sand; as the play progresses the sand gradually mounts to her neck. Yet all the while she keeps chattering away, applying lipstick, inventorying the items in her purse and otherwise filling her time with senseless activity. Dialogue in Beckett's plays often takes the form of meaningless chatter or of the kind of "cross talk" engaged in by vaudeville comedians. In recent years, however, he seems to have become increasingly mistrustful of language and the amount of dialogue has decreased. One of his most recent short plays, in fact, contains no dialogue at all and is entitled, *Act Without Words*.

Ionesco's approach to theatre is different but no less absurd. The most immediate thing that strikes one about Ionesco's plays is the total meaninglessness of the language and the almost total breakdown of logic. This is heightened by the fact that his characters move and act in ordinary middle-class surroundings that could be presented on stage with Ibsenesque realism. One of the most famous is *The Bald Soprano*. In it, we find Mr. and Mrs. Smith, an English couple, sitting in their living room while Mr. Smith reads an English newspaper and Mrs. Smith darns English socks. After a bit the English clock strikes seventeen strokes. Eventually, they are visited by another couple, Mr. and Mrs. Martin, who, after a long conversation in which they discover that they came on the same train, live in the same city, on the same street, in the same house, sleep in the same bedroom and have the same child, decide that they must be husband and wife. Throughout the play ordinary logic is undercut in a number of ways. In one bit of conversation, for example, Mr. Smith offers the insane analogy that if a captain goes down with his ship, a doctor should die with his patient. This follows a conversation about a family in which all the members are named Bobby Watson. At another point the doorbell rings, but when Mrs. Smith goes to answer it there is no one there. This happens three more times. Mrs. Smith therefore concludes that on the basis of empirical evidence there is no one there when the doorbell rings. The bell rings a fifth time and after an argument Mrs. Smith goes to the door again. This time the Fire Chief is there. Conclusion: sometimes when the doorbell rings there is no one there and sometimes when the doorbell rings there is someone there. The play ends with the four principal characters and the Fire Chief standing in a circle angrily screaming nonsense words and phrases at each other, whereupon it begins again, this time with the Martins saying and doing the same thing the Smiths were doing and saying at the beginning. In *The Chairs* an old man and an old woman live alone in a castle on an island. The old man has just discovered the secret of life and has invited all of the dignitaries of the world to hear it. When the guests arrive, however, they are imaginary. More and more chairs are moved in for these invisible guests until the stage is so crowded that there is almost no room to move. The old man has engaged a professional speaker to communicate his message and when the orator arrives the old man and the old woman jump out of the window into the sea. The orator now turns to the crowd to speak. He is a mute. All he can get out are garbled, incoherent sounds. In *The New Tenant* a man rents an apartment and begins to move in his furniture. But more furniture arrives and more, and more until at last the stage is stacked almost from floor to ceiling.

There are some obvious differences between Beckett and Ionesco. First of all, Beckett's plays tend to be set in an ambiguous time and place, while Ionesco's usually take place in relatively ordinary and recognizable locales. Beckett's plays take place in an empty world, while Ionesco's dramatic world is full, almost overfull, of things. Beckett's dialogue is perhaps not quite as nonsensical, though there are times, listening to Ionesco's characters when we feel that they should make sense. We are lured into thinking that we are listening to realistic conversation and are therefore all the more frustrated because we cannot make sense of it. Both playwrights' work, however, defeats logic and sense and suggests the theme that life is absurd.

There are a number of other playwrights who are classified with the Absurdists and tend to be similar in their styles. The foremost of these is a Spaniard living in exile in France, named Fernando Arrabal. His two best plays are probably *The Automobile Graveyard* and *The Architect and the Emperor of Assyria*. There is also a very interesting Polish playwright whose work probably belongs in the same group though he precedes the others by at least twenty years. His name is Stanislaw Witkiewicz and the two plays that perhaps most clearly reveal his relationship to Beckett, Ionesco and company are *The Madman and the Nun* and *The Water Hen*. In English speaking theatre, few playwrights have gone as far as the continental absurdists. In England, N. F. Simpson's *One Way Pendulum* might be considered Absurdist, while in America Arthur Kopit's early play, *Oh, Dad, Poor Dad, Mama's Hung You In The Closet and I'm Feeling So Sad,* also fits this category. Kopit's later work, however, especially *In-*

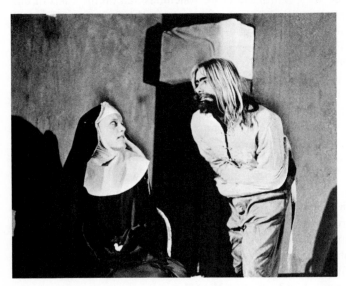

Figure 11–2. Witkiewicz's *The Madman and the Nun,* a Polish forerunner of the theatre of the Absurd. (St. Olaf College, Patrick Quade, director, and Dave Boelke, designer.)

Figure 11–3. Theatre of the Absurd in Eastern Europe. Slawomir Mrozek's satire on Communist society in Poland, *Tango*. (Eastern Montana College, Frederick K. Miller director, designed by James A. Bernardi.)

dians, seems to have moved more in the direction of the theatre of confrontation. The Englishman, Harold Pinter, and the American, Edward Albee, are also occasionally mentioned in this context. Both have written plays that could be considered Absurdist, but both also seem to have their roots more strongly in realism than do Beckett, Ionesco or Arrabal.[11]

There is one other French playwright that probably also should be included among the writers of the theatre of chaos, though he is probably not, strictly speaking, an Absurdist. Indeed, some people feel that he has come closer than anyone else to realizing Artaud's theatre of cruelty. The man in question is Jean Genet who, in addition to being an extremely gifted playwright, is an admitted homosexual and a convicted criminal. Genet's dramatic technique involves the turning upside down of traditional ideas of good and evil and of playing with various kinds of reality. In *The Balcony* we find a group of ordinary citizens in a brothel where they are permitted to act out their fantasies of power as king, bishop, judge, and general. Outside of the brothel, however, a revolution is going on and when the revolutionists win they find that in order to restore order among the people they must bring back to life the authority figures they have just executed. So the pretenders in the brothel assume publically the roles they have played in their fantasies, with Irma, the madame, taking the role of the queen. Implied here, first of all, may be a judgment about the real nature of those public figures whom we are supposed to respect. Second and more important is the notion that all of life may merely be a series of pretenses or arbitrary and false roles. This idea is borne out in

215

another of Genet's plays, *The Maids,* in which two maids act out the symbolic murder of their mistress and in which Genet desired the roles of the maids to be played by men. It is also seen in *The Blacks* which depicts one layer of pretense or illusion heaped upon another: blacks as seen by whites, blacks as they wish to be seen by whites, whites as they think blacks see them, whites as they are actually seen by blacks, etc.

The theatre of chaos, with the possible exception of Genet, tends to end in despair, pessimism, or nihilism. Indeed, it is sometimes difficult to understand how someone so committed to an image of total futility can continue to write plays at all. Nevertheless, this theatre clearly reflects the disorientation and disillusion which so strongly affected European society, especially after World War II.

THE THEATRE OF CONFRONTATION

The theatre of confrontation may be just as cynical and pessimistic about man's past and present, but it takes a different and more hopeful view of his future. The fundamental premise underlying this theatre is that both man and his conditions can be changed, though that change may require a violent restructuring of society. If the theatre of chaos had antecedents in Dada, this theatre found them in that branch of German Expressionism which was concerned with political and social questions. The two men who can be said to be most influential in creating it, however, are Erwin Piscator and Bertolt Brecht. What came to be known as Epic Theatre was founded on the assumption that the theatre should function not merely as a place of entertainment but as a lecture platform or a pulpit. It should teach; it should change attitudes and stimulate action, and the action it should stimulate is social change. As Piscator recounts the generation of this idea in his own mind, it occurred during World War I when, as a soldier in the German army, he was trying to dig a foxhole under fire. A sergeant bellowed at him to get down and asked his name and occupation in civilian life. As he replied, "Actor" Piscator was struck by the revelation that being an actor is a silly and useless thing. This led him to the conclusion that the theatre should be committed to something more important than merely making people laugh and weep, and that the actor could, therefore, become a socially useful human being.[12] Brecht seems to have come to somewhat the same conclusion while working in a German army hospital helping to care for the maimed and wounded that were brought back from the front. When the war was over and the two men returned to the theatre they, independently at first, and later as short-lived collaborators, began to work out a theatre designed to change the unsatisfactory conditions which they felt had brought the war about.

Piscator was primarily a director and some of his early work was done with the plays of the Expressionists. His own account of the beginning of the concept of Epic Theatre says that it began when he was directing a play called *The Cripple* in 1920. The scene designer did not get the scenery ready for opening night and after a long delay Piscator decided to start the play without it. About halfway through the first act the designer arrived carrying the scenery and called out, "Stop, Erwin! I'm here." An argument developed, with Piscator saying that the show must go on and the designer arguing that it could not go on without his scenery. At last Piscator turned to the audience and gave them the opportunity to vote on their preference. They agreed to stop the show, put up the scenery and start again from the beginning. The crucial point here is not whether there was or was not to be scenery, but rather the new actor-audience relationship in which the audience become collaborators rather than spectators and in which they make a judgment about what they see on the stage.[13]

Out of this simple beginning, then, developed a new kind of theatre. According to Piscator's widow, this theatre was to have five characteristics. It was to be:

1. A theatre of political and social nature. An attempt to reach all people.
2. A collective ceremony, an invitation to learning, conscious that it must lead to a communion.
3. A rejection of the naturalistic style and the Aristotelian unities.
4. A theatre with a particular bias for technical innovation, drawing upon other arts and other civilizations.
5. A theatre for vast audiences, a theatre of action, whose objective it is to bring out the stirring questions of our time and to bring about a total re-education of both men of the theatre and the audience.[14]

To accomplish these aims Piscator, and others whose work led to the development of Epic Theatre, made use of more than just the resources of the stage itself. They aimed at a kind of "total theatre" making use of music, machinery, placards, films, etc., in order to strengthen the political message. In his production of Ernst Toller's *Hurrah, We Live!,* for example, Piscator used a newsreel which depicted the events that had happened in the outside world during the years Toller's hero spent in an insane asylum. In one of his most famous productions, *The Good Soldier Schweik,* he had Schweik marching on a treadmill, getting nowhere, while he was passed by long lines of cardboard cut-out soldiers.

If Piscator was the pioneer director in this form, there is no doubt that Brecht was the pioneer and most important playwright and theorist. Indeed, together with Artaud, Brecht is one of the two most important figures in twentieth-century theatre. His earliest work tended toward Expressionism, especially that of Frank Wedekind, whom Brecht had known and admired in his early years in Berlin. Later, however, he became deeply involved in a theatre with a political outlook and adopted a whole new approach to the writing and staging of plays. Essentially, this approach can be summed up in one word that Brecht coined — *Verfremdungseffekt.* This word is sometimes translated as "alienation," sometimes as "estrangement" effect. The latter is probably the better translation. In the sentimental theatre that was still popular in Germany the audience was led to identify with the action, in the sense of sharing it or feeling into it. When the play was over they could go home emotionally satisfied, having had a good thrill, cry, or laugh, but otherwise unchanged. Brecht scornfully referred to this kind of thing as "culinary" theatre, implying that the audience was merely fed, that it had had its appetite for sensation satisfied. Having been fed they quickly forgot what they had seen and did not think of the events of the play as having any particular relevance for their own lives. Brecht felt that the blame for this had to be placed upon the emotional identification with the characters and events.

By contrast, he wanted the audience to think about what they were seeing on the stage, to evaluate it, make decisions about it, and then go out and change the unsatisfactory conditions they had seen there. In order to do this they had to be prevented from identifying and this Brecht proposed to do by making the events "strange," — i.e. constructing the play and the production in such a way that the viewers were jolted out of their complacency. First of all, he objected to the creation of the illusion of real life on the stage. People should be made aware that they are watching a play. To that end he proposed to make the scenery obviously theatrical, to allow the lighting instruments to show rather than hiding them behind scenery or curtains, to use, as had Piscator, films, sound effects, music, and placards, periodically to break any illusion that might be developing, and even to employ a different style of acting in which the actor suggested, outlined, or sketched in the character rather than trying to assume his identity. Along these same lines, Brecht argued that people ought to be allowed to smoke in the theatre, because a man with a cigar in his mouth cannot be deceived, and that they ought to go to the theatre with pretty much the same attitude with which they attended a sporting match. Brecht's own plays were deliberately written to achieve the *Verfremdungseffekt,* though critics have argued that they did not always succeed. Sometimes, as in *The Private Life of the Master Race,* they have no plot continuity but are only held together by the fact that all of scenes deal with the same general subject, in this case, life in Nazi Germany. In other instances they treat serious events with a broad, burlesque form of comedy and interrupt the action with direct address to the audience and with music and song. The music is often estranging in itself, in that harsh or crude lyrics may be sung to a very pretty, sentimental melody. Both of these characteristics are to be found in Brecht's most famous work in America, *The Threepenny Opera.* Furthermore, Brecht insisted that the actors who were cast in that show, and required to sing, should not be able to sing.

In another case, *The Caucasian Chalk Circle,* he uses an old Chinese play as a basis, and also employs a Chinese theatre convention. In this play two groups of Russian peasants are arguing over the ownership of a collective farm, which had been taken over by the Germans. The first group had been driven out and when the Germans in turn had to give it up a new group of peasants took it over. The dispute between the original owners and the new is settled by a story teller who begins to tell an old Chinese tale which is then acted out and forms the bulk of the play. After the tale is concluded the story teller states the moral,"Property belongs to those who care for it." In another of his plays, *Mother Courage,* discussed briefly in Chapter 4, Brecht attempts to depict the horrors and stupidity of war by telling the story of an old peddlar woman who profits by traveling about selling various goods to both sides in the Thirty Years War, and continues to do so even though the war costs the lives of her three children. In this case, he argued that we are not to sympathize with or admire Mother Courage, but to judge her and the social conditions which made her. Some critics, however, argue that here the estrangement effect fails; we do sympathize despite Brecht's intentions.[15]

Both Brecht and Piscator were Communists, though in part, perhaps, because the Communists seemed, after World War I, the only group to protest against social conditions in defeated Germany and later were the only party that seriously resisted Hitler. Both, therefore, had to flee Germany and both eventually wound up in the United States. Brecht returned to East Germany after the war and established the Berliner Ensemble, one of the most influential of contemporary theatre groups. Piscator went back to West Germany in 1951. Piscator had given up Communism at about the time of the Hitler-Stalin pact in 1938; Brecht never did. It is interesting, however, that he was greatly upset when Russian tanks forcibly put down workers' rebellions in East Germany and

Figure 11–4. Brecht's *Mother Courage.* (Westminster College, directed by Earl Lammel, designed by Douglas Vander Yacht.)

considered leaving at that time. He died in the Spring of 1956, only a few months before the Russians even more brutally suppressed a revolution in Hungary. Some people who knew Brecht feel that had he lived he could not have tolerated that act and would have defected to the West.

Epic Theatre, then, had a political aim. Its intention was to confront audiences with social conditions as they are, to make them look at and think about those conditions, and to leave the theatre with the desire to change them. Brecht's work has influenced a good many playwrights, especially in the German speaking world. The most important of these is probably Peter Weiss, who in some ways could also be said to belong to the theatre of chaos. His most famous play, outside of Europe, is undoubtedly *The Persecution and Assassination of Jean Paul Marat as Performed by the Inmates of Charenton Asylum under the Direction of the Marquis de Sade,* more commonly known as *Marat/Sade.* It is set, as the title indicates, in an asylum for the insane during the era of Napoleon. The inmates are performing a play written and directed by the French nobleman whose name and exploits have given us the common psychological term for the uniting of sexual pleasure with the inflicting of pain — sadism. This play within a play depicts the events of the French Revolution leading up to the assassination of one of the Revolutionary leaders who was responsible, at least in part, for the mass executions during the Terror. Thus, insane people are acting out the events of a period that might be described as an orgy of collective insanity. The play is almost impossible to describe. At one level it takes the form of a debate between de Sade, who argues that if one is going to kill people one should do it with passion, and Marat, who contends that execution and murder should be carried on cold-bloodedly as a matter of public policy. Marat insists that order can be created by reason and force; de Sade argues for man's passionate and irrational nature. The latter's point seems to be vindicated when the play ends with the patients completely losing control and attacking the director of the asylum and his family, their keepers, the nuns, and each other, while de Sade stands in the middle of the stage laughing. The use of the madhouse as a scene for a play about history may suggest that all of human history is one long attack of madness. In writing the play Weiss claimed to be following Brecht. When Peter Brook directed it, with the Royal Shakespeare Company, he attempted to combine the ideas of Brecht and Artaud. That he succeeded in achieving a kind of theatre of cruelty is suggested by the fact that audiences were usually made uncomfortable by his production, and sometimes upset and angered by it.

Weiss has asserted that his work has always been political. *Marat/Sade* was a debate between the superindividualistic de Sade and the revolutionary folk-hero, Marat, which expressed his situation at the time. Since then, he says, he has moved in the direction of Marat's point of view or even farther to the left.[16] Since the writing of *Marat/Sade* Weiss has adopted a technique he calls "documentary theatre." It is a clearly political theatre which unabashedly takes sides and which, Weiss says, reacts

Figure 11–5. One version, of Peter Weiss's *Marat/Sade*. This version was done at Rocky Mountain College. (Directed by Daniel Rogers, and designed by Bob Morrison.)

against the contemporary situation and demands explanations in the same way as does a street demonstration. In form it consists of actual documents — news stories, letters, statistics, reports, transcripts, speeches, etc. — put together in various ways, but unaltered or edited in content. For example, *The Investigation*, written in 1964–1965, was based on selected excerpts from the transcripts of the Frankfurt War Crimes Trial which attempted to place the blame for the atrocities at Auschwitz. Its first German production was directed by Erwin Piscator. *Song of the Lusitanian Bogey* (1966) dealt with the Portuguese suppression of a native uprising in the African state of Angola, in the form of a political cabaret, with music and song. *Viet Nam Discourse,* finished in 1968, is also in the form of a revue, recounting the history of Viet Nam in two parts, up until 1954 and from 1954 to the present. It employs quotations from Churchill, John Foster Dulles, Kennedy, and Johnson. Weiss's intent, then, is clearly political and he uses many of the same devices as did Brecht.[17]

In Switzerland both Max Frisch and Friedrich Duerrenmatt are in the Epic tradition, Frisch perhaps more clearly so. His most famous play is probably *Biedermann and the Fire-Bugs*. The plot revolves around a proper middle-class businessman named Gottlieb Biedermann who lives in a town that is plagued by arsonists. Nevertheless, he allows two strangers to talk their way into his home, puts them up in his attic, and even looks the other way when they bring in fuses and barrels of gasoline. At last he becomes a bit worried and invites them to a lavish dinner, hoping

Figure 11–6. A second version of *Marat/Sade* performed at Slippery Rock State College. (Directed by Orley I. Holtan, and designed by Dale Melsness.)

that by winning their friendship he can keep his house safe. In spite of his efforts they burn it down and even talk him into giving them the matches with which to do it. The play can be interpreted in various ways, but most critics see it as an allegory of the Nazi rise to power in Germany.

Epic Theatre has had a great influence on modern theatre especially through such techniques as projections, films, music, breaking the illusion and the mood, and using the theatre as a lecture platform. Not all of the plays that employ Brechtian techniques are necessarily political; we can find examples in such popular musicals as *The Fantasticks* and *Man of La Mancha.* Primarily, however, this theatre has aimed to confront the audience with a political point of view and with a social situation which needs changing.

The theatre of confrontation in recent years has gone even farther than did Brecht in provoking not a later and considered response, but sometimes an immediate one. Such groups as the Living Theatre, the Bread and Puppet Theatre, the Free Southern Theatre, El Teatro Campesino, and the San Francisco Mime Troupe can all be considered theatres of confrontation, though some of them, especially the Living Theatre, have moved in the direction of the theatre of communion. The Free Southern Theatre and El Teatro Campesino are or were clearly revolutionary in the sense of making people aware of injustice and prompting them to do something about it. The former was started during the height of the civil rights movement of the 1960s and was aimed at Southern rural Blacks. There has subsequently been a rapid growth in Black theatre with similar aims, some of it performed in ghetto streets and some of it in regular theatres. The latter is aimed at Spanish speaking migrant farm workers **222** and is connected with Cesar Chavez's attempts to organize those workers. Similar groups have also been active in connection with the women's movement and with the antiwar movements of the 1960s and early 1970s. In its extreme form it involves direct confrontation through argument and sometimes even physical contact with the audience. Typically it rejects the traditional theatre in favor of parks, meeting halls, abandoned warehouses and streets. In some instances it actually involves the spectators in the action. The aim is to provoke a response, even if it is a hostile one. The people involved in such theatre usually argue that it is better that the audience should react, even by throwing rocks, than that they should merely say, "Wasn't that a nice play?" Theatre of confrontation, then, can be understood in two senses. One the one hand it confronts the audience with a problem or what the players perceive to be a problem; on the other it confronts them verbally and physically in the sense of a challenge, a threat, or a demonstration.

THE THEATRE OF COMMUNION

There is much overlap between the theatre of confrontation and the theatre of communion. Indeed, some of the groups that began as conscious political radicals eventually made a switch as they began to feel that the problems were deeper than political and economic forms. A solution to the problems of anomie, alienation, and the specific social ills that resulted therefrom required, they felt, something more than a mere political change. It required, to employ a somewhat overused phrase of the 1960s, an alteration of consciousness. There are two significant differ-

Figure 11–7. "The Firemen's Chorus" from Max Frisch's *Biedermann and the Firebugs.* (Slippery Rock State College, directed by Orley I. Holtan, designed by Frank Magers.)

ences from the other two theatres we have so far discussed, and each may result from a different influence.

The theatres of chaos and confrontation, at least in the forms of the Absurd and Epic, had retained the idea of plot or story. Even in such plays as Beckett's which do not contain plot in the conventional sense, there is still a feeling of a progression of events in time and of some connection among them. The typical play, of almost any period prior to the last ten or fifteen years, tends to do three things: (1) It presents us with a time-space-situational matrix or with what Stanislavsky called given circumstances. We see characters in a place, in a time frame, and in a situation that the play at least partially defines for us. (2) It is cumulative in terms of the information given. In other words, in most plays what we learn in the beginning adds up to and contributes to our understanding of what follows, though this may not be quite so true of the Theatre of the Absurd as it is of other forms. (3) It involves impersonation. That is, it presents us with imaginary or real characters who are impersonated by actors. The theatre of communion tends to reject all three of these conditions. In part taking its cue from a shortlived experimental movement called happenings, which was in turn influenced by Dadaist manifestations, it presents us with a time/space dimension that is here and now, while we are watching. The people we see are not actors being someone else; they are themselves. The thing they are doing does not lead up to anything nor have any special significance outside itself. It is simply a thing being done. Not all of the theatre of communion follows this tack completely but to a degree most such groups dispense with plot or story as it is commonly understood. Even if they use a written script, which, given the above conditions, is clearly unnecessary, they may alter it, adapt it, rearrange the scenes, or use it merely as the base line for a series of improvisations. Frequently members of these experimental groups will speak of "violating" the text, "confronting" the text, or "playing against" the text, their argument being that the standard repertory of plays have become so encrusted with habit and tradition that we no longer see them. Thus, we must be forced to come to them with fresh eyes.

The second change was an almost complete breakdown of the separation between actor and audience. The groups who constitute the theatre of communion tend not to use conventional theatres at all, but to play in all sorts of environments in which they and the audience share the same space.[18] It is here that the element of communion is directly involved and this too derives from several influences. One of the basic premises of this theatre, as with the other two, is that theatre is not merely a form of entertainment. Neither is it, however, a mere depiction of futility nor a political diatribe. Rather, it is something holy; it is a means of self-discovery; it is a coming together; it is a group celebration. Clearly the influence of Artaud is felt here. These actors take as their starting point the theory that the theatre originated out of ritual, that such things as an Indian rain dance or a primitive puberty rite are proto-theatre. They argue, then, that the farther theatre got away from ritual the more vitality it lost and that the only way for the theatre to be reborn is for it to go back and rediscover its sources. Extending the argument, they might say that civilization is to blame for the ills of the twentieth century, that the farther modern man gets from his primal sources the more he loses his vitality. Ritual does not, at least in its early stages, involve a group of performers and a group of spectators; it involves participation by all the members of the tribe. How this works in practice is considered later in the text.

Jerzy Grotowski is an individual who has had a fundamental influence on these movements in modern theatre; though he does not adopt all of the attributes of the theatre of communion as it has been described above he has a close affinity with it. Jerzy Grotowski operates a laboratory theatre in the Polish city of Wroclaw, formerly Breslau and began with the aim of discovering what theatre basically is. To do this he followed a reductive method and asked himself a number of questions. Can we have theatre without lights, scenery, and costumes? Yes. Can we have theatre without written plays? Yes. Can we have theatre without actors and audience? No. What is finally essential to the theatre, then, is the confrontation between the live actor and the live spectator. Indeed, if the aim of theatre is to create the illusion of reality, especially through technical means, the film can do it much better, by shooting in the actual locations. The one thing that the film and television cannot do, however, is to give us that living contact. Consequently, Grotowski proposed to strip away all of the nonessentials, leaving what he called a "poor theatre." But what is involved in this living confrontation? What is its purpose? As Grotowski states in his seminal book:

> The actor is a man who works in public with his body, offering it publicly. If this body restricts itself to demonstrating what it is — something that any average person can do — then it is not an obedient instrument capable of performing a spiritual act.[19]

Grotowski argues that for the actor to exploit his body for money or for the audience's approval is the equivalent of prostitution. This, he says, is what the theatre has become. What, then, does the actor do with his body?

> If the actor, by setting himself a challenge publicly challenges others, and through excess, profanation, and outrageous sacrilege reveals himself by casting off his everyday mask, he makes it possible for the spectator to undertake a similar process of self-penetration. If he does not exhibit his body, but annihilates it, burns it, frees it from every resistance to any psychic impulse, then he does not sell his body but sacrifices it. He repeats the atonement; he is close to holiness.[20]

From this Grotowski derives the concept of the "holy actor," the actor who will put himself to the most rigorous demands in order to reveal his most secret and painful self in the process of performance. To become such an actor requires extreme dedication and the most strenuous of training. In his training process Grotowski employs exercises taken from Yoga, from Chinese classical ballet, from Indian Kathakali dance, and a series of vigorous gymnastic movements he has developed himself and calls *exercises plastiques.* According to Grotowski, his actors also learn, though it is difficult to see how it can be done, to project their voices through the tops of their heads, the middles of their backs, and other unlikely places. Grotowski and his actors have visited the United States twice. Each time the audience was arbitrarily limited to a very small number, but those who have seen the group say that his people can do amazing and unbelievable things with voice and body. They are particularly loud in their praise of his leading actor, Richard Cieslak.

In order to bring about this penetration into self within the audience, Grotowski says that the performance must involve a probing into "the collective subconscious . . . the myths which are not an invention of the mind but are, so to speak, inherited through one's blood, religion, culture, and climate."[21] In this sense, Grotowski's thinking seems to be close to that of Artaud, and of Jung.

Grotowski has been and continues to be of enormous influence. He does not, however, go as far as have some of the experimental groups in the United States and other countries, in wiping out the line between actor and spectator. The theatre of communion as practiced by such groups as the Firehouse Theatre, formerly of Minneapolis, the Living Theatre, and the Performance Group, invites the audience in and occasionally actually includes them in the performance. This may start with the way they are seated but it goes farther. In performing various ritual acts, the players may encourage the audience to join in. Indeed, some critics have complained that they were not only invited or encouraged, but almost compelled to participate. The Living Theatre's *Paradise Now,* for example, concludes with a large pile of nude and seminude bodies on stage, actors and audience all intermingled in a heap. Richard Schechner's *Dionysus in 69,* involved two rituals, one a symbolic birth based upon an actual ritual performed by New Guinea tribesmen, and the other a death ritual, in each of which the audience was free to participate.[22]

In this theatre the playwright tends to diminish in importance. The most radical of these groups follow Artaud's suggestion and reduce dialogue to a minimum; what little dialogue there is is often improvised or spoken spontaneously. Singing, chanting, animal noises, groans, sighs, and screams are all a part of the sound structure of the performance, and dancing, acrobatics, physical contact, and frequently nudity are part of the visual scheme. The whole experience is designed to put the members of audience first into contact with themselves and second with the other people around them and, thereby, to alter their consciousness.

In spite of the lessening of importance of the playwright a few exciting new scripts have come out of group improvisations or collective creations. The most famous of these is undoubtedly *Hair* which was first conceived by Jerome Ragni in a workshop of Joseph Chaikin's Open Theatre and received its first full scale production as the opening effort of Joseph Papp's Public Theatre. Later, it was moved to Broadway, revised, polished and, in the opinion of some people, ruined. Chaikin's Open Theatre has also produced Jean Claude Van Itallie's *America Hurrah* and *The Serpent* and Megan Terry's *Viet Rock*. Other new playwrights to have come out of such groups are Rosalyn Drexler, Rochelle Owens, and Sam Shepherd.

Here, then, we have three attempts to deal with the problems and changing realities of the twentieth century. Each deals with the outside world in a different way. The first asserts that the world is chaotic, insane, meaningless, and seems ultimately to advise an acceptance of the chaos. The second identifies the problems of the world in human institutions and attacks and vows to change them. The third sees the problems neither in the universe, nor in social institutions as such, but in man himself, in his isolation from himself and his fellow beings. It attempts to bridge this gap of separation through communion, sought through self-penetration, a return to ritual forms, and a theatre of participation.

If the foregoing has suggested that the modern theatre is in a somewhat confused state, it has not been entirely unintended. An outstanding characteristic of this part of the twentieth century has been the bewilder-

Figure 11–8. A production of *Hair.* (Memphis State University, Keith Kennedy, director.)

ing speed and variety of change in all phases of human activity. The student who is likely to read this book was at most two years old when the Russians sent up their first Sputnik in 1957. Since then men have walked on the moon and Mars may be the next step. The fathers of today's students may have been about twelve years old when the first atom bomb was dropped on Hiroshima. Their grandfathers may have lived to see horse and buggy transportation be replaced by the automobile, the airplane, and now the jet aircraft. This rate of change has even given rise to a new term to describe its effects—future shock. It is not surprising, therefore, that the theatre, though it is one of man's oldest insitutions, should also find itself in a state of flux.

Today, in America at least, we can be said to have at least four theatres: the theatre of pure entertainment which constitutes most Broadway offerings and the bulk of the fare offered by community theatres; the classic theatre, consisting of masterpieces of the past kept alive primarily in regional repertory companies and on college and university campuses; a more serious modern theatre, located Off-Broadway and also occasionally in regional and university companies; and the experimental groups, largely self-supporting and attempting to strike off in new directions. The movements we have just described may be the forerunners of a totally new kind of theatre, unlike anything we have seen before, or they may be passing fads and fancies. Indeed, the Theatre of the Absurd is already somewhat outdated and some of the others show signs of dying. Throughout its history, as these last four chapters have attempted to point out, the theatre has adapted to deal with new ways of seeing and experiencing. It will undoubtedly continue to do so, for if it does not, it will die. And, despite various gloomy predictions, the theatre has thus far continued to live. How much will be retained from the past, how much will be adopted of the new, what totally new directions it will take in the years ahead cannot be predicted. Grotowski is right in saying that it cannot dispense with the actor; beyond that basic element there may be a vast array of options. Many people are put off and offended by the new developments in the theatre, while others are extremely excited by them. Some of the former would like to close their eyes and hope that these movements will go away, while many of the latter are willing to hail them as the wave of the future, perhaps the salvation of the arts and of mankind. Whatever theatre we would prefer, those of us who are interested in the theatre and the arts, which is another way of saying those of us who are alert and alive, must at least consider and try to understand what is happening.

Notes

[1]In recent years a German playwright, Rolf Hochhuth, has written a powerful indictment of those, especially the Catholic hierarchy, who ignored the Nazi terror until it actually resulted in war. His play, *The Deputy,* obviously represents one point of view and Catholics have vigorously protested it, but the fact remains that there were many people who simply stood by and watched.

[2]For many years America had been able somewhat to escape the more severe shocks of the European experience. In recent years, however, with Vietnam, the assassinations of political leaders, riots, demonstrations, and social unrest, Watergate, etc. Americans have come to share some of the European sensibility.

[3]She has made this point in various lectures, articles, and television interviews, as well as alluding to it in *Culture and Commitment: A Study of the Generation Gap* (Garden City, N.Y.: Doubleday & Co., Inc., 1970).

[4]Various philosophers and social critics have commented upon the phenomenon of alienation. A particularly good discussion of it is to be found in Eric Fromm's *The Sane Society* (New York: Holt, Rinehart & Winston, 1955).

[5]That other is Bertolt Brecht whom we discuss a little later.

[6]Antonin Artaud, *The Theater and Its Double,* trans. Mary Caroline Richards (New York: Grove Press, Inc., 1958., p. 31. © 1958 by Grove Press. Reprinted by permission of Grove Press Inc. and Calder and Boyars Ltd.

[7]Ibid., p. 79.

[8]"Metaphysics and the Mise-en-Scene," in *The Theater and its Double,* p. 41.

[9]The best biography of Artaud is Bettina L. Knapp, *Antonin Artaud: Man of Vision* (New York: David Lewis Inc., 1969).

[10]One of the best discussions of the existentialist philosophy is William Barrett's *Irrational Man* (Garden City, N.Y.: Doubleday Anchor Books, 1962).

[11]The Absurdist movement has been discussed in detail by Martin Esslin in *The Theatre of the Absurd* (Woodstock, N.Y.: Overlook Press, 1973). Esslin is, in fact, responsible for the categorical term.

[12]This story is recounted in Maria Ley Piscator, *The Piscator Experiment* (New York: James H. Heineman Inc., 1967), pp. 1–2.

[13]Ibid., pp. 11–12.

[14]Ibid., p. 13.

[15]Brecht's theories and the details of his life have been discussed in a number of sources. The best single one for his ideas is John Willet, ed. *Brecht on Theatre* (New York: Hill & Wang, 1964).

[16]In an interview published in the Swedish journal *Ord och Bild* (June, 1972).

[17]The concept of documentary theatre is discussed at some length in a piece by Weiss entitled "The Material and the Models" published in *Theatre Quarterly, I* (January–March, 1971).

[18]In this connection see Richard Schechner's *Environmental Theater,* New York: Hawthorn Books Inc., 1973).

[19]Jerzy Grotowski, *Toward a Poor Theatre* (Copenhagen, Denmark: H. M. Bergs Farlag. © 1968 Jerzy Grotowski and Odin Teatrets Farlag.), p. 33.

[20]Ibid., p. 34.

[21]Ibid., p. 42.

[22]The production of *Dionysus in 69* is described in a book by the same name published by Farrar, Straus and Giroux in 1970. The book contains numerous photographs and is as good a way as any, short of seeing a performance, to familiarize yourself with this theatre. Other helpful material can be found in *Environmental Theater,* cited above.

Suggested Readings

Books:

The works listed as Suggested Readings for Chapter 10 are also helpful here.

CORRIGAN, ROBERT W., ed. *Theatre in the Twentieth Century.* New York: Grove Press, Inc., 1963.

ESSLIN, MARTIN. *The Theatre of the Absurd.* Woodstock, N.Y.: Overlook Press, 1973.

GROTOWSKI, JERZY. *Toward a Poor Theatre.* New York: Simon & Schuster, 1968.

KIRBY, MICHAEL. *Happenings: An Illustrated History.* New York: E. P. Dutton and Co., 1965.

WILLET, JOHN, ed. *Brecht on Theatre.* New York: Hill and Wang, 1964.

The interested student should also see various issues of *The Drama Review.* It is probably the best single source for keeping up with the most advanced developments in modern theatre.

Plays:

BECKETT, SAMUEL. *Waiting for Godot.*

BRECHT, BERTOLT. *Mother Courage*

GENET, JEAN. *The Balcony.*

IONESCO, EUGENE. *The Bald Soprano.*

TERRY, MEGAN. *Viet Rock.*

VAN ITALLIE, JEAN CLAUDE. *America Hurrah.*

WEISS, PETER. *Marat/Sade.*

Perhaps of more value than the published script is the excellent recording of Weiss's play done by the Royal Shakespeare Company.

PART FOUR

EVALUATING THE THEATRE

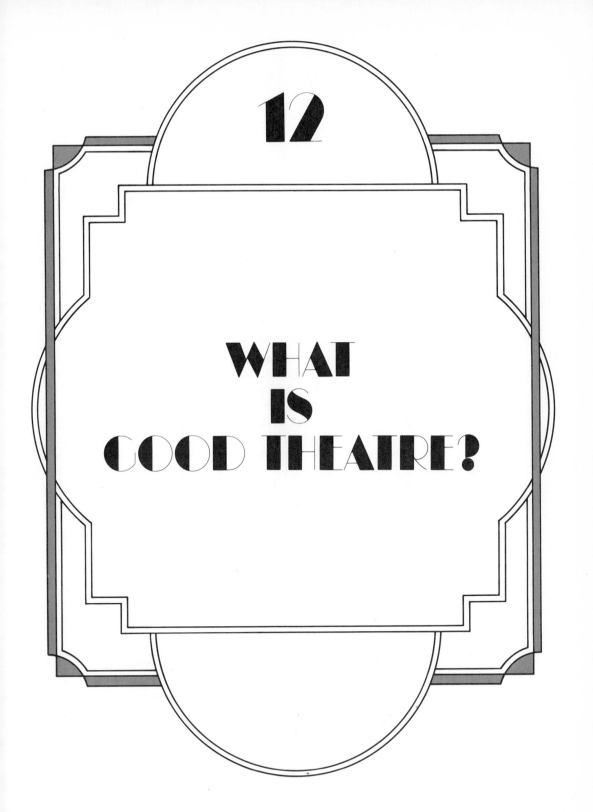

12

WHAT IS GOOD THEATRE?

THROUGHOUT THIS BOOK we have had a good deal to say about theatre—the elements that make it up, the way in which it operates to reflect or to portray reality, the ways in which it has changed as social realities and our concepts of existence have changed. To summarize all of this we could say that theatre, through enactment, recreates an image of human experience in time. In the way in which it presents this enactment it says something implicitly or explicitly, about the life that we all share, about human nature, about existence and the ways in which man responds to it. It differs from literature in that its medium is enactment and from such related arts as film and television drama in that the enactment is live, not pre-packaged, but worked out while the audience watches. We have not, thus far, said anything about the criticism of theatre or, in other words, about what is considered to be good theatre.

Critics are not always popular with theatre artists. They are often viewed as outsiders who write or talk about a subject which they do not practice. The corollary of this objection, of course, is that only those who practice the art are qualified to talk about it. Yet theatre is done for audiences and everyone who goes to the theatre is in some sense a critic. In theatre lobbies during intermissions one hears many critical comments ranging from the simple and uninformed to the quite sophisticated and intelligent. A sound reason, then, for concerning ourselves with criticism is that it is a natural part of the artistic experience. Not only can we not help responding positively or negatively to plays we see, but we naturally tend to talk about that response, and a part of the pleasure of the experience is the chance to talk about it afterward.

THE CRITICAL ACT

All criticism, not only of theatre but of other phenomena, the other arts, football games, food or fashion, tends to fall into two categories. The first is the simple statement of preference or response—the "I like it" or "I don't like it" type of statement. Such a statement is usually based on an immediate subjective response and as such may not be open to discussion or argument. No one, after all, can convince you that you should like something you do not like. Such judgments, however, may change with time, with more frequent exposure to the thing in question, and with more

234

knowledge and understanding of it. This brings us to the second category which is the value judgment. In a value judgment we go beyond the mere statement of preference and attempt to assign a place to the phenomenon on the scale of goodness to badness. Here we make statements such as "*Death of a Salesman* is a good play." or "Jones's performance was better than Smith's." Such statements involve two steps: (1) the discovery of criteria by which the thing is to be judged and (2) the application of those criteria to the specific item in question. Thus, before we can say that *Death of a Salesman* is a good play we must have in mind some criteria that define what we mean by "good play." One such criterian, of course, may be the "I like it." statement, i.e. it is good if you like it, bad if you do not. We can readily recognize, however, that that is a naive and probably invalid criterion, at least in many cases. It is perfectly possible to like something that is bad or not to like something that is good, and furthermore we are apt to find totally opposite reactions to the same phenomenon. If that is the only criterion it silences discussion as soon as it has been expressed. More intelligent criteria are developed through experience with the thing in question and knowledge about it. Thus, the more we know about the problems and skills of playing quarterback and the more quarterbacks we have seen, the better we are able to evaluate one. Obviously, the same applies to theatre. The more we know about what the theatre artist is trying to do, the better we understand the processes and problems involved in doing it, and the more plays we have seen, the better we are able to judge and evaluate each new play we see. Intelligent critical judgement is based upon a set of standards derived from knowledge of and experience with the thing we are judging. Of course, no critical judgment is 100 percent true or correct. There is almost always room for argument at both stages of the process. That is, we can argue about the correctness or validity of the standards, or we can argue about whether those standards really fit the specific case we are evaluating. Even very intelligent and sophisticated critics disagree about the same play or production. However, in contrast to those who base their statements entirely on personal preference, they are able to talk about the bases of their disagreement.

The second stage of the critical act, as described above, involves four somewhat overlapping operations. The first of these is *cataloging* or *description*. It consists of taking inventory or recounting what is in the work. In the case of a play, this involves a description of what happens— who does what to whom. It must also, of course, take into account performances by the actors, the work of the director, and the various technical artists as they reveal themselves in the finished performance.

The second step is *formal analysis* in which the critic goes beyond mere description to consider how the work is put together. With a drama this involves the kind of formal analysis discussed in Chapter 4 and perhaps a classification of the drama into types such as those considered in the four preceding chapters. In performance, the critic may deal with such things as acting styles, styles of scenery, appropriateness of the design to the play's theme and intent, pacing, and the way in which the director has handled his actors in order to communicate the structure and the theme.

The third operation is *interpretation*. This involves explaining the work, trying to discover its meaning or meanings and the relevance of the theatrical experience to our lives and to the human situation in general. Here we run into difficulties, for the determination of what a play means and the significance of that meaning can be a very difficult and subjective activity. For this reason some critics, such as Susan Sontag, have argued that we should not even attempt to interpret a work of art, but should simply experience it.[1] The problem with this point of view is that human beings seem by nature equipped with a desire to discover and interpret meanings; we have minds and we cannot simply turn them off as we could an electric bulb. We should, however, approach the task of interpretation with caution.

The fourth operation is *judgment* — deciding how good a work is and giving it a rank in relationship to other works in its class or of its type. Inherent in the evaluation of a work of art is comparison with other works that we know, usually within the same general type. This is one reason that the evaluation of a totally new type is so difficult. Nineteenth-century critics, for example, faced with Strindberg's *The Dream Play* had no basis for comparison because they had seen nothing like it before. Judgment also involves evaluating originality and the craftsmanship or technique with which the work was done.

The good critic consciously engages the work at the first three levels before he gets to the final operation and most of us, insofar as we approach a work of art seriously, do so at least subconsciously. One of the problems faced by the journalistic critic is that in the rush to meet his deadlines for the next day's newspaper he simply does not have time adequately to consider the work at all four of these levels.

To summarize, then, the informed critic does not simply make a snap judgment based upon his personal like or dislike. Rather, he attempts seriously to consider the value of a work in the light of a set of criteria which he has derived through training and experience. Where theatre is concerned the critic ought ideally to possess experience not only of theatre but of life, for the art of the theatre, as we have said in the preceding pages, is intimately related to life. Much of this book has been devoted to providing information that will be helpful to the playgoer in developing his own criteria for judgment. That information, however, must be supplemented by seeing plays and by attempting to evaluate them. Certain formulae may be of use to the novice critic as he attempts to engage a work. One of these consists of three simple questions: (1) What was the artist trying to do? (2) How well has he done it? (3) Was it worth doing? Another and perhaps more sophisticated formula is based upon Kenneth Burke's approach to rhetoric or communication, which he has in turn borrowed from theatre. It consists of five terms: (1) Act — what was done? (2)

Agent — who did it? (3) Agency — by what means? (4) Scene — where and when, in what dimension of time and space? and (5) Purpose — to what end?[2] Thus, as we approach a play we keep in mind the interaction of these five terms — the relationship of the artist or artists to the thing done, the relationship of both to the means of doing, the relationship of the previous three to the place and time in which it was done, the relationship of all four to the purpose of the act.

PROBLEMS OF THEATRE CRITICISM

We have discussed the nature of the critical act and provided a couple of formulae to serve as the basis for a generalized approach to criticism. There are, however, a number of problems that relate to the criticism of art in general and to that of theatre in particular.

The first problem is the question of where we derive the criteria for judgment. At the risk of oversimplifying, we could say that there are two broad approaches to this problem. One point of view holds that the standards for judging a work of art are essentially subjective or at least historically and societally bound. In other words, the standards vary from person to person, historical period to historical period, society to society. This is the attitude that underlies Artaud's feelings about masterpieces of the past. Another point of view suggests that there are certain universal standards, good for all times and all peoples. It implies also the existence of an ideal form toward which all actual works of art aspire. Thus, either in reality or in the collective minds of artists, there is a perfect sonata or a perfect tragedy, and everyone who writes a sonata or a tragedy is attempting to realize that perfect form. Each of these points of view has its disadvantages. Subjectivism or relativism carried to its logical extremes would mean that we must agree with Artaud and discard all works from the past as being irrelevant and substitute for any general standards the simple question of effect on the individual viewer. Thus, we are brought full circle to "I like it." as a final test of value. The other approach, which could be labelled idealism, can lead to a sterile attempt to copy supposedly perfect works of the past and to an inflexibility toward new works that take different approaches. The really perceptive and open minded critic probably applies both approaches to varying degrees as he attempts to determine how good a work is and what value it has for him and for others who might see it.

Another problem, related specifically to theatre, is that of script or written text versus performance. Throughout our history we have tended to treat plays, especially those of the Greeks and Shakespeare, as primarily literary works and often to ignore or downgrade performance. Certainly a "good" script does not guarantee a brilliant performance, nor does a "bad" — i.e. nonliterary — script necessarily mean a bad performance. Many plays, those of Sophocles, Shakespeare, Shaw, Ibsen, etc.,

are good literature—that is, one can derive a good deal of the pleasure they have to offer from reading them. Yet a play is meant to be acted
and the movements and vocal inflections of the actors, the work of the
scenery, lighting and costume designers and the work of the director
should enhance that pleasure and make it greater. By the same token
many plays that provide an exciting evening in the theatre may not necessarily be good literature. Indeed, as we have pointed out in previous chapters, an exciting performance need not necessarily be based upon a written script at all.

The third problem is related to the observation that in judging a
work we compare it to others of its type. Throughout its long history
theatre has occupied an ambiguous position between art and entertainment. The term is used to encompass everything from the tragedies of
Sophocles and Shakespeare to the clowning of the burlesque comedian.
Indeed, the nineteenth-century live theatre tended to fill somewhat the
same role for the mass audience that is today played by movies and television. The problem this poses for the critic is what standards to apply. If
we apply the criterion of pleasing the audience or attracting large crowds
at the box office we can certainly evaluate plays and productions, but in so
doing we may find that by that standard a simple farce, thriller, or musical
comedy is "better" than Sophocles or Shakespeare. On the other hand, if
we apply the artistic standard universally we run the risk of condemning a
play for failing to do something that it never intended or attempted. We
are thus in the position of criticizing a mule for not being a racehorse. The
critic, therefore, must attempt to judge a thing in terms of what it is rather
than in terms of what he would like it to be. A commercial Broadway
farce or a musical must be judged by standards applicable to that type of
theatre. Indeed, a play which honestly sets out only to entertain and does
it well, may be "better" than a play which sets out to make a serious point
and fails.

SOME CRITERIA FOR JUDGMENT

Throughout this book we have emphasized the point that theatre reflects
reality—that it tries to say something about the life we all share. A beginning point, then, in trying to answer the question, what is good theatre,
might be to focus on the ways in which it reflects reality. To do so, we
shall discuss a series of questions which can be asked about any play and
production. These are, of course, not the only possible questions, and an
experienced and sophisticated critic might go well beyond this level. They
will, however, serve as a springboard for further thought about what is
good in dramatic art.

We might begin with the question, *is it true?* Truth, in this context,
does not necessarily mean resemblance to surface reality nor does it mean
literal truth in the sense that the events depicted really happened. By far

the majority of plays depict imaginary events and persons and even those which are based upon real situations often alter the historical facts as we know them. The "truth" in question here has to do with whether the events, characters, and emotions of the play correspond to what we know about human nature and about the way life really works. Even in such non-logical forms as the Theatre of the Absurd we should be able to recognize the element of truth upon which the exaggeration or caricature was based. Even if we do not accept Beckett's pessimistic assessment of life in *Waiting for Godot,* for example, we do know that all human beings spend a great deal of time waiting for things and attempting to fill the time while they wait. If we listen a bit we can hear conversations in life that are not significantly more sensible than those in Ionesco's *The Bald Soprano.* Truth, moreover, is not merely a function of the script. Through lack of understanding or lack of skill actors and director can falsify what, in the written text, is a basically true situation. Of course, what we are likely to perceive as true will be somewhat dependent upon our experience of life and our willingness to consider ideas and situations that go against our prejudices. Married people are, for example, more likely to recognize the truth behind the extreme relationship of George and Martha in *Who's Afraid of Virginia Woolf?* than are people who have never been married. By the same token, if we insist upon the fairy tale ending, "they got married and lived happily ever after," we may be reluctant to accept Albee's play as true.

Second we can ask, *is it honest?* This is related to truth in several ways but it is not quite the same thing. Many plays use easy, perhaps we could say cheap, tricks to manipulate our responses. They may play upon our sentimentality about such things as children, puppies, and Christmas; they may try to shock or excite us with horror, violence, nudity, sex or obscene language; they may play upon our desire for happy endings by providing last minute rescues or reformations, etc. Again, however, we must offer a caution. In some sense all theatre is trickery or, to use a more respectable term, illusion. It has occasionally been referred to as a lie that seems like the truth. The great film director, Alfred Hitchcock is a master of such trickery and frankly admits it. In such cases, however, a part of the pleasure of the experience lies in our awareness that we are being tricked and in our attempts to avoid it. Such tricks are part of the convention of thrillers, whether on film or on stage, and are so accepted. In more serious plays, the intent of the illusion is to reveal truth and *dis*honesty lies in trying to make us accept the false as true or the insignificant as important. One form of theatrical dishonesty is the "soap opera technique" in which Mary Jones's divorce or young Johnny's dropping out of school is treated with a degree of seriousness more appropriate to the outbreak of World War III. Another type of dishonesty is the incredible sugar coating with which certain plays endow life. Many of the typical "high school plays" fall into this category. In the world of such plays there is no death, no divorce, no serious conflict between parents and children, no war, no

serious crime, no poverty or unemployment, no racial or minority problems, no drugs or alcohol — in short, none of the things that make up a considerable part of the reality of the world in which most of us live. Even if,
in such a play, a problem does arise it is not a serious one and can usually
be solved by the application of a little love and a slice of apple pie. This is
not to say that a play must be pessimistic or sordid in order to be honest,
but it should attempt to deal forthrightly with people and situations and
not take the easy way out. Again, there are various ways in which a play
can be dishonest in production, deliberately or through carelessness. An
actress, for example, may insist on being glamorous even though she is
playing a kitchen maid, or a supposedly poverty stricken family may have
clothes and furniture that they could not possibly have afforded.

Closely related to the question about honesty is another; *is the play
predictable*. Most plays, of course, are predictable to a certain degree.
They set up expectations that are later fulfilled. We know early in *A Doll's
House* that Nora's forgery will be revealed and that this will be a severe
blow to her marriage. We do not, however, *how* the forgery will be revealed, the exact nature of its effect, nor that Nora will decide to leave her
husband. The play that is predictable in the bad sense is the one which is
done according to a formula so obvious that if the play were stopped mid-
way in the second act the audience could write its own ending and stand a
90 percent chance of being right. To illustrate let us play a little game that
was used as an examination question in a course in mass communication
taught at a large university. In order to illustrate this idea of predictability
in popular films certain "deathless lines" were supplied and students were
asked to reconstruct the plots. Here are some samples:

> Sir, these men have been through hell. They're half dead from exhaustion. I
> can't send them into the line again!
> I've tried to fight it, but I just can't stay away from you, Marge!
> Gee, Ed, there's a kid in the chorus that could play that part.

Though we might differ slightly in details we all recognize these films and
would pretty much agree on the basic plots. Though we have used films as
examples, they are no more guilty of this sort of thing than many commercial Broadway plays and musical comedies.

A play may also be predictable in terms of character. Earlier we
pointed out that melodrama and farce tend to use a set of stock characters, only changing the names from one play to another. In fact, formula
plots and formula characters tend to go together. Again, let us play a
variation on our game. Visualize the World War II story from which the
first line above may have been taken and try to list the members of the
infantry rifle squad around whom it revolves. There will be a tough kid
from Brooklyn, a farm boy from the Midwest, away from home for the
first time, a man who was almost too old for the draft and is called Pop by
the others, the hard-boiled sergeant who fights for his men and takes it

hard when one of them gets killed, etc. All of this is not to say that the formula play is always bad or that it is not occasionally fun but the formula is often used by the popular playwright as an easy way out, a quick ticket to success, or a way to avoid struggling with the complexities of real people and real events.

Fourth, we can ask, *is it significant?* Does it say anything very important, does it increase our insights into ourselves and other human beings, does it throw any light on the human condition. All plays have a theme of some sort and like the plots, characters, and dialogue we have just discussed, these themes can be trite. How many hundreds, perhaps thousands, of plays, for example, have been built around themes such as "Love conquers all.," "Evil is always punished.," or "Money isn't everything." This is not to say that these themes may not be true but they are not really very profound and furthermore, they tend to be done to death. It may be true, as some scholars and critics have suggested, that there are only a very few basic plots and themes. Even so, one aspect of significance involves the way the playwright and the performers handle the material. Human freedom, for instance, is a fairly common theme in drama, but it can be handled significantly or tritely and superficially. What strikes us as significant, of course, may be a matter of experience and exposure. What seems earth-shakingly important to a child of ten may seem relatively unimportant to an adult. Similarly, upon first exposure one of these themes may seem quite significant, but by the time it has been encountered for the thirtieth time it has become trite. Significance may also be a matter of situation or context. The social plays of the Great Depression, for example, may not be as significant in times of prosperity and may gain significance in a period of economic distress.

Finally, we must ask, *did it entertain?* Immediately, however, we must add that by "entertain" we do not necessarily mean make you laugh or feel good. Too often when people say that they go to the theatre to be entertained they mean that they go to be amused, to laugh, to escape, and not to have to think. Of course, there is nothing wrong with entertainment thus defined. All of us occasionally want to be amused or to escape, just as all of us may occasionally eat cotton candy. Most of us, however, would tire of a steady diet of either one. Entertainment in the context of this question refers to the play's ability to grip an audience, to involve them, to keep them interested, to provide them with a rewarding experience. No play ought ever to bore. Certainly individuals may be bored by any play and performance, but a good play will usually involve the vast majority of the audience and if scattered individuals are bored the fault may be theirs rather than the play's. The capacity to entertain, involve or hold interest is to some extent written in by the playwright, but it is perhaps even more a factor of production. The best script can be destroyed by a deadly and uninspired performance while a very weak one can often be made to seem better than it is by a lively and energetic performance. Evaluating performance as separated from the material performed is a rather difficult activity and depends a good deal upon wide experience with many kinds of plays by many different theatre groups. As a rule of thumb, however, we can say that a performance that holds the audience's interest throughout and in which no one element strikes them as out of key with the others, is probably a good one.

To summarize and conclude this list of criteria, we might ask two more questions: (1) *How long did the play stay with you after you left the theatre?* and (2) *How many times do you think you could go back and see it again?* If the only thing you are thinking about when you leave the theatre is your drive home or where you can get something to eat, the play may not have been a very good or significant one. The good play tends to come back to you in the form of memories—perhaps a scene, a snatch of dialogue, or a bit of acting—long after you have seen it. Furthermore, if the play was a good one there is probably a strong desire to think about it and to talk about it with your friends. The good play also continues to deliver rewards upon repeated viewings. A common characteristic of most products of the popular arts is that they tend to wear out rather quickly, whereas the good work of art is likely to have as much or perhaps more to offer when we go back to it.

SOME IRRELEVANT CRITERIA

The questions posed in the preceding section were designed to focus on criteria that are relevant to the judging of plays and productions. There are, however, some irrelevant criteria which many of us, even experienced critics, occasionally apply to plays. They have little or nothing to do with the evaluation of the piece as a work of art. As before, the following list is not necessarily complete, but it does provide an indication of some standards by which a play should *not* be judged.

One such irrelevant standard is the demand for *traditional form*. All of us have become used to certain patterns which we expect plays to follow and probably the majority of the plays we see do follow those patterns. In our present age and in Western culture the traditional form tends to be realistic, to tell a story and to work itself out in cause-effect sequences and in a forward progression in time.[3] Such plays "make sense" to us; we can follow them with relative ease. One important aim of the artist, however, may be to induce you to perceive reality in a new way, to alter or widen your way of looking at the world. In fact, one contemporary critic has argued that this is the primary aim of so-called *avant-garde* art.[4] In order to do so it may be necessary for the artist to modify or distort traditional form or even to invent a totally new one. Chapters Ten and Eleven dealt at length with such attempts in our century. It is easy to become so tied to tradition that we automatically shut out or dislike new forms without even trying to discover what they have to say to us. In seventeenth century France artists were forced to create within the limits of certain narrowly defined traditional forms and could lose their financial backing or get into worse trouble if they did not. Such an attitude is probably shortsighted. We must be willing to approach each new work on its own terms and try to assess its merits. Of course if the lack of traditional form is not necessarily a fault, neither is it necessarily a criterion of value. Something is not good merely because it is new and unusual. The crucial test is whether what the playwright and the performers wished to say about life could best be said through that new form.

Closely related to the above is the demand that the play be *easily understandable*. There are people who feel that if the full value of a play cannot be grasped upon the first viewing there is something wrong with the play. They do not wish to have to put forth any effort to understand what the artists are saying. An obvious problem here is that our ability to understand also varies with age, experience, and knowledge. The twentieth-century American watching one of Shakespeare's history plays may have a great deal of trouble understanding it since the average American is simply not very familiar with English history. Similarly, the very young may have difficulty completely understanding or empathizing with a play that deals with the problems of the aged. Such problems can, of course, be remedied through learning and they are located in the observer not in the play. In short, it is rarely a good idea to reject a theatrical experience simply because you do not, at first, understand it. Again, however, we must point out that while difficulty of understanding does not make a work bad neither does it necessarily make it good. We may occasionally be led to believe by our professors that if we understand a work of art too easily we are missing something or the work is not a good one. It *is* possible for an artist or a playwright to be confused, obscure, or to lack the skill to make his message clear. Perhaps by going back to the earlier question, "how long did the play stay with you?" the problem can be put in perspective. If the play is difficult to understand but stimulates you to continue to talk and think about it, it may be a good one.

Another irrelevant criterion is the demand that the play be *pleasant* — or you may substitute the words, "uplifting," "wholesome," or "moral" and mean essentially the same thing. Many human beings exhibit what we could term the ostrich syndrome; they would rather hide their heads in the sand than face unpleasant truths. The artist who forces them to face these truths is not likely be very popular. There is no necessary value in deliberately upsetting, offending, or disturbing an audience by forcing them to wallow in unpleasantness unnecessarily, but there are things in our society or in any society, or in life experience in general, that are unpleasant, grim, sordid, and depressing but that, nonetheless, we need to think about. Frequently a play can do more than speeches or pamphlets to bring about necessary change. In the nineteenth century, *Uncle Tom's Cabin*, both as a novel and a play, is said to have had a considerable impact upon public thinking about slavery and thus may have been a causative factor in the Civil War. The people of Athens did not like Euripides' antiwar play, *The Trojan Women*, but in the context of the war then going on it may have needed to be written. The crucial tests are the two questions, "is it true?" and "is it significant?" The drama of escape, of course—the thriller, the farce, the musical comedy—has its place. No one is always in the mood to see a serious drama about war, poverty, prison conditions, or alcoholism, and all of us, at one time or another, prefer to escape the unpleasantness of life. But we should not, if we are mature, expect *always* to feel good, warm, cozy, and comforted when we leave the theatre.

Often when people say that a play is unpleasant they merely mean that it *does not agree with conventional ideas and attitudes*, whether political, social, religious, or moral. Again, this is an irrelevant criterion. No one can deny others the right to refuse to see a play with ideas of which they disapprove. Some of those people may go on, however, to attack the play on irrelevant grounds and even to demand that it be closed or banned. The argument offered is usually one of protecting someone or something from damage or corruption. The problem with this attitude is threefold. First, it exhibits very little confidence in one's fellow man and his ability to withstand corruption; second, it exhibits a desire on the part of the critic or the citizen protestor to impose *his* ideas upon everyone; third, it fails to take into account the fact that ideas, values, and attitudes change. Not long ago, Ibsen's *A Doll's House* was shown on prime time television. When the play was first done in the 1880s it was condemned in parlors and from pulpits all over Europe and America as grossly immoral. The play did not change in less than a century; our attitudes and values have. The theatre-goer is under no obligation to like or to agree with the ideas expressed in a play, but he may be under some obligation to give them a fair hearing, to weigh them on their merits, and to allow others to do the same.

Finally, it is irrelevant *to judge an actor's performance on the basis of his beliefs or his personal life*. Whether he is a Communist, a Republican, a Democrat, a vegetarian, how many times he has been married, whether he beats his wife, what he drinks and how much, are all irrelevant to the quality of his performance. There is a real problem here, for actors have occasionally served as models for behavior, especially among the young and immature. We are perfectly free to disapprove of his offstage behavior if we wish, but we must not confuse that judgment with an evaluation of his work. Furthermore, an actor must not be confused with the roles he plays. He may play nothing but villains onstage and offstage be the most mild, softspoken, and moral of human beings, or he may play the all-American boy in show after show and offstage be completely dissipated. We must not confuse the performer with the role and we must not confuse the personal life with the work unless the one interferes with the other.

Thousands of books have been written about theatre criticism and the debate still goes on about what is bad, what is good, and what standards to apply. Even professional critics do not always agree on a particular play. It would be presumptuous, then, to say that in a few pages, or even in the entire book, the subject has been completely dealt with. At best this book has provided an introduction, a few insights, and a starting point for further thought, discussion, and experience.

It is probably safe to say that most people in America today have got out of the habit of theatre going, and it is just for that reason that courses like this are taught. The tendency not to go to the theatre can be explained by a couple of factors. First of all, the live theatre in this century has tended more and more to be centered in New York and, except for college and university productions and occasional community theatres, large sections of the country have had no live theatre at all. In the last dozen years, probably beginning with the founding of the Tyrone Guthrie theatre in 1962, that trend has been reversing. Many smaller cities now have professional repertory companies, some independent and some, such as the Hillberry company, associated with universities. Dinner theatres have also multiplied around the country and, though their dramatic fare is typically light, they have encouraged more people to go to the theatre. Many people predict that the trend will continue. Second, especially in New York, but in other parts of the country as well, the professional theatre has tended to price itself out of the market. As ticket prices have risen people have been more and more reluctant to risk six to ten dollars for what might be bad production or the same kind of fare that they could see on television for nothing. European countries, especially in Scandinavia, have tried seriously to solve these problems by providing generous government support for theatres and theatre artists, even in the very remote locations near the Arctic circle, so that ticket prices may be kept within reason. Whether or not something similar is the answer for the United States is open to debate, but many people feel that a nation owes it to itself and to its people to support its museums, its art galleries, its concert halls, and its theatres. In respect to both of these difficulties college students are fortunate. Colleges and universities frequently provide a considerable variety of high quality theatre offerings at no or negligible cost to the students.

Not long ago, at the time of this writing, a well-known actress was interviewed on a Pittsburgh television channel and asked, "Why should people go to the theatre?" Her answer began "First of all, because it's such marvelous fun!" Theatre going *is* fun, not only in terms of the play itself, but in the communal interchange between performer and audience and among the members of the audience. In that latter sense it provides a pleasure that other similar media cannot provide. But the values of theatre going, as this book has tried to suggest, go considerably beyond fun.

Two thousand years ago Aristotle said that man has an instinct for imitation and a natural delight in seeing things imitated. We even enjoy seeing unpleasant things imitated because through such imitation we learn. Echoing Aristotle in this century, the sociologist, George Herbert Mead, has said that it is through role playing, both in the theatre and in everyday life, that we learn who and what we are.[5] In the theatre we learn to know ourselves by seeing ourselves reflected in others, we learn how to deal with realities by seeing them dealt with in imagination, we learn what is good and valuable by seeing values tested in action.

Two things make man unique among animals says Joseph Bronowski in his book and television series, *The Ascent of Man*. The first is his marvelous curiousity and the second is his ability to manipulate symbols. The first quality led him out of the caves to begin with, led him to range over the earth, to invent tools, and to adapt himself to a variety of environments. The second made it possible for him to create societies, to work together with other men, to preserve and transfer what he learned and, most importantly, to conduct a continuous search for truth. He has sought truth through a variety of instruments—religion, philosophy, science, and art. Theatre is one such instrument. The truth it has sought and still seeks is not the truth of the laboratory or of the classroom, but the truth of experience, of feeling, of life, of the human soul and spirit.

Notes

[1]See her essay, "Against Interpretation," in the book by the same title (New York: Farrar, Straus and Giroux, Inc., 1966).

[2]This formula is discussed at great length in Burke's *The Grammar of Motives* (New York: George Braziller Inc., 1955) and *A Rhetoric of Motives* (New York: George Braziller, Inc., 1955).

[3]Actually several "realistic" plays violate this time pattern. For example, we typically think of Miller's *Death of A Salesman* as a realistic play, though it alternates freely between Willie's dreams and memories and the real present.

[4]See the title essay in Michael Kirby, *The Art of Time: Essays on the Avant-Garde* (New York: E. P. Dutton and Co. Inc., 1969).

[5]Mead discusses these concepts at length in two works, *Mind, Self and Society* (Chicago: University of Chicago Press, 1934) and *Philosophy of the Act* (Chicago: University of Chicago Press, 1938).

Suggested Readings

Books:

BARRY, JACKSON G. *Dramatic Structure: The Shaping of Experience*. Berkeley: University of California Press, 1970.

COLLINGWOOD, R. G. *The Principles of Art*. Oxford: The Clarendon Press, 1938.

NICOLL, ALLARDYCE. *The Theatre and Dramatic Theory*. New York: Barnes and Noble, 1962.

SHANK, THEODORE. *The Art of Dramatic Art*. Belmont, Calif.: Dickenson Publishing Co., Inc. 1969.

Students may also wish to look at some collections of criticism such as:

BRUSTEIN, ROBERT. *Seasons of Discontent*. New York: Simon & Schuster, 1965.

GOTTFRIED, MARTIN. *Opening Nights*. New York: Putnam's, 1969.

LAHR, JOHN. *Up Against the Fourth Wall: Essays on the Modern Theatre*. New York: Grove Press, Inc., 1968.

INDEX